# The Compl
# Insider's G
# Romania

# 2013

# TABLE OF CONTENTS

# The Author

*I stood there next to Bogdan, both of us quiet and contemplative, gazing down at the scene before us, endless fields of waving green fading off into the darkening twilight. I had told him, finally and with much trepidation, of my plan to write a guidebook about his country.*

*Finally, he cleared his throat and patted me on the back and said, "România este o țara frumoasa. E un păcat ca sunt locuitori".[1]*

Through a complicated series of concatenating events, I found myself on a plane headed for Romania in the spring of the year 2000. At the time, I spoke only one word of Romanian[2] and not only did nobody know I was coming but I also had no idea where I was going.

Somehow, I made it. I had a wonderful and surprisingly fabulous time and over the next few years, continued to visit until finally one day I decided to move here. Despite the fact that I was born and raised in the United States, I now consider Romania my home.

Although I have been traveling and living in various countries all over the world since my childhood, Romania was quite an overwhelming experience to me, especially coming into it as unprepared as I was all those years ago.

It took me 10 long years to learn to speak Romanian well enough to pass for a native but the effort was worth it as it opened many doors that remain shut to outsiders.

During my many visits and now residence here, I've met many tourists, expatriates, missionaries, volunteers and other foreigners here. Having lived here so long, I realized, to my own surprise, that I've become something of an expert on what to expect in Romania, explaining and

---

[1] "Romania is a beautiful country, it is a shame that there are people living in it". While this may sound like a darkly pessimistic view to hold, it is altogether quite common here, one of the many things I came to learn during my time here.
[2] "Opt" or the number eight.

1

decoding the mysteries, making comprehensible a land that sometimes seems baffling, mysterious and taciturn, if not occasionally frightening and overwhelming.

But to tell you this story of why I finally decided to sit down and write this book, I've got to tell you a story about Spain first.

To begin with, Spain is a really wonderful country. The weather is gorgeous, the sun shines in a very special and heart-gladdening way, the food is delicious, the music is enchanting and the people are kind. I've met many, many, many people throughout my life who have been to Spain and not one was every sorry that they went.

I used to live in Spain, myself. I strolled around town eating *tapas* and listened to the *flamenco* music and took my fair share of *siestas* and yep, even went to a genuine bullfight. Definitely a wonderful country and I'd love to go back any time.

After I no longer lived there any longer, I read the book Iberia by James Michener. Like all Michener books, it was long, it was thorough and it was what they call "sweeping" – it really transported you to the place. Unlike many of Michener's other fine books though, Iberia is a work of non-fiction – it's a true account of his real travels and adventures in Spain (and Portugal).

Every town in Spain has (at least) one *feria*[3], which is essentially a city-wide party and festival, where all work ceases and all the town residents from ages 8 to 88 get together and celebrate. How each town does it is unique. I think most people are familiar with Pamplona's running of the bulls and you might have heard of the *Tomatina*[4] in Buñol as well, where everyone gathers in the street for the world's largest food fight with tomatoes.

Where I lived in Spain, the *feria* took place on an enormous plot of land near the river. The rest of the year this land stood empty, despite its potential commercial real estate value, and looked like a parking lot at the world's largest Wal-Mart or something. But as the *feria* drew closer, the lot would start filling up with *casitas*, literally "little houses", gaily-colored square tent-like structures with a wooden platform base.

A long, long time ago, this *feria* began as a market event where horses were traded. In this giant lot nowadays, no cars or motorized vehicles are allowed but horses are permitted and you will see very colorfully decorated horses prancing around with their riders often in elaborate get-up as well.

---

[3] http://en.wikipedia.org/wiki/Feria
[4] http://en.wikipedia.org/wiki/Tomatina

The action, however, mostly takes place inside the *casitas*, inside the large tents. Many, many drinks are consumed, music is played and people get together to tell jokes and laugh and dance and meet old friends and a wonderful time is had by all. The *feria* coincides with the harvest of a special kind of grape that is made into a kind of wine that isn't aged – it is made and consumed only within a short period of time. During the *feria*, it flows like water.

If you read Iberia, you know that Mr. Michener went to this *feria* as well. But he had one major problem – all of those thousands of *casitas* with merry-making Spaniards inside of them are *privately owned*. You cannot just walk into them uninvited because they won't let you in. There's only a handful of *casetas* where the owner lets the general public in, and those are usually sponsored by political parties.

So there was Mr. Michener, this awe-inspiring writer, this inveterate traveler and all he could do was walk up and down the rows of the *casetas* and catch glimpses of the fun going on inside and nothing else. Without an invitation, without an "in", there was just no way to make it beyond the entrance. Despite his stature and earnest intent, he was forced to remain an outsider looking in.

At the time I was living in Spain, I was living with a Spaniard so I had my invitation. I was inside of those *casetas*. My girlfriend's father was somewhat of a local bigwig and through his graces, I was invited in to many other *casetas* and many hands were shaken and many glasses of the special wine were raised and toasted. Heck, I might have even danced a little, I don't remember.

What I do remember though is reading Iberia and realizing that there is a tremendous difference between visiting a place and actually living there, from being on the outside and peeking through the tent flaps and catching brief views of the "real" place and being on the inside, speaking the language, shaking hands and telling jokes and being welcomed in the festivities.

Yes, I've traveled to many places. And yes, I've had the privilege of actually parking myself in a few places for a while and living there and getting past the museums and the big churches and the old castles and the shopping districts downtown and the restaurant or two wherein I sampled a dish that I'd never tried before and hoisted a few beers or soft drinks with a friendly local who spoke excellent English. And it's always surprised me just how much *more* there always is when you live in a place.

A few months ago I went to a nice bar in town with a tourist who had just arrived in Romania. To get there, you have to walk down an ordinary street and see a large gate leading to a very dark alley. Inside that alley they were doing some kind of digging or something so there were two men in dirty overalls working in a trench. We had to walk past them, go up a flight of stairs (completely covered in graffiti) and turn a corner and voila – a very nice, warm and inviting bar.

The tourist turned and said to me, "You know, I never would've known this place was here," and it's true. There's absolutely no sign outside and no indication that there's anything but a dark and dirty alley there. Locals just know it's there and so I guess there's no need to advertise its existence. And it was that exact comment that prompted me to write this book because it's true, if you don't live here, you'd *never know it was there*.

That is sort of my "mission" here, so to speak, to take you inside the metaphorical tent flaps of the *casitas* of Romania, to get past the Dracula menus and the castles and the wow ZOMG[5] people still use horses here for basic transportation and the woe-begotten filthy gypsy beggar children and show you the Romania I know and love from the "inside".

For better or for worse, as the saying goes, this is the land where I live. I guess, just like a spouse, sometimes we have our bad days but overall it's a place that I've come to really get to know and appreciate.

Spain is a wonderful country but there are many countless fine writers singing and extolling its praises. Romania? Not so many.

This book is my humble effort to do this wonderful country a little justice and let you see it through my eyes, the eyes of a half-foreign and now half-native person.

## Why You Should Read This Guide

Quite honestly, in the very best of situations your typical guidebook will be written by a talented writer who has probably written other travel guides to unrelated countries and is therefore an experienced writer.

The author is usually paid a fee upfront to spend a few weeks in the country, eating out at restaurants, sleeping in hotels and tabulating basic tourism information.

---

[5] Meaning "Wow oh my goodness" ;)

At worst, the average guidebook is written by a hack who blew through a country at top speed, barely noticing or experiencing anything, akin to taking a picture of the Eiffel Tower through the car window as they raced by.

Unfortunately, this leaves anyone relying on such a guidebook with little more than some encyclopedia facts, hotel phone numbers and a couple of restaurant reviews.

With the advent of the internet, a lot of that information can be collated online. In fact, this entire book is written in such a way that it can be easily meshed with online resources.

Paper, printed books of the standard guidebook variety certainly have their usefulness but when their information changes, you're suddenly out of luck. And let's be honest, if you truly want a lengthy discourse on Romanian history, that's what Wikipedia was invented for.

For me, what would've been far more useful all those years ago as I first set foot in the country was a guidebook teaching me how to navigate this country, not just in terms of bus lines and hotels but also in terms of understanding the culture, the mentality and what to expect here.

Even if you've never set foot in Romania before, by the time you are finished with this book you will be quite prepared and ready to understand this mysterious and special land.

## The Internet In Conjunction With This Book

Unlike many other European countries, there is wi-fi or cabled (Ethernet) access to the internet almost everywhere you go in Romania.

Bring your own wi-fi device and you can skip either the crappy, shared computer at the hostel or else a dingy "internet cafe", which are becoming increasingly scarce.

A second-hand netbook or a low-end tablet computer goes for almost nothing and is both light and extremely portable. Spend the 100 bucks or whatever it takes and get one that has no moving parts like the one I have[6] and the thing is almost indestructible.

The best idea is make sure it has some kind of microphone option so you can use Skype (or some other kind of VOIP) to contact the loved ones at

---

[6] http://en.wikipedia.org/wiki/Eeepc

home. Calling cards to dial overseas using regular phones are available in Romania but they are far more expensive. Much better to sit at a nice cafe sipping that perfect cup of coffee and chatting with the folks at home on your computer.

Furthermore, if you can handle the small screen, many "smart phones" and tablets sold these days have wi-fi access capability (iPhones, etc). Again, since wi-fi and internet access is both common and usually free in Romania, you can use your smart phone to stay in touch.

A few places that'll usually always have wi-fi:

- Nicer hotels, including their lobbies
- International fast-food chains (Starbucks, McDonald's, KFC)
- Cafes, especially nicer ones or ones in downtown (city centre/**centru**)
- Quite a few hostels, esp. those in bigger cities
- Bars which cater to university students
- Any place which has a decal on the door saying it has wi-fi (duh)
- Inside major downtown (city centre/centru) squares

The best part is it's almost always free!

But what about more rural areas? Or perhaps you'd like to be connected to the internet all the time, not just from a hotel or café, what then?

The first thing you can do is check and see if you can turn "roaming" on for your phone (or other internet device) for data. This is possible in some countries but you need to check with your data carrier at home first.

The other option is pre-paid internet, which is available to anyone, tourist or citizen alike, in Romania. It uses a USB "stick" modem that can be plugged into any computer using a mainstream operating system (Windows or Mac).

These are available from all three of the mobile telephone providers in Romania – **Orange**, **Vodafone** and **Cosmote** for a relatively modest fee. Check their websites (www.name-of-company.ro) for current pricing (look for the little British flag for information in English).

I can tell you from personal experience that the modem will pull in a signal from just about anywhere in the country and this is probably your only option for more rural locations.

Since many things in Romania change constantly (such as restaurants and nightclubs), throughout this book you will see many internet references in the footnotes. Using these will allow you to gain the timely, useful information when you need it, yet another reason to make good use of the internet.

**Twitter**

An increasing number of Romanians use Twitter and they can be an invaluable resource to you. Twitter is a great way to contact locals in real-time through virtually all forms of digital media, including mobile phones.

Note: Currently only the mobile phone company **Vodafone** allows its users to communicate with Twitter via SMS, however all three companies sell mobile data plans.

Additionally, you can find me (the author) on Twitter at @**lifeinromania**.

# GPS

The number of usages for a GPS whenever traveling in a foreign land are incalculable but I rarely see people using them, so I will enumerate some of the advantages.

For one thing, you will never get lost (again). It's a heck of a lot easier to set your hotel as "home" on the device and then wander around, free of worry that you won't be able to make your way back.

It's also a portable map in every town you go to, allowing you a much easier time of finding monuments, museums and places to eat than relying on a collection of static, paper maps.

A good GPS device is also fantastic whenever you're traveling by car, bus, taxi or tram because you can see where you are going, ensuring you don't head off into the wrong direction or the taxi driver taking you on a wild goose chase.

I've sat in the front seat of many a taxi, GPS device in hand, allowing me both to watch the route as well as orient myself. It's also great for telling the driver *where* to go, especially when the destination is unpronounceable. All you do is key it in and show it to him and off you go.

Although some smart phones often have a GPS receiver and some sort of mapping application, the small screens can be difficult to use. I highly recommend a dedicated GPS device, if possible.

At the moment, Google Maps (and other applications which use this data) has fairly correct and detailed information inside most *cities*. At the moment, the Apple map application is less accurate. For more rural information, there is still a lot of detail lacking for both these mapping services and I wouldn't depend on it for a trek into the wilderness.

But for city streets, especially large ones like Bucharest, Google Maps works extremely well and also has a lot of useful information such as subway (metro) stops, restaurants, etcetera. Also the "Street View" in most cities (where you can see a 360 panoramic view) is now active in Romania.

Nokia maps seem to be about on par with Google in terms of the accuracy of their data in Romania.

Since Romania is now part of the European Union, most GPS devices sold with maps of "Europe" usually have maps of Romania included. The best thing you can do is check your device before you leave home as usually it's possible to download new maps for free (on registered devices).

Inside Romania itself, you can buy GPS devices (with maps for Romania of course) for anywhere between the equivalent in the local currency of 85 to 400 euros.

# Weather

Romania has approximately three large geographic zones (see page 248) but they all have roughly the same weather. Obviously higher elevations (mountains) are going to be colder year-round and have more snow, and generally the southernmost locales are warmer.

Romania has a true four-season "continental climate" that rarely gets extremely cold or hot for long periods of time.

Generally speaking you can expect the following when planning your trip/move to Romania:

### Fall/Autumn

Roughly starting in September and lasting until sometime early in December, the temperatures are often quite crisp and cool at night but still fairly warm in the daytime.

Definitely too cool to go to the beach (minus a few brief warm days in early September) but snow is quite rare. The leaves begin to turn and cheeks start to redden but a far cry from the true depths of winter.

## Winter

Due to the fact that Romania is at a (relatively) high latitude, the days are incredibly short and the air is often incredibly cold during winter, approximately December through February. The snowfall usually kicks in right around the end of the year and while rarely voluminous it can be quite persistent.

This and a combination of cold rain, icy rain, slush and sleet can make winter a very, very dreary and brutal experience. The only reason to come to Romania in winter is to partake in winter sports.

## Spring

Approximately running from March through May, the sun begins to lift its head and breathe life into the planet once again but warmer temperatures are a long time coming. Considering how cold and dreary winter can be, a small rise in temperatures feels good but it's still often quite blustery and cold.

Usually there's one last "surprise" snow storm at either the end of March or beginning of April.

## Summer

Almost always serendipitously on May 1 (see page 117), the summer sun peeps its head out and the air truly warms up enough for T-shirts.

Nonetheless, very few locales in Romania get truly, blazingly hot until around the early part of July, with the "dog days" (Rom: **canicula**) of August being particularly brutal. This period usually (thankfully) lasts only a couple of short weeks.

The inverse of winter, the days of summer in Romania are usually quite sunny and long with daylight lasting over 14 hours at some points.

## When to Visit

In terms of weather for visiting, anytime from May to mid-July would be absolutely perfect in terms of it being warm, the sun shining and yet not so hot as to sap your spirit.

Romania is an amazingly fertile country and this is partly a result of regular precipitation year-round. Therefore it can rain (or snow) at just about any time of year yet it is rarely onerous.

For current weather conditions in Romania I highly recommend Weather Underground[7], which has data in both metric (Celsius) and American (Fahrenheit) as well as in multiple languages.

If you click on a city, the site also has a nice feature called "History and Almanac" where you can find out the weather in years past, allowing you to fairly accurately gauge what to expect if you're planning a trip here in the future.

# Dracula – Separating fiction from reality
## Vlad Țepeș, the real Dracula

I used to tell people that I lived in Cluj[8] and they'd say, "Huh?" Then I'd tell them that Cluj was a city in **Romania** and they'd scratch their head with their mouths hanging open. Then I'd say, "It's in Transylvania" and they'd grin and slap me high-fives and reply, "Sweet, *vampires!*"

Well first of all, to dispel all rumors to the contrary, I've been living in Transylvania for a long while and I've yet to see even one vampire – not a baby one, not a glittering one, nothing. Sadly, nobody drinks blood around here or anything either, only Coca-Cola and fruit juice mostly.

So who was the "real" Dracula aka *Vlad The Impaler*? He truly was a real person in history but most of what you (probably) think you know about him is wrong. Time for a little impromptu history lesson.

Vlad's sort of "nickname" if you will really *was* Dracula but it has to do with the fact that his dad belonged to a creepy Christian Freemasonic Illuminati type cult called the "Order of the Dragon" and "Dracul" is Romanian for "the dragon". Therefore the son became "Dracula" or "Little Dragon".

Starting around the year 1460, the real *Vlad the Impaler* ruled over mostly what would be southern Romania today (Wallachia). And he spent most of his time wheeling and dealing in old skool European politics, aka murdering brothers and half-cousins and scheming to get on thrones and get back on thrones and all that sort of late medieval nonsense.

---

[7] http://www.wunderground.com/global/RO.html
[8] See page 175.

10

At the time, the two big superpowers in the region were the Turks and the Hungarians and so Vlad was quite busy playing one off against another and variously pledging undying loyalty and then turning around and stabbing them in the back and treacherously raising armies to conquer their territory and then breaking down and crying and swearing he'd never break his promises again and so on and so forth.

So why does everyone know his name and not the other 500 princes of Romania? Well for two historical reasons. Despite what your mother may have told you, Vlad "the Impaler" didn't get his nickname because he liked to aggressively eat little squares of cheese with toothpicks.

Whenever anyone royally angered him (and he was a short-tempered fellow) he would bend you over and jam a long wooden stake up your rear end with the tip coming out of your mouth. Vlad would then leave you there to wriggle around for a few days as a "warning" to anyone else who even thought about making fun of his mustache.

But what he *really* did to get remembered forever and ever as one nasty prince was that Vlad got into a dispute with some Germans (see page 206), who at the time ran a little town called **Braşov** (see page 142).

The way the story goes is that these meddlesome German merchants were giving Vlad a real headache so he decided to invite them to a huge feast in **Braşov**. When they showed up, Vlad served them a real nice dinner, probably with lots of sausages and beer. After the dinner was over, Vlad cackled and twirled his mustache and gave the Germans the old "what for" and had all the rich, fancy merchants impaled on sticks outside the town walls.

The surviving relatives in **Braşov** were none too happy about seeing Fritz and Helmut and the gang come to such an inglorious end and wrote long, anguished letters in run-on sentences and compound nouns to their relatives back in the "old country". As this was right around the time another German[9] had just invented the printing press, the story got printed up in a series of pamphlets and passed around.

It was, in effect, the first horror story of the modern printing age and so it got copied (and embellished) in different languages and passed from one side of Europe to the other until the whole world knew that in Romania lived one fearsomely diabolical dude.

---

[9] Johannes Gutenberg

Interestingly enough, to Romanians (even today), Vlad is a national hero up there sort of where George Washington is for Americans or Ned Kelly is for Australians. In no way is he considered an "evil" or "bad" guy.

After all, Vlad spent most of his time running around fighting off people who tried to keep Romanians down and there are many local folk tales of him imposing a harsh but fair rule on his subjects.

## Dracula by Bram Stoker

The reason why "everyone knows" vampires come from Transylvania, however, is because of the book Dracula written in 1897 by Abraham "Bram" Stoker, an Irishman who never once set foot in Romania.

If you're familiar with the book (or one of the many film versions), you can see how Bram Stoker grafted the name "Dracula" and the fearsome reputation of (the real) Vlad the Impaler together, combining it with some Balkan legends about the undead in order to write his thriller.

Even today, many tourists come to Romania strictly to see the "sights" from the book. One section of the story concerns the protagonist (Jonathan Harker) spending a night in a hotel in the town of *Bistriz*. That's the German name for the modern Romanian town of **Bistrița**[10], which is located in central Transylvania, a very real place.

For a long, complicated reason I'm not going to get into here, I once had to spend the night in **Bistrița** and it was a last minute thing so I just walked around until I found the first hotel I could find. That hotel was the "Golden Crown" Hotel[11], which is a real hotel but is named specifically for the hotel in the book (which again, is fiction). I thought that was cute but didn't pay it much attention.

However the next morning when I woke up to eat breakfast, I noticed they have a special menu so that you can order the same foods that Jonathan Harker "ate", if you so desire. Therefore there's a real hotel named after a fictional hotel in a fictional book wherein the hero eats a fictional breakfast that you can really order in the real hotel.

Also, even more confusing is that *Vlad the Impaler* (the real guy) was an ethnic Romanian but Dracula the fictional vampire was a Szekler (see page 199), which is a kind of special Hungarian.

Oh and Vlad the Impaler (real guy) had a Hungarian wife.

---

[10] http://en.wikipedia.org/wiki/Bistrita
[11] http://www.hotel-coroana-de-aur.ro/index.php?lang=english

So "Dracula" the vampire = totally fictional and a Hungarian and not from Transylvania.

Vlad The Impaler = real Romanian but named Dracula and married to a Hungarian and was never the ruler of Transylvania.

Also, the fake book Dracula mostly isn't set in Transylvania at all and the real Vlad The Impaler barely spent any time in Transylvania either, interestingly enough.

Again though, the reason why the real Dracula was notorious was because of his actions in **Braşov** (which *is* in Transylvania) that got written up in the newly invented German press.

It should be noted that the infamous stories of **Elizabeth Bathory** (see page 255) clearly had a role in the author's conception of what vampirism was all about.

## Real Vampires and the Undead

The famous *Dracula* book essentially mixed up a few items about Vlad and then added the concept of vampires, which really do exist[12] in Romania, as do other forms of the undead.

Every year there's always some news story from some remote village about the "superstitious peasants" who dug up Uncle Bogdan's corpse because he was a vampire and the Romanian government and media always try to downplay it because they find it embarrassing.

Personally, I've been to some pretty spooky places in Romania so I'm keeping my mind open about this kind of thing, to be perfectly honest with you.

Romanian vampires don't really prowl around doing all the blood drinking though. That is based on the super creepy and true story of Elizabeth Bathory (page 255), who was a Hungarian noble accused of some of the most bone-chilling acts in history.

## Dracula/Vampire Tourism in Romania

Although there have been several proposals to build large scale fun parks in Romania with a Dracula/vampire theme, so far none of these have come to fruition.

---

[12] http://en.wikipedia.org/wiki/Strigoi

In general, the locus of vampire tourism is the hotel in **Bistriţa**, the two castles considered to be "Dracula's castle" (see page 169 and 171) and the real Vlad's birthplace in **Sighişoara** (see page 155) as well as Dracula's last stop in **Galaţi** (page 161). Lastly, there is a tombstone in **Snagov** outside **Bucharest** that is reported to be mark the final resting place of Vlad Tepes.

Not so fun fact – There are some people out there who just find the whole blood drinking vampire thing super "cool" and get quite obsessed with it, sometimes to the point where they save up their money and come to Romania in search of vampire adventures and whatnot.

They engage in some pretty creepy stuff sometimes, especially on Halloween (see page 123), which has nothing to do with Romania OR vampires. You might run into one of them if you ever come here. I know I have and I pray I never do again as that's really not my thing.

The most famous actor to play Dracula in Hollywood films was a guy named Bela Lugosi, who was an ethnic Hungarian but was born in (what is now) Romania.

Although many Romanians (and some foreigners) say that advertisements and other media that use Dracula or vampires is "everywhere" and quite tacky and cheaply commercial, all I can say to counter that is to note the prevalence of Coca-Cola logos everywhere in this country. For some reason that one particular company seems to have a tremendous advertising presence in Romania everywhere you go, including the very home of Dracula himself in **Sighişoara**.


# Tourism Basics
### Visas

For absolutely the most current (and legally valid) information, look online for Romania's embassy in your country.

That being said, generally speaking, if you're a citizen of the **European Union** then you have free right to unlimited travel, work and residence in Romania.

If you're from a country that is a major economic powerhouse (United States, Canada, Japan, Australia, etc) or other "important" country then generally you can enter Romania as a tourist and stay for **90 days without a visa** obtained beforehand.

At the moment, Romania is not currently part of the **Schengen Zone**, (scheduled to have happened in early 2012 but still hasn't happened as of this writing and it is highly doubtful that it will happen before 2014 due to systemic political problems) which is useful information for those people on extended tourist visits to Europe from non-EU countries[13].

If you're not sure whether or not you need a visa to be a tourist, see the Romanian government's official Ministry of the Interior website[14], which is a confusing, bureaucratic maze to negotiate.

For information on longer-term visas for living in Romania or other non-tourist activities, see page 226.

## Poverty

Mercy! Over all the years I've lived here I think the one consistent topic that I continually hear being discussed is poverty (**sărăcie** – *sah-rah chee-eh*). It's something people who live here obsess over and it's often one of the first thing visitors remark upon.

Heck, I know I did the exact same thing. Many moons ago when I first came to Romania, my plane glided in to Otopeni Airport (see page 102) and out the window the very first thing I saw was a rusted, burnt-out hulk of a plane parked right next to the tarmac. It was clear it had been sitting there for years.

As our plane taxied off the runway, it struck me that the only reason you'd leave an old rusty plane sitting next to the tarmac is if you were too poor to move it, chop it up for scrap, recycle it or anything else.

Is there poverty in Romania? Of course there is. But even Romanians themselves misunderstand a lot of it. I've seen so much change in this country over the (relatively) brief period that I've been here that it's made my head spin. For example, the year that I saw that rusty hulk of a plane on the tarmac, almost nobody in this country had a washing machine or a microwave in their home. Now Otopeni is completely modern (and free of abandoned planes) and everyone I know has a new refrigerator, washing machine *and* microwave, plus tons of other electronic junk.

---

[13] Most European countries in the Schengen Zone allow you to be in the country for only 90 days and then stay away for another 90 before you can re-enter. Therefore if you wanted to share time between living in France and Romania, for example, you could spend 90 days in Romania then 90 in France and then back to Romania. This kind of behavior, I should mention, is highly discouraged by most governments.
[14] http://www.mai.gov.ro/engleza/Home_eng/english.htm

Yet I distinctly remember sitting in the kitchen of a Romanian woman in **Baia Mare** (page 157), listening to her tell me how "poor" she and her family were. My elbow was literally resting on the *second* brand-new washing machine in her house while I was asking if she'd been just 50km to the north (to Ukraine[15]) and of course the answer was no. Romanians are determined to be fixated on the fact that they're "poor" and there's nothing you can do to convince them otherwise.

How does one even measure poverty? Cash in the bank? Yet we all know that in countries like the USA where credit cards and other loans are easy to get, most people are in debt up to their eyeballs. Who is richer, a Romanian peasant with no debt or a Londoner with a nice car and thousands of pounds of debt?

Certainly wages, in terms of absolute measurements of monetary value, are much lower in Romania. A school teacher's salary in Romania would barely keep a homeless person in New York fed. There's no question about this.

Yet again, I have to ask, what does poverty even mean? If we try another metric like "how many of your people are going hungry", which country is poorer, the United States or Romania? I can tell you the answer is obvious when you learn that 36 million Americans, including 13 million children, have serious issues concerning lack of (proper) food.

How many Romanians are hungry, as in truly hungry? Thankfully, far, far fewer than in many other countries, including Britain and Spain and all those other countries that Romanians imagine are some kind of paradise.

And what value do we place on the *quality* of food? After all, we *are* what we eat. Is there such a thing as food poverty? As in those concoctions we call "food" are so impoverished in terms of taste and nutrition – does such a thing exist?

Just about every visitor to Romania remarks on how attractive a lot of Romanians are[16]. And it's true. But does anyone ever stop to think that perhaps it's because they're eating wholesome, nutritious, homemade foods on a regular basis?

Let me ask this question. If your salary is too low to afford eating fast food[17] every day (especially at McDonald's or KFC) so you eat less of it and eat more home cooked meals, are you *actually* poorer than someone who wolfs down french fries and a Coke every day?

---

[15] У мене є всі повагу і любов до українців :)
[16] For much more on this, see page 27.
[17] For much more on fast foods in Romania, see page 64.

And if gasoline (petrol) being ludicrously cheap allows you drive everywhere by yourself, is that actually making you "richer" than someone in Romania limiting their trips and car pooling or riding public transportation or even walking due to financial restrictions?

And all those peasants with their horses and wooden carts, at first glance they *seem* poor. Of course! They have neither cash in the bank nor all the wonderful toys that credit can buy. Yet they're raising organic crops by hand, transporting them using completely Earth-friendly horses and homemade wooden wagons made of almost entirely recyclable components.

Is a smog-filled urban metropolis in some "richer" country really better than fresh air and the clip-clop of hooves?

Poverty is how you measure it and there are certainly people in Romania who live hard lives filled with struggle and strife. Yet I challenge anyone to name a place where this is not also true.

I know (and hear about) a lot of elderly people in Romania who are too old to work and yet receive a very low stipend from the government every month. Even with some government food assistance, it's really not enough to live on and so they are dependent on their children and family to take care of them.

That's certainly a tough spot to be in, no doubt about it. But I have to ask two questions. How did they even manage to live long enough to be here today to be in this position? I meet a lot of "senior citizens" and they're quite healthy, in general (especially compared to my own relatives in America).

Secondly, what value do we assign to having a family nearby? Most Romanians I know have a large, well-connected family with almost all members living fairly close by. Every Romanian you meet has a cousin, uncle and two cute little nieces also living in the same city. What's that worth? And are you impoverished when your family is spread all over the place?

Romania is a different country, there is no doubt about it. Some things here are shocking to see simply because they don't exist elsewhere. But not everything is what it seems to be at first glance and that includes poverty.

That Romanian lady you see on the side of the road with a toothy grin peeping out of her simple woolen clothes may not own a brand new digital SLR camera or an X-Box 360 but she's heading home to make a home-made meal with fresh vegetables from her garden for her large, close-knit family.

She just might be richer than either of you realize ;)

**Dangers**

Romania is certainly a unique and amazing country but often times visitors get mixed up on where the dangers lie.

I'll start off by saying unequivocally that <u>Romania is an incredibly safe country</u> in every sense of the word. Violent crime is almost non-existent[18], there is almost no civil unrest, the food and water are of high quality and even small children walk around town unaccompanied without any trouble whatsoever.

That being said, of course there are dangerous things in this country.

**Periculos** (*perry-cole-ose*) – This word means "dangerous".

**Pericol** (*perry-cole*) – This means "danger" in Romanian.

**Interzis** (*inter-zeese*) – This means "forbidden" in Romanian.

If you see any of these three words, be careful!

The number for all emergencies (fire, police, etc) is **112** which can be dialed from any telephone, including public phone boxes (bright orange).

<u>High Risk</u>

By far the most dangerous thing you can do in Romania is drive at nighttime between cities, either behind the wheel yourself (page 106) or on some form of inter-city transportation like a **minibuz** (page 92).

Many of the roads are poorly illuminated with multiple hazards including people, animals, carts and abandoned or parked vehicles on the roads. Also, many drivers are operating poorly illuminated or completely dark vehicles or carts. Other drivers are extremely tired or inattentive.

There is simply nothing else in Romania you can do that is as dangerous as being on the roads at nighttime.

<u>Medium Risk</u>

Probably the greatest risk you need to worry about is being tricked out of your money. A wealthy tourist is going to be pretty obvious to spot and some people have a plan in place to separate you from your money.

---

[18] The vast majority of the violent crime that *does* occur in Romania is nearly always domestic – between two people who know each other quite well and usually live together.

Some visitors report being scammed or tricked by taxi drivers. It's pretty easy to avoid problems by knowing a few basics. For the complete guide on taxis, see page 109.

Tricks with the bill and mysterious charges in restaurants and bars are fairly rare these days but still do occur. The law in Romania states that a detailed, itemized bill must be generated for every purchase. If you have any doubts, ask for a copy of the menu and compare the prices.

For a more detailed guide on eating out, see page 221.

Please be aware that it's not a "trick" but hotels often list (and quote) their prices without the tax included, which can be quite hefty[19] indeed. For more on this tax (called **TVA**), see page 40 but just be sure to ask or inquire about it to avoid unpleasant surprises.

Hotels and hostels usually quote their prices in euros, which may or may not be converted at the optimal rate (see page 41).

I'm hesitant to include pick-pocketing under the "medium" risk heading but since it is something that can and does occur in some places, I will mention it. As someone who has been pickpocketed myself, it certainly is a risk that exists in Romania, particularly in crowded areas like train stations. That being said, it's very easy to protect yourself simply by carrying valuables and money in a secure location like an inside pocket or a money belt.

Another item to include in the "medium risk" category are poorly marked hazards, whether potholes in the road or else excavations in the middle of a sidewalk. A lot of repairs, construction and remodeling is done in Romania that is very poorly marked, identified or otherwise been "made safe" for the clueless, wandering visitor. Falling into a hole that's poorly marked (or sometimes not marked even at all) is a genuine risk[20] in this country.

Always be alert to your environment. When walking, avoid stepping on anything metal, especially hatch covers and gratings.

Low Risk

Violent crime of any kind, whether rape, robbery or assault, is extremely uncommon. Does it ever happen? Of course it does, but so infrequently that it's not truly an "issue". It's certainly possible to start a fistfight at a bar if

---

[19] It currently stands at 24%.
[20] I once fell headlong into a ditch that was completely unmarked. I laugh about it now but an accident like this could really mess you up.

that's what you want but walking down the street minding your own business and being unexpectedly assaulted or robbed is almost unheard of.

Driving in the daytime can be quite an adventure (page 106) but is generally safe. Just be attentive!

I've heard from a lot of people that they are concerned about "fake police" or shakedowns by real police officers.

I've been traveling all over Romania for years and never seen a fake policeman, never. Not ever. Never even heard of it secondhand from other tourists or visitors. Never seen it mentioned in the newspaper. I assume it has happened at one time or another but it seems to be equivalent to worrying about a lightning strike – those happen too but hardly on the top of the list of dangers to be concerned about.

If you ever have some kind of "confrontation" with police, legitimate officers or "fakes", do not show them any ID, **do not give them anything**, don't sign anything, don't take anything from them (tickets, fines, whatever), do not do jack squat with them. If they insist on something, **go with them to the police station**. Period. If something truly and honestly is going on and it somehow involves you, go to the station. Walk into the big building with the word "Politia" outside and deal with whatever it is there.

Police in Romania only throw on the handcuffs and put you in the squad car when something very major has happened, and in that case, you should be well aware of whatever it was. The rest of the time they just talk to you. Stand there and talk it out however long it takes and you should be fine. They spend all their time harassing gypsies and their fellow Romanians, not foreigners, so you should be fine.

If anyone in a uniform, police officer or railroad official or bus inspector or anyone else wants money from you, **do not give it to them, ever**. There are no fees for entering or exiting Romania. There is absolutely no legitimate reason to pay any Romanian official who is not working inside a government building, period. Are we clear on this? Good, I hope so.

Especially in some rural areas, the electrical wiring can be a little erratic and power surges and spikes can occur. This is an issue with sensitive electronics (like computers) so be careful. In the cities and nicer hotels, the electrical systems are modernized and work just fine. For more on electricity, see page 22.

Having your luggage "messed with", especially on forms of public transportation (including the train), is very rare. I see a lot of visitors are incredibly fretful about this issue and I'm here to tell you it's really not something you need to worry about.

And despite the fact that several "western" governments warn their citizens about public demonstrations or strikes becoming violent, that is also a very rare occurrence here in Romania.  Strikes *do* regularly occur however, especially in **Bucharest**, as that is the capital.  This may severely impact transportation at times.  Protests and demonstrations also do occur but are almost never violent.

While it is customary to have minor "stomach troubles" when visiting a foreign country, the water in Romania is safe to drink.

I'm going to come right out and say this – there is no extra risk in catching any kind of diseases here any more than wherever you (probably) come from.  Communicable diseases of a fatal or severe nature are quite rare here in Romania although cases do occasionally occur, of course.

In other words, you don't need any special shots, injections, vaccines or anything else specifically because you're coming to Romania.

There certainly are a lot of computer savvy Romanians so basic computer safety and internet use is recommended.

A lot of people ask me about the dog situation.  The good news is that the packs of roaming, feral dogs are no longer a threat.  There are however still a lot of "street" dogs or loose, outdoor dogs and it is important to avoid being bitten.  For the complete guide on dogs, see page 215.

A lot of Romanians (especially women but men also) enjoy wearing perfume and sometimes a *lot* of perfume.  If you are sensitive to these kinds of things, be aware that the odor of perfume in certain crowded situations (page 129) can be quite intense.

Last but not least, talking to Gypsies (for much, much more on them, see page 200) is always going to carry a low amount of risk.  Why?  Because a large part of their culture concerns how to wheedle or otherwise separate you from your money and valuables.  I say that openly without rancor or prejudice.

While some sticky fingers might slide into your pocket, having a group of Gypsies suddenly physically assault you is extremely uncommon although, like all things, it does occasionally occur.

Almost No Risk

Again I hate to say that none of these things will *ever* be dangerous or ever occur but generally speaking, you don't need to worry about it in Romania.

- Showing, displaying, counting or otherwise "flashing" cash
- Carrying around an expensive camera or phone
- Walking by yourself at night
- Using a laptop or tablet computer
- Drinking the water and eating the food
- Riding public transportation
- Police brutality

**Handling Your Passport**

From the United States' government travel advisory on Romania:

> ***Foreigners are required to carry identification documents at all times.*** *Americans who obtained a temporary or permanent stay permit must be able to present the document upon the request of any "competent authorities." Foreigners who do not have a stay permit should present their passports. The Embassy recommends carrying a copy of the relevant document.*

Romania is a land of 10 million laws and not a whole lot of enforcement of them. It's a strange dichotomy until you get used to it.

Therefore the only time you need your passport is either to **exchange money** or else to **check into a hotel**[21]. The rest of the time you don't need to carry it and it's far, far better to get stopped by the police (or "competent authorities") and not have your passport than it is to lose it or have it get stolen.

If any police stop you and "demand" your identification, basically tell them to go to hell (in your native language). If it's actually some kind of genuine emergency situation, they'll either take you down to the police station or escort you back to your house/hotel to get the dang thing. And that's about as likely to happen as you getting hit in the head by lightning.

No. Don't carry your passport around unless you truly need it and there's just about no time that the police need to see it unless something extremely serious has happened.

---

[21] And entering and leaving the country, of course.

Furthermore, a really good idea is to carry a Xeroxed copy of your passport (or main ID) around with you. It makes it about a million times easier to get it replaced if sadly you do lose your passport. If you feel pressured into showing some ID, show them the Xeroxed copy and not the original document.

## Electricity and Batteries

All electricity in Romania is 220 volts, the standard across Europe.

The plugs used to power electrical devices in Romania follow the continental European standard, i.e. two identical, parallel prongs that fit into a round hole. Therefore any electrical device bought on the European continent (Germany, France, Italy, etc) should work just fine in Romania.

Electronic devices from Britain, the USA, Hong Kong and other systems will need some kind of adapter in order to function in Romania.

I should warn you that there are occasionally current fluctuations and spikes in some rural electrical systems so extremely sensitive devices (like a laptop) should only be used in conjunction with a surge protector. Electricity in the cities, however, is generally as reliable, steady and constant as in any other modern country.

Batteries are generally ubiquitous and easy to find almost anywhere, provided they are of the AA (sometimes called R6) or AAA variety. The good brands are sometimes fairly expensive but in this case worth it as many of the knock-offs are of extremely low quality.

## Nudity, Dress Codes and Bare Skin

There are various modes of dress in Romania, ranging from some very conservative outfits in some rural areas to the very revealing, nearly nude styles worn in some urban and other areas.

Generally speaking, in rural areas, a more conservative approach to dress is be found, with older women often covering their hair with a kerchief in addition to wearing full-length skirts or dresses.

Decorous and respectful dress is the norm[22] inside of churches, monasteries and nunneries, other houses of worship and in some rural areas.

During the summertime however, in urban areas and at vacation resorts across the country, very revealing clothing and/or a lot of bare skin is quite

---

[22] And may occasionally be actively enforced.

normal on people of both genders and all body types. This means that you may equally see an old man with a tremendous belly with little to no clothes on as you may see a gorgeous young woman equally unashamed[23] about her body.

Some people find this shocking and/or offensive or perhaps against their personal and/or religious or ethical beliefs. If that applies to you, you are now forewarned.

Other people, especially men, sometimes find that their attraction levels shoot through the roof for the women here during the summertime. If that's the case for you, see page 182 immediately.

Furthermore, the general sense of open mindedness about how one can dress plus public displays of affection (see page 127) may be quite a lot for some people to handle. If this kind of thing is shocking to you, please brace yourself (mentally) ahead of time.

Complete nudity in public situations is usually limited to just a handful of specifically delimited beaches (see page 160) although it isn't likely that someone would get in trouble for laying out for tanning purposes in other settings.

That being said, it is a general custom that very young children often go completely naked at beaches, water parks and similar places.

**Useful Languages To Know And When To Use Them**

Although many Romanians enjoy watching Spanish-language *telenovelas* or soap operas, they rarely can speak or understand Spanish beyond a very limited level. Understanding and reading Spanish words will only be useful in deciphering Romanian about a third of the time and is not really that helpful.

There are many Romanians who speak English and these are generally people under the age of 30, with a much higher prevalence found in cities and urban areas. Very few rural Romanians will speak English.

If you are a monolingual English speaker in a Romanian city, the best person to approach for directions or other help would be a young adult aged 18-25.

---

[23] I've noticed a lot of foreigners become shocked that less than perfect people often become partially or completely disrobed here and it's okay and no one is judging them or freaking out about it. Get over it.

That being said, there is a lot of English being spoken (and understood) quite poorly in Romania, so don't be surprised if you are occasionally misinterpreted. If you find a Romanian who professes to speak English, speak to him/her slowly and clearly without the use of a lot of slang, jargon and euphemisms.

Romanians are often a shy people and speak/understand foreign languages better than they say they do.

After English, German is the most commonly learned and spoken foreign language, especially in the historically German areas of Romania (see page 206).

Together, German and English are considered the prestige languages.

French was once the prestige foreign language to learn in Romania and many older Romanians can still converse in it on some level. There are also a few younger people still learning French but it isn't a language I'd rely (solely) upon to navigate in Romania.

While Italian's strong similarity to Romanian makes it fairly easy to decipher (especially when written), few Romanians actually feel comfortable enough in Italian to speak it beyond perhaps a few memorized phrases although many Romanians have worked in Italy long enough to be able to converse in the language.

There are a great number of foreigners in Romania (see page 210) who speak all kinds of other languages from Arabic to Norwegian and so you will find Romanians studying and speaking these languages as well. Nonetheless, these form a very small group.

Speaking the Hungarian language is certainly extremely useful when interacting with (ethnic) Hungarians but it is such a difficult language to learn that if you already speak it, you're almost definitely an ethnic Hungarian yourself and therefore know all of this already.

That being said, learning a few words of Hungarian will certainly be appreciated by Hungarians and it can be a useful skill if you're planning on spending a lot of time in a majority Hungarian area (see page 197).

Since almost all signage is required to be in the Romanian language, you won't need to learn any Hungarian in order to get around - it's purely optional.

Although Russian was mandatory for some Romanians during the Communist era, the Russian language is almost never used in Romania and most people avoid it like the plague, with the one exception being the **Lipoveni** (page 209).

## Hotels and Lodging

For information on hotels and lodging in cities, see page 219.

For information on inns and rural places to stay, see page 224.

For a list of relevant phrases, see page 271.

There are no specific recommendations for hotels, villas, hostels or other lodging in this book. This is because they are relatively easy to find and it is far more useful to know *how* to find good lodging than a (possibly outdated) list of places to stay. Check for the internet for current information and reviews about the best places to stay.

## Telephone Numbers

A few years ago, the government re-arranged telephone numbers in this country to make them a lot simpler to use. Nonetheless, it can sometimes be confusing.

To understand, let's look at a real telephone number, that of the mayor of **Cluj**, the city where I live:

**+40 264.592.301**

To begin with, the **+40** is Romania's country code, so this phone number has been written in such a way that anyone *outside* the country can dial it.

Depending on where you are, there is a code to dial international. In the United States, this is often (011). Therefore, if you were in the U.S. and wanted to call the mayor for a chat, you'd dial 011-40-264-592-301.

But what if you were in Romania already? What is the mayor's phone number?

Turns out it's **0264-592-301**. That's right, it's exactly the same minus only the very first 4.

All Romanian phone numbers begin with 0. Every single Romanian knows this yet they always give out their numbers emphasizing that (mandatory) first zero.

Therefore minus the obligatory zero, the phone number is: **264-592-301**.

The first three numbers (or four if you count zero) are always composed of a code that tells you what kind of telephone you're dialing.

During the Communist era, the only telephones available were the "land-line" kind, hard-wired cables running under the ground and in the air. This is known as a **telefon fix** (*feeks*) in Romanian. It's sometimes known in English as a "house phone" or an "office phone" but in all cases means a telephone plugged into a cable in the wall.

Every city's **fix** telephones have their own prefix, always beginning with a **2**. In **Cluj** this is **264**. **Braşov** is **268**. **Bucharest** is the only city with multiple **fix** phone codes but they always begin with **21**.

Therefore looking once again at the mayor's phone number, we can see a) it's in **Cluj** (no surprise) and b) it's a **fix** phone or a cabled telephone, presumably in his office.

Occasionally you will see "short" numbers in Romania, especially for businesses, consisting solely of six numbers, for example perhaps **592-301**. This is presuming you know it's a **fix** number in that town, therefore (assuming this is Cluj) I myself know to add the **0264** when dialing it.

Due to deregulation, the former government telephone monopoly allowed other companies to sell **fix** phone services. To differentiate, their **fix** numbers are the same only they begin with a **3** instead of a **2**.

Therefore if the mayor's **fix** number was through a different company, it would be **0364-592-301**.

Romania, like many other countries, had relatively few **fix** phones in place by the time mobile telephony took off. Therefore mobile (cell) phones are extremely common with excellent coverage just about anywhere.

There are currently three mobile telephone providers in Romania and their subscribers are assigned different numbers. Since telephone calls between people on the same network are often far cheaper than between networks, it's important to know at a glance which telephone numbers correspond to which company.

**0720** to **0739** – Vodafone

**0740** to **0759** – Orange

**0760** and up – Cosmote

Now let's assume that the mayor has a public mobile phone number (he doesn't) with the company Orange. What could his phone number be?

Answer: **0745-592-301**.

I just made that up, by the way, so don't consider that a real number. The point here is that mobile phones don't show which city the person is in, only who their carrier is.

You might have noticed I have been writing the telephone numbers xxx-xxx while earlier you saw xxx.xxx style. Romanians tend to write telephone numbers in a variety of different ways, but tend to say them orally in pairs.

A Romanian saying out loud the mayor's **fix** number: 0264 59 23 01.

Note: Taxi companies often use special phone numbers.  For more information on this, see page 109.

Note: Due to recent deregulations, people can now "keep" their phone numbers and switch providers, therefore everything written above will one day be obsolete although this has just begun and is therefore still quite rare.

**Making/Receiving Phone Calls in Romania**

If you already own a GSM mobile phone with a removable SIM card inside, you're set. All three of Romania's mobile networks sell pre-paid cards that anyone can use for about 8 euros (roughly 35 lei).

It is critical to remember that *incoming* calls (someone's calling you) from any number worldwide are free in Romania. If you are here in this country and have wealthier family or cherished ones wanting to call you from abroad, this is a great way to stay in touch.

If you want to buy your own telephone here as well, your best bet is any store called **telefoane second hand**, which surely you can guess specializes in cut-rate used mobile telephones. That plus a SIM card (Rom: **cartela SIM**) from one of the three mobile providers will get you in business right away.

If you prefer, check with your current mobile phone provider to see if they support "roaming" in Romania before you come here.

## SMS

This is what's known as a "text message" in some places. Sending these is usually incredibly cheap, including internationally and are a great way to stay in touch for not much money.

As with voice calls, receiving an SMS is always <u>free</u> in Romania.

## City/Town/Village

All inhabited places in Romania are divided into three types:

**Oraş** (*oh-ROSH*) – City

**Comună** (*co-MOO-nuh*) – Town

**Sat** (*sot*) – Village

By government definition, there are 172 "cities" in Romania but this is because an inhabited place with 5,000 residents (or more) is officially a city[24].

**Bucharest,** the capital, is an immense city of about 2 million inhabitants and has all the accoutrements of a large municipal area, an extensive public transportation system (including a subway/metro), multiple airports, onerous traffic congestion, a wide variety of entertainment venues and a breathtaking number of beautiful parks.

Due to Romanian demographics, Bucharest's inhabitants represent approximately 20% or one-fifth of all urban dwellers in the country.

Six other cities, **Cluj-Napoca, Constanţa, Craiova, Galaţi, Iaşi** and **Timişoara** have a population of over 300,000 residents and are likewise modern and well-developed.

Another 20 cities have a population of 100,000 or more.

Most of Romania's 172 "cities" however are far, far smaller and have a population of under 50,000.

A town meanwhile (*comună*) is by definition even smaller than a city, and often is between 1,000 and 3,000 residents. Usually in a *comună* you can find at least one bar, one *magazin mixt* (see page 132) and an ATM/cash point/**bancomat**.

---

[24] Actually there are a few other requirements, including the condition of the streets, number of buildings, etc, but the minimum population of a city in Romania is indeed just 5,000 people.

The village (*sat*), being smallest of all, can simply be three or four houses in close proximity to each other. Because they are so small, most villages are administered politically through the nearby *comună*.

**Neighborhoods - (Cartier)**

Although most Romanian "cities" are extremely small, they all usually have a significant geographic feature, a series of internal divisions, each one called a **cartier** (*car-tee-AIR*) or a "neighborhood".

All Romanians who live in a city will know exactly where these neighborhoods (plural: **cartiere**) are. Most bus routes are designed (and marked) by which neighborhood they go to.

For example, in **Cluj-Napoca** there is a bus that runs through the *Buna Ziua* neighborhood, which you might know[25] means "Hello" or literally "Good Day". So if you know your destination is in *Buna Ziua* neighborhood, you can hop on that bus knowing that it will get you close to your destination.

Furthermore, a lot of road signs inside the city point to the different **cartiere** or neighborhoods. Since Romanians are genetically prone to being the world's worst ethnic group at giving directions, usually they don't know where anything is but generally they *do* know where the various neighborhoods are.

Oddly enough, however, on a minor digression, Hungarians seem to be genetically the complete opposite, being outstandingly talented at giving concise, accurate directions. It's almost a perfect shibboleth to determine one's ethnicity in this country, interestingly enough.

Anyhow, the big problem for you, the traveler/visitor is <u>exactly where these neighborhoods are is never marked or written down anywhere</u>. It's also rarely on any maps. It's utterly bizarre. For example if you're in a car, you'll see a sign to turn right to enter *Buna Ziua* neighborhood. Fine. You make the right-hand turn. Are you in *Buna Ziua*? <u>You will never know</u> because you're just "expected to know". You'll basically never see a sign saying, "Hey you are in X Neighborhood."

It's insanely confusing furthermore because often the exact border between each neighborhood is only *loosely defined*.

It's almost impossible to find paper maps (or maps online, even) with the neighborhoods marked and you'll rarely, if ever, see any kind of written sign or other indicator to ever tell you which neighborhood you're in.

---

[25] For a complete list of greetings, see page 284.

In **Bucharest** it gets even more complicated because the city proper is divided into a number of sectors (which thankfully are sometimes marked on street signs) which then is furthermore divided into neighborhoods or **cartiere**, the most notorious of which is **Pantelimon** in Sector 2, sometimes considered Romania's only true "ghetto".

The default **cartier** in every city is known as **centru** (*chen-true*), which means "downtown" if you're American and "city centre" for everybody else who speaks English. Since this is often where most of the things you came to see are located, it's important that you get a feel for where **centru** is in every city.

Additionally, the borders between cartiere in Romanian cities are often composed of a **piața** (plural: **piețe** – *pee-EHT-zay*) meaning a "plaza" or "square". This is not to be confused with the food market (see page 63), which is also called a "**piața**".

Hint: These "squares" or **piețe** are therefore incredibly useful as landmarks with which to orient yourself.

If you're coming to Romania and planning on doing some unguided exploration inside cities, I highly recommend you bring a dedicated GPS device (see page 7) with you as this will make orienting yourself and finding destinations about a thousand times easier.

Otherwise your best bet is to get a good map and learn how to find *friendly* locals (especially Hungarians) to give you directions, assuming you don't have a host Romanian guide/family to help you.

For a list of basic phrases, especially on how to ask for directions, see page 135.

**Nightlife**

The sun is steadily fading over the horizon and night is descending. Yet you aren't tired; in fact, the opposite. You feel a nervous rhythm in your blood and a strange excitement. You want to go out! But what is there to do in Romania?

Well my friend, if "going out" at night to public places, especially ones with loud music and lots of alcoholic drinks is your idea of fun, you have hit the jackpot in Romania. Despite the fact that geographically this country is in Eastern Europe, at times you would think that you have arrived in Ibiza. Simply put, Romanians love to party!

The norm amongst frequented clubs and bars is that the facility stays open **până la ultimul client** or literally "until the last customer leaves". When is this? Quite often 4:00, 5:00, 6:00 and yes, even 7 o'clock in the morning is when the last bleary-eyed drunk will stumble out of the bar. I know this because I too have sometimes *been* that customer.

But before we get ahead of ourselves, let's work our way up.

For starters, most *comune* (towns) and some *sate* (villages) will have just one or two bars at most, the only nightspot available, usually a "regular" bar during the day and then a place for dancing and revelry as night falls. The music in these smaller venues will almost universally be **manele** (see page 178), which is fairly unpalatable to most foreigners.

Many smaller cities (50k to 100k residents) on the other hand, will have a few dedicated clubs that open at night. In general, these clubs are similar in concept and operation as the ones in larger cities, so let's look at the definition.

To begin with, **night club**, written just like that in English, <u>always, always</u> means a "gentleman's bar" or "strip club" or "titty bar" or whatever you wish to call it (see page 182). Always!

A "regular" club for dancing and drinks is called a club, disco, discotheque or bar.

A standard Romanian club (disco) however always consists of these same elements:

- Alcohol is served liberally
- It's loud as hell
- Filled with dense clouds of smoke
- Dancing regularly occurs whether there's a specific "dance floor" or not
- Skimpy/revealing clothes is normal (often called "looking your best")
- The music is often high BPM "techno"

Since most of these same elements also occur in bars, the only difference is that slightly more dancing occurs in quote unquote "clubs" than bars.

If there is enough of a crowd and enough alcohol has been served, Romanians will then enter a particular state known as the *club frenzy*. This is the magic moment of the night when an invisible hand seemingly pushes a button and the entire crowd goes wild.

This is when people start dancing on tables, grinding each other and yes, occasionally taking their clothes off. The flashing lights and blasting music and undulations of the crowd distort your perception of time and space and for a moment, you lose track of yourself.

In larger cities, there are clubs open seven days a week. In cities like **Bucharest, Cluj, Timişoara** and **Iaşi**, there are enormous numbers of university students so you can get lost in a *club frenzy* every day of the week if that's your kind of thing.

Smaller cities with fewer university students, such as **Braşov**, rarely have a *club frenzy* more than once or twice a week.

In the larger cities only, you can find another alternative kind of nightspot, known as the Rocker Bar (or club) in Romanian (or *bar pentru rockeri*), although it is almost never labeled that way.

This is going to be populated almost entirely with young people wearing black clothes, including a lot of T-shirts with heavy metal bands on them. The music can be anything from a combination of Nirvana, Rammstein and Metallica to some Romanian music (especially the band *Vama Veche*) and "classic rock".

Romanian "rockeri" are rarely what's considered either "goth" or "emo" in some other western countries but are more "grunge" than anything else, as in the early 90's "Seattle style" grunge. Also especially common is (white) people with dreadlocks in their hair, for some reason, as well as a lot of tattoos and/or body piercings.

And yes, even *rockeri* occasionally engage in a *club frenzy*, but rarely.

**Bucharest**, being such an immense city, has every kind of nightlife imaginable, up to and including openly gay-friendly bars (see page 182).

If drinking and dancing aren't what you're in the mood for, almost all larger Romanian cities have Communist-era theaters and opera houses with quite busy concert schedules. Or you can mix and match them, seeing *Le Figaro* before heading out to get plastered and dance in the club.

The other kind of nightspot that's growing in popularity in Romania is **bowling**, spelled that way but universally pronounced *boweling* as in (disem)boweling someone, which always makes me smile.

These too will also serve alcohol, often be quite smoky and have loud music blasting. From my experience, the clientele is usually quite young, as in high school or younger, so if you don't mind hanging out with the kiddies, it can be fun.

Less common and only in some bigger cities are pool (billiards) halls and places to play darts although these are growing in popularity.

The rarest nightspot to be found in Romania is a bar where it *isn't* deafeningly loud so you can actually meet people and strike up conversations. If you find a place like that, hang onto it!

So how does one go *about* finding the local hotspot? By far the easiest thing to do is simply *ask* someone, whether the receptionist at your hotel, a Romanian friend or heck even just stopping locals on the street – I've done all three.

For the top 10 largest cities in Romania, there are two useful and well-known entertainment guides, one being **Şapte Seri**[26] (literally "7 nights" and having somewhat of an English-language option) and the other being **24-Fun**[27] (Romanian only). These guides list not just bars and clubs but also themed parties, musical exhibitions, concerts and plays and is a great way to see at a glance what's going on.

Both of the websites default to **Bucharest** listings but you can click and navigate to local listings in other cities.

Generally speaking these (and other guides) are also printed out on paper and distributed free at most bars, cafes and restaurants. They usually are stacked near the end of the counter somewhere and are full of advertisements.

**Rural Life**

Because roughly half of all Romanians live in rural areas, the country's long history and implementation of traditional agriculture and lifestyles are still in use today.

A lot of Romanian mores, beliefs and mindsets are still a direct legacy of the country's long history of pastoral living and it is still more common to see the country life encroaching on cities rather than the other way around. In other words, don't be surprised to see someone herding a group of pigs across the street, even in downtown **Bucharest**, as I myself have seen with my own eyes.

---

[26] http://www.sapteseri.ro
[27] http://www.24fun.ro

A visit to a true Romanian village, where the only sounds you hear are the gentle creak of wooden wagons, the soft lowing of cows and the sharp cries of a rooster is definitely worth the experience.

Although Romania's villages are priceless gems of living history, they can often be difficult to get to due to the lack of public transportation, poor road conditions and lack of accommodations for visitors. It is also a little incongruous to suddenly stop your car on the side of the road and approach a startled villager.

The good news though is that there is starting to be a developed network of rural tourism organizations, one of which is called ANTREC[28], although it could stand to be a lot better. Unfortunately, the government's official tourist website[29] has only a little information in this regard.

If you are in Romania and being hosted by a local, your best bet is to ask them to take you to the village where one of their relatives live as most Romanians have family in the countryside.

Many, many people who visit Romania are simply blown away by the amazingly beautiful countryside that exists here, from luscious fields of brilliant sunflowers to some of the kindest and most down-to-Earth people you'll ever meet.

Even though many of the cities are amazing and definitely worth visiting, I would not consider any trip to Romania to be complete without at least one visit to the countryside.

## Camping

One of the delightful things about Romania is that there are an enormous number of parks, nature preserves, and protected wildlife zones. Many of these can be visited and a partial list of these, including their corresponding websites, can be found online[30].

Camping inside parks is regulated by the park rules in place. In smaller parks or designated natural areas, you can usually camp (providing your own equipment) just about anywhere for free, provided you follow commonsense rules.

Many parks and natural areas often rent out small cabins or **cabane** (*kah-bahn-eh*) for a small fee provided you bring your own sleeping gear. Usually

---

[28] http://www.antrec.ro/en-antrec.html
[29] http://www.romaniatourism.com
[30] http://www.romaniatourism.com/national-parks.html

these are quite tiny, little more than small, wooden sheds big enough for you to sleep inside and stay dry without any other amenities provided (like electricity) unless otherwise specified.

Many Romanians also "free camp", setting up tents and grills (and loud radios – see page 176) anywhere there is an uncultivated piece of greenery, sometimes even on the outskirts of a city. This is due to the Romanian cultural propensity for *iarbă verde* (see page 130) but the long and short of it is, anyone can camp where they want to provided they're not disturbing the neighbors.

Camping on the beach is generally prohibited anywhere on Romania's Black Sea coast with the exception of **Vama Veche** beach (see page 160) in the extreme southeastern part of the country. Due to its anarchist past, free camping is not just permissible there but considered a fundamental right.

## Castles And Palaces

Even today, Romania has a king (see page 254) and the country was ruled for centuries by a combination of nobles, princes and kings. Several of their castles and palaces still exist in Romania.

For information on **Bran Castle**, see page 169.

For information on **Peleş**, see page 170.

For information on **Poenari**, see page 171.

For information on **Hunedoara Palace/Castle**, see page 169.

For information on **Elisabeta Palace**, see page 170.

If you're interested in Roman ruins and fortifications, see page 167.

## Museums

There are many fine museums through Romania and generally they charge just a nominal entrance fee (**3-10 lei**).

That being said, they do often get a little carried away with tacking on extra fees for permitting photography or video. It's far easier to not pay these and just do what you want, protesting innocence or giving a generous tip to any museum employee who might interject.

Generally speaking, most museums in Romania are closed on the weekends as well as Mondays.

**Medical Care**

Probably one of the most misunderstood things in Romania is the quality of medical care, especially thanks to some movies[31] that got international attention.

Medical insurance, obtained in your home country prior to departure, is always recommended.

While care for unusual or severe cases of chronic illness may be hard to obtain in Romania, if something does unfortunately occur during your visit, you will be okay. All Romanian cities have clinics and hospitals that do an excellent job of treating trauma injuries and many illnesses.

Many doctors and medical personnel in Romania also speak English (and other foreign languages).

For a much lengthier description of the medical system in Romania, see page 238.

The emergency number to call in Romania is **112**, including for medical emergencies.

If you feel more comfortable with a doctor speaking your own language, contact your embassy in Romania as usually they have a list of recommended physicians.

"House calls" where the doctor comes to visit you at home (or at your hotel) are usually available in cities as well. If you're staying at a hotel or *pensiune*, ask the receptionist for more information.

Generally speaking, medical fees in Romania are quite low[32]. For lengthier or more expensive treatment, you'll need to consult with your insurance provider for a transfer to your home country.


# Money
**Basic Introduction**

Romania's currency is called the **leu**, the plural of which is **lei** (*lay*) and literally means "lion(s)".

---

[31] *Moartea domnului Lazarescu* or "The Death of Mr. Lazarescu"
[32] For example, a friend of mine came to visit me in Romania and her severe asthma flared up. We walked in a city clinic, got seen almost immediately and the doctor spoke flawless English. The total cost of the consult plus the medicine from the pharmacy was **24 lei** or about 8 USD.

Each **leu** is divided into 100 **bani** (*bawn*).

Prior to 2005, the currency had four more zeroes on every bank note and so occasionally you will see the old prices (like a bottle of water for 20,000 lei) but in general, the majority of the country uses the new currency.

Currencies fluctuate all the time but generally speaking:

**1 U.S. Dollar =** 3 lei

**1 Euro =** 4 lei

**1 UK Pound =** 5 lei

For information about the (exact) current exchange rates, see the *Bancă Naţională ai României* (central bank)'s official website[33].

All Romanian bank notes (bills) are made of plastic, which adds to their longevity and durability, and come in the denominations of 1, 5, 10, 50, 100, 200 and 500 **lei**.

Coins are either gold or silver in color, in the denominations of 5, 10 and 50 bani. **100 bani = 1 leu.**

For some unfathomable reason, there does exist a **1 ban** coin (equivalent to an American penny) but it is rarely, if ever used. In nearly all cases, prices are rounded up (or down) to the near 5 **bani** despite what the cash register may say.

A picture of all Romanian bank notes and coins can be found on the central bank's official website[34].

**Changing Money**

It is extremely important to understand that Romanian **lei** are impossible to buy or sell anywhere outside of Romania itself.

Places to change money can be found almost everywhere in Romania and are known as **schimb de valutari** (*skeem day vah-loo-TAR*), which always have their rates posted nearby.

Almost every bank likewise has a currency exchange window, often marked as the **casa de schimb.**

---

[33] http://www.bnr.ro/
[34] http://www.bnr.ro/Monede-si-bancnote-in-circulatie-724.aspx

Generally speaking, banks offer the least favorable exchange rates but they are always safe, trustworthy and reliable.

Private commission booths may offer a better rate but sometimes balk at accepting non-Romanian forms of identification (such as passports).

If you decide to change money at a non-bank exchange window, be very sure to count your money and look for a sign saying, "**Nu percepem comisioane**" which means they do not charge any additional fees.

A list of currencies that can be exchanged in Romania:

- American dollar
- Australian dollar
- Canadian dollar
- Euro
- British pound
- Hungarian forint
- Japanese yen
- Scandinavian currencies (kroner)
- Swiss franc

Be aware that currencies from neighboring countries (Serbia, Ukraine, Bulgaria and Republic of Moldova) with the exception of the Hungarian forint cannot be exchanged in Romania. Likewise, any other currencies besides the ones listed above cannot either be sold or purchased inside Romania.

Be also aware that Romanian money cannot be exchanged anywhere outside of the country. If you don't spend/convert all of your **lei** before you leave then you'll have some interesting souvenirs to give to your friends and family.

If you have a bank card (debit) from a major "western" bank, you can however choose to use it in any ATM or "cash point" in Romania, known here as a **bancomat** (*bonco-maht*) to withdraw money from your home account, which will be dispensed to you in Romanian **lei**.

If you're not sure whether your card can be used in Romania, check with your bank before you leave home!

Almost all Romanian banks have **bancomate** and they can be found in all cities and towns (see page 29) in the country.

## Spending Money

Romania is almost an entirely cash economy and so you're going to have to get used to handling and managing large numbers of coins and notes during your stay here.

For a long time, there was a shortage (or perceived shortage) of coins and so cashiers are often quite fussy over providing the exact change for purchases.

Be aware that prices in Romania are always shown with the tax included, called **TVA** in Romanian[35]. This means that if the price tag says **5 lei** then that's what it will cost at the register[36]. Only in certain, specified situations is the tax not included in the price.

Observing Romanian cultural sensitivities, it is extremely important that you never touch someone else's hand when exchanging money (like when you're buying something).

Therefore, do not hand money directly to someone. Most cash registers have a small, plastic dish nearby precisely for people to lay their money on. The cashier will then place your change in the same dish.

If there is no dish, just set your money down on the counter somewhere near the register. If you absolutely must exchange money hand to hand, it is best to do so in a way that your skin never actually touches their skin.

If you are giving money to someone you know (a friend, etc) it is considered politic to put cash money in something else, such as envelope, before exchanging it.

Note: Sometimes Romanians use the English word "cash" (pronounced *kish*) and sometimes use the word **bani gheața** (*bawn-gay-otza)* for "cash", literally meaning "ice money".

Occasionally the formal word **numerar** will be used to mean "cash".

## Lending Money

I will keep this section extremely short and bittersweet. <u>Do not lend money to a Romanian ever</u>. There is a very different mentality in play in this country concerning money, debts and financial obligations and it is very difficult to understand for the outsider.

---

[35] This is the VAT tax in English.
[36] As far as I am aware, only the United States does that thing where you have to wait until you're at the cash register to realize what the "real" price will be.

If you wish to *give* money to someone, whether a beggar on the street or a friend you meet here, that is entirely up to you.

If you are a foreigner in Romania (as I'm assuming you are, else why are you reading this?) then you may be (accurately) perceived as being rich and therefore some people will ask you for loans or other financial generosity.

Spend your money however you wish but do not lend or "front" money to anyone with the expectation of getting it back.

**Credit Cards**

Again, Romania is largely a cash-based society so credit cards are less useful here.

The only place I'd feel comfortable using a credit card in Romania is at a luxury hotel although upscale restaurants in bigger cities and shops in the mall are now fairly safe places to use a credit card as well.

While some stores and restaurants now accept credit cards, there always remains the risk of having to sort out fraudulent use, delays in reporting or even innocent errors weeks or months afterwards with your bank, an unpleasant experience.

In Romania credit cards are just called a "**card**" using the English word.

**Why are some prices in Euros?**

Although the Romanian currency has been stable for a few years now, there was a long period of inflation and volatile price shifts and so many people got used to marking prices in a more stable currency, especially the euro.

In almost every case, <u>when you see a price in euros you are expected to pay in Romanian lei</u> (at that day's exchange rate) although very expensive hotels in large cities usually take euros directly for payment.

A few things that are commonly priced in Euros:

- Hotel/hostel room rates
- Real estate (rent or buy)
- Cars and automobiles (including renting them)
- Mobile telephones (and their cards/plans/rates)

If you see almost anything else priced in euros (especially restaurants or transportation), this is a sure sign that you're entering a *tourist trap*, where the prices have been inflated.

For a complete guide to eating out, see page 221.

## Tipping

There is little to no tipping as a common practice in Romania unless you are given extraordinarily good service.

Tipping taxi drivers is not necessary beyond rounding up to the nearest whole **leu**. For more information about taxis, see page 109.

Whether at restaurants or cafes, tipping is never mandatory although the waitress (or waiter) may bring you back your change rounded up to the nearest whole **leu**.

## The Concept of "a-la-carte" Pricing

Many first-time visitors to Romania are confused when goods and services are priced and sold separately by *individual component* rather than being bundled together.

For example, in a restaurant (or fast-food) the purchase of a sandwich is one cost but additional items like condiments (ketchup, mustard, etc) may be sold separately.

Other services, such as a haircut, may be broken up into individual prices, with a shampoo and wash being a separate cost from the haircut itself.

Or a hotel or inn might quote one price for the room but then "renting" the remote control for the television might be an additional price.

Furthermore, most medical care is "sold" a-la-carte as well, meaning that the cost of admission does not necessarily include food, clothing, medicine or other services that might be provided in other countries. For a longer look at medical care in Romania, see page 238.

On a restaurant menu, occasionally there may be some confusion as the price is listed "per 100 grams" but the portion you may be served is larger, therefore becoming more expensive than you expected. Read all menus carefully and be prepared to stand up for yourself (see page 221), if you suspect any trickery is afoot.

The good news is that with everything being sold separately, you can get exactly what you want sometimes and not have to pay for what you don't want. This includes buying pills at a pharmacy, where you can get just 1 or 2 and not have to buy an entire box.

In general, be extremely prudent when inquiring into prices and make sure they include the goods and services you want.

# Food

Although often derided by idiot foreigners who write guidebooks as "non-existent", there most definitely is a distinct Romanian cuisine. It is however, largely "peasant food" or simple, hearty staples that have been enjoyed for centuries in this country.

Generally speaking, most Romanian food is not spicy but quite often flavorful, with an abundant use of herbs and spices, most definitely including garlic.

Romanian food is often given short shrift because there is a huge gulf between what's cooked and eaten at home versus the (often much lower quality) dishes served in restaurants, pizzerias and fast food eateries.

### Traditional Romanian Food

### Mici/Mititei

Clearly one of Romania's most popular and enduring dishes, **mici** (*meetch*, literally "small ones"), sometimes known as **mititei** (*meaty-tay*), are generally referred to in English as "skinless sausages".

Unlike most of the concoctions you will find at a fast-food restaurant (see page 56), **mici** truly are a Romanian domestic creation. Many years ago a well-known restaurant in **Bucharest** ran out of casings and so had to create a "sausage" right there on the spot to feed their hungry customers, thus inventing **mici**.

In general, any sausage is a combination of ground meat and spices mixed together and then injected into a casing, originally animal intestines but today sometimes made of a kind of edible plastic (I know). What makes Romanian **mici** unique is that they have no casing – they are simply blends of meat and spices formed into a small "log" and grilled or pan-fried.

Because no casing is necessary, it's rather easy to make **mici** at home[37].

If you look closely at the recipes, you see that the majority of the meat in **mici** is surprisingly beef, specifically cuts from the **ceafă** (*chah-fah*), which

---

[37] http://student.maxwell.syr.edu/irsa/cookbook/mici.html

means the "back of the neck", more commonly known as "chuck" in English and the source for (high-quality) hamburgers, amongst other things.

It is then mixed with a smaller portion of lamb meat (and sometimes pork) as well as critical amounts of garlic and cumin, which give **mici** its unique flavor.

**Mici** are the "hot dog" of Romanian culture, the most ubiquitous form of "the common man's meat" and are generally extremely inexpensive to buy, often sold in large packs (in grocery stores) precisely so you can cook them on your grill for a summer picnic.

It is extremely common to eat **mici** with a healthy dollop of "plain" yellow mustard, usually served on the side so that the eater can swirl each bite of **mici** in the sauce as desired. If you ever order **mici**, whether at a fast-food or "proper" restaurant, mustard will always be served with it.

**Mici** are often served as "festival food", eaten at concerts and summertime events. It is much rarer to find **mici** served at fast food restaurants, although some do, especially those who cater to the poorest customers (such as those who flock around train stations).

If you consume meat, I heartily recommend you try some **mici**, especially hot off the grill and swirled in mustard, accompanied by a beer of your choice.

## Chiftele

Pronounced *keef-tay-lay*, these are fairly "standard" meatballs, usually consisting of a combination of ground beef and lamb meat mixed with egg and spices and formed into little balls.

## Cremvurşti

Generally speaking, this is one of the most common Romanian sausages, which does including a casing (unlike **mici**) and is the meat most similar to an American hot dog, although in Romania they are usually eaten plain alongside other food and not in a bun.

Many Romanians boil and eat **cremvurşti** (*krem-voorsht*) for breakfast. These are rarely found for sale in fast food restaurants and are primarily something eaten at home or packed for picnics.

## Mezeluri

Romanians have a great fondness for cured meats and sausages, collectively known as **mezeluri** (*meh-zeh-lure*). Many shops specialize in this and nothing else.

Additionally, if you see the word **brânzeturi** (*brun-zeh-tour*), this means aged or smoked cheeses are also sold along with the cured meats, a common occurrence.

## Slănină

If you travel to Eastern Europe and the Balkans area, sooner or later you're going to run into it so time to learn about it NOW.

The very first day I was in Romania, I spent a few hours in the home of a Romanian couple that didn't speak English. They poured me many fine shots of very strong alcohol (see page 73) but they also fed me many delicious and varied Romanian foods.

They also gave me a slice of **slănină** (*slah-nee-nah*). At the time, I had no idea what it was. Sitting on my plate it looked like one very oily and severely undercooked French fry. I took a bite of it, thinking it was some kind of potato, and found it to be cold, loathsome and hideously greasy.

My host kept saying, "**Slănină, slănină**" and I looked in my pathetic guidebook and there it was: **slănină** – pork fat.

Imagine taking a pig and slicing off thick slabs of pure fat. You take this fat and either smoke it or salt it or both. Then you leave it to hang somewhere dry for a long time and this is what **slănină** is. It isn't "bacon" in any sense of the word because proper **slănină** is about 99% fat and no meat.

These days, I don't even eat animal products anymore, but regrettably I got introduced to **slănină** the wrong way – when you're not expecting it to be a hot, crunchy French fry, it's actually pretty good.

The most common way to eat **slănină** is to throw it on the grill and get it nice and toasted and then eat it with (raw red) onions. Recently, I was talking to a friend of mine who had just gone to a "barbeque" slash cookout and I asked her if she had eaten any **slănină** and onions. She looked at me as if I had asked her if the sky was blue. "Of course!" was her reply.

Another popular method to eat it is to impale a slice of **slănină** on a wooden stick, roasting it over a campfire until it begins to melt and then catching the drippings on a piece of bread.

I know to many western sensibilities, **slănină** seems a little "wrong" in the sense that it's all, you know, *pure fat*. But really it's just a cousin of ordinary bacon. And if you DO eat meat and you DO like bacon, give **slănină** a try. I think you'll really like it.

## Mămăligă

Ah yes, time to talk about the single most important Romanian food of all time – **mămăligă** (*mama-league-ah*).

Any time I ever mention this food, *ever*, anywhere, within hearing range of an English-speaking person born anywhere on the planet, they immediately say, "Oh yeah it's just like polenta". No! No, no, no and no.

Folks, polenta and **mămăligă** are <u>very similar</u> but they are not the same. Polenta has its own merits and qualities and is used in Italian cooking and is delicious and I wish you many happy meals of polenta in your journeys to Italy or in your fancy dinners at Italian restaurants in America (or wherever) as you dream of summers in Tuscany and all that but polenta and **mămăligă** are not the same.

Neither is **mămăligă** something called "corn mush", eaten in the southern United States. I've eaten corn mush before and it's a lot closer to the Romanian food but it's still not the same.

So what is the real deal 100% Romanian food **mămăligă**? Well quite simply put, it is boiled corn meal. That's it. I know, right? After all that razzle-dazzle, you were expecting something amazing and jaw-dropping and complicated but it's not. It's an *extremely simple food*.

To understand Romania and to understand **mămăligă**, you have to understand that food here is what's known as peasant food. It's food so simple, so readily available, so affordable that even the poorest guy out there in his simple little house can come home after a hard day working in the field and eat it. And that, friends, is **mămăligă**. In fact, there's an old Romanian expression "the guy is so poor he doesn't even have **mămăligă** to eat".

Because it is such a simple dish to prepare, I'm going to tell you how to cook your own **mămăligă** and then how to serve/eat it.

<u>Ingredients</u>

1 x corn meal
4 x water

Materials

1 pot (big enough to hold everything – duh)
1 long handled spoon (preferably wooden to be Authentic Romanian)

Yep, that's it. If you want to use one cup of corn meal, add 4 cups of water. If you want to use 1 gallon of corn meal (hey, you might be REALLY, REALLY hungry) use 4 gallons of water. Just whatever *volume* (not weight) of corn meal you're planning on cooking, add four times the water.

**Step 1**

In a pot, any old regular pot you've got in your kitchen, of any make, model, material or condition, add the water. Get said water to boil.

**Step 2**

After water is boiling, reduce heat to the lowest possible setting on your stove that's still "on" and producing heat.

**Step 3**

Begin pouring in corn meal *slowly*. Don't just dump it in there but pour it in there slowly. Meanwhile keep stirring. Stir, add some more, stir, add some more, stir, add some more until all the corn meal is now in the water.

Note: whether you use a whisk or a spoon, be sure that sucker has a LONG HANDLE. The vapors coming off the pot are going to be hot so you really don't want to cook your fingers while stirring, do ya?

**Step 4**

Keep stirring occasionally. You don't have to stir non-stop but if the pot looks like one of those mud geysers that's burping out wet, farty blurps like a volcano, it's time to stir some more. If someone rings your doorbell, you can walk over to the door and answer it and let them in but just say hello and come back and keep stirring. The main thing here is to keep it from burping a big wet mash of hot corn meal all over your kitchen wall.

**Step 5**

It's done being cooked. How do you know? Well two ways. One is, as you are stirring, you will notice it begins to stick to the side of the pot before collapsing back into the mix. The second way is take a spoonful and put it onto a plate. If it gels up and looks semi-rigid within 60 seconds, the **mămăligă** is done.

## Step 6 – Serving it

I told my mother how to make this recipe and then she went nuts and decided to make it super fancy and a meal unto itself and added eggs and cheese and meat and I don't know what else. Certainly you're free to do this yourself as I can't stop you but in my opinion **mămăligă** is best when it's *kept simple*, a kind of "bread" to accompany some OTHER main dishes of your meal.

In fact, **mămăligă** is quite filling UNTO ITSELF so if you jazz it up with a ton of dairy and meat and whatnot, your stomach is probably going to explode (but you'll die happy, so that's a plus).

I've eaten **mămăligă** all over Romania so there are 50 million ways to eat it so below are a few ideas on how to serve it:

Simple American style

Spoon out a layer of **mămăligă** on the bottom of a plate/dish. Add a layer of shredded cheese (note: shred your own cheese as pre-shredded cheese is a nastiness beyond description) OR if you want to go buck wild, use some feta cheese (highly recommended). Spoon out another layer of **mămăligă** on top of that. The "icing" on this **mămăligă** cake can be either plain yogurt (lower fat) or sour cream (better tasting).

Let this "cake" cool for 2-3 minutes and you will see it "gels" to the point where you can eat it with a fork and it holds together.

Simple Cluj style

Again make the "cake" as above but use **telemea** cheese (see page 68) and add homemade (sliced) pickles on the top along with the sour cream.

Simple Moldovan style

Don't even bother making the "cake", just keep your **mămăligă** separate on one side of the plate (adding a little salt) and then have the soft cheese of your preference (**brânza** – *bruhn-zah*) on the other. Mix and match bites using your fork.

Simple vegan style – my favorite

Again, make the "cake" but for the layers you want a good **mujdei de usturoi** (*mooj-day day 'ooster-oy*). This is the world's simplest sauce so I'm going to tell you how to make it right here because it's very tasty.

- ❖ 6-10 cloves of garlic, peeled and then mashed/smashed into tiny bits
- ❖ pinch of salt
- ❖ some oil (sunflower in Romania but anything BUT olive oil works great)

Put it all in a cup and stir it like crazy with a spoon until it's well mixed. You don't need to make 20 liters of this ahead of time – just make as much as you need. It's going to be extremely garlicky, which is true, but it goes wonderfully with **mămăligă** like you can't believe.

As I mentioned before, keep **mămăligă** simple – at least at first. It's meant to be something on the side you eat WITH a main meal, not **mămăligă** all unto itself.

**Mămăligă** is completely fat-free, cholesterol-free and sodium-free until you begin to add other ingredients so it's a great way to get that "filling bread feel" along with a main dish of your choice. I personally recommend some **mămăligă** along with a good soup as a wonderful lunch. Romanians tend to eat it with just about anything else around for lunch and dinner.

If you own one of those accursed devices known as a "microwave" then let it be known that **mămăligă** re-heats extremely well if you have any leftovers for another time.

Note: In Hungarian, this dish is known as **puliszka**.

**Sarmale**

If there is one national "comfort food" in Romania, it has to be the dish **sarmale** (*sar-mall-eh*), inherited from the long centuries of Turkish rule.

Simply put, **sarmale** are cabbage leaves[38] which are folded around a special filling into little "packages" and then (further) cooked.

Because this is a Balkans-wide dish, there are many variants of *sarmale* but the Romanian version generally has two different methods.

Method one is using (pre-)pickled cabbage leaves. That is to say, the whole cabbage leaves were previously allowed to ferment in a similar way that cucumbers are pickled.

Method two, assuming you don't have/want pickled leaves is to briefly blanche the cabbage leaves and then add **borş** (*boarsh*). This sounds a little bit like the Russian soup *borscht* but in Romania it has nothing to do

---

[38] Occasionally grape or other leaves are used.

with that. **Borș** is instead a liquid concoction you can buy here that is very sour. It is essentially "pickle juice" made from fermenting sugar beets.

Either way, the dish **sarmale** is never complete without some kind of souring agent, as it adds a nice tang to the filling.

Again, the filling varies from household to household and region to region but generally consists of rice, tomato (paste) and some kind of minced meat, often pork.  The filling is cooked and prepared and then spooned into the cabbage leaves, which are tightly rolled and placed in a dish. The dish is then (partially) filled with liquid and cooked further, sealing in all the juices and goodness.

When served (piping hot is best), the most common thing to do is add a dollop of sour cream right on top just before eating. And yes, the most popular side dish to accompany some delicious sarmale is the other Romanian classic, **mămăligă** (page 46).

Because making **sarmale** takes a lot of work, usually these are saved for special occasions (especially Christmas) so you're in for a real treat if someone makes you homemade **sarmale**. In fact, this is probably your only chance to get some in Romania as they are rarely sold in restaurants.

There is also a vegetarian version called **sarmale de post**, eaten during the Lenten season (see page 71) wherein the filling is chiefly composed of rice and mushrooms.

The heartiness of the cabbage roll and the rice and meat (or mushrooms) mixture gives every **sarmale** a solid weight and a good, warm feeling in your belly. Do not miss out on this national treat!

**Pizza**

It seems just about every visitor to Romania ends up noticing the vast plethora of pizza restaurants in this country – simply put, they're everywhere.

The quality of pizza you will find ranges from barely edible to absolutely heavenly and it's fairly likely that you'll end up sitting down in a restaurant and ordering some while you're here.

Since this dish is served a little differently in Romania, it can be confusing to some. The first thing to understand is that most of the time all pizza orders are for a "one person" pizza – i.e. each person orders their own separate pizza.

Sometimes you'll get your choice of sizes, usually listed in the menu by their weight (in grams), often called **mic** (small), **mediu** (medium) and **mare** (large). But if you don't see any mention of sizes, assume that all pizzas are "one person" size. The law states that the weight of each pizza must be included on the menu although in some cases it isn't.

**450 grams = 1 pound**[39]

Secondly, in about 99% of all cases, the crust (dough) will be very, very thin, also known as Neapolitan (from Naples, Italy) or "old skool European" style, and quite often crunchy. As far as my brain can remember, the multinational chain *Pizza Hut* is the only place I've ever seen a thicker, chewier crust option for pizza in Romania.

What's always been odd to me is rarely does the customer (you!) get to choose the toppings in Romania. Instead, the menu will list a variety of pizzas by name and then list the ingredients below in Romanian only, or if they feel like being fancy they'll also write them in Italian.

If you see a pizza you like but it has one ingredient you don't want, just tell the waiter/waitress **fără x** (*fuh-ruh*) where **x** is the ingredient you don't want. It's far easier (and comprehensible to your wait person) if you order a pizza *minus* some toppings than a pizza *plus* some specific toppings.

Below are a few names of the most common pizzas and their ingredients. You may notice most of them are in Italian. Again, this is how Romanian pizza restaurants look "cool". Often the spelling of the Italian is horrendously mangled.

**Piadina** – Just the crust with olive oil and some herbs on it and neither red tomato sauce nor cheese.

**Margherita** – Your basic pizza: crust, cheese and red tomato sauce. Theoretically it's supposed to have basil sprinkled on top but it almost never does in Romania.

**Quattro Stagioni** – Literally means "four seasons" so each quarter of the pizza has different toppings, consisting of meat, mushrooms and other vegetables.

**Quattro Formaggi** – Literally means "four cheeses" and theoretically *should* be made with four layers of different cheeses but in your lower end (crappier) restaurants, you might just get two layers of the same cheese.

---

[39] For some basic conversion tables, see page 308.

**Canibale** – You guessed it, related to the word "cannibal". Always a lot of meat toppings, consisting of a combination of sausages. If you want a lot of meat on your pizza, this is a good choice.

**Prosciutto** – This means ham, sometimes written in Romanian: **şunca** (*shoon-kah*).

**Prosciutto e Funghi** – Exactly the same as above except it also comes with mushrooms. Rarely but occasionally written in Romanian as **şunca şi ciuperci** (*she chew-perch*).

**Funghi** – This is a vegetarian pizza that is a **margherita** plus mushrooms. Be extremely careful however as sometimes you'll get the pizza above (ham and mushrooms) instead.

**Tonno (E Cippola)** – This means "tuna fish" and usually also has onions as well.

**Vegetariană** – Every vegetable in the restaurant on top of your pizza – often including eggplant, green peppers, mushrooms, peas, corn, onions and olives. Quite often the heaviest pizza on the menu and by far your most economical (price per weight), good to know for the budget traveler.

**Diavola** – Literally means "Devil" pizza. Usually the only pizza you can get anywhere that is remotely approaching spicy, as in *picante*. The toppings are a variety of spicy sausages.

**Salam(i)** – You guessed it again! This pizza's main topping is salami, which is very similar to or identical to what's known in some countries as pepperoni, which occasionally you will see as a separate pizza choice.

**Hawai'i** – Ham and pineapple.

**Fructe de Mare** – One of the few names almost always written in Romanian, this means "seafood" and can be just about anything.

And those are your most basic ones. Every restaurant has other pizzas as well with different toppings but for those you'll just have to decipher the ingredient list (see page 262). For sure you will usually find lots of combinations of pork, as that is the ingredient Romanians are insatiable for.

Probably the oddest ingredients for (some) visitors is usually there are several pizzas with corn (**porumb** – *poh-room*) as a topping as well as some with sour cream (**smântână** – *smun-tuna*).

Be aware that nine times out of 10, when a pizza comes with **măsline** – (*musleen-aye*) these are whole black olives with the stones still inside, perhaps just three or four per pizza.

Now let's talk about condiments.

Throughout Romania, it is quite popular to use ketchup as a condiment but usually you have to order it and pay for it separately.

I'm sure that upon hearing that, many of you will have the same reaction I did when I first came into contact with this practice – I shuddered in revulsion. I was imagining a thick, red sweet paste similar to the Heinz 57 version, something I rarely ever ate except with potatoes.

Ketchup in Romania is completely different. Ketchup in this country is much thinner and less tangy and more similar to the sauce on your pizza than the Heinz 57 variety.

Most Romanian pizzas come with very little tomato sauce. Therefore the ketchup is a way to add a little more sauce on top of your pizza. It often comes in both **dulce** (sweet) and mildly **iute** (spicy) varieties (see page 53).

In some cases the restaurant may have **sos iute** (*sauce you-teh*), a spicy sauce, or **sos cu usturoi** (*ooster-oy*), a white garlic sauce.

In just about every case, however, the wait staff will bring a small condiment tray to your table that has salt, pepper, oil and vinegar on it. These are free to use and many Romanians like to put oil on their pizza as a topping. Occasionally at some places you can get **ulei iute** (*ooh-lay*), which consists of hot peppers steeped in oil.

Very few other condiments are usually available, even at a separate price, including oregano, parmesan cheese or hot chili peppers.

The very tastiest pizzas in the world (including in Romania) are made in a special purpose oven, which has a very distinct, round shape. The fuel used to cook the pizza is wood and it has a delightful aroma.

In Italian this is written as **forno a legna** and in Romanian as **la vatră** (*la vatrah* – the name of a traditional peasant oven). Many restaurants use one or the other of these terms (or a combination) to let you know that they serve this kind of pizza.

The easiest thing to do is simply walk towards the back of the restaurant and take a peep at the kitchen. Pizza ovens are usually so huge (and put out so much heat) that they are easy to spot. In fact, quite often they're put on display front and center.

In most cities of decent size in Romania, pizza restaurants often have delivery services, known as **livrare (la domiciliu)**, literally meaning "delivery (to the domicile)" or house.

It's quite rare to get someone on the phone who speaks English, so your best bet is to ask a Romanian to order for you. If you're staying in a hotel/hostel, the easiest thing to do is ask the person at the front desk to order it for you. Sometimes they'll give you a song and dance about how they can't do it because it's "against the rules" but just blink your puppy dog eyes at them and usually they'll relent.

Be aware that it is sometimes common in smaller cities for the restaurant to deliver your pizza via taxi[40], which means you'll also have to pay the driver the normal fare (see page 109) on top of the price of the pizza. Even when the restaurant has their own vehicles, there's quite often a delivery charge except for large orders.

In the very biggest cities there are a few restaurants (including with food besides pizza) that have websites where you can place an order. This quite often will result in someone calling you to confirm your order, so if you don't speak Romanian well just say "**da**" (yes) a lot.

As everywhere else, all orders should be paid for in cash. A small tip for prompt service is appreciated but in no cases is it ever mandated, although rounding up to the nearest **leu** is standard practice.

Be aware that if you have a pizza delivered or want to take some uneaten pizza home from the restaurant, you have to pay for the box or container, usually referred to in Romanian as **ambalaj** (packaging) or sometimes **cutie** (box).

### Langoşi/Placinte

While some people consider **langoşi** (*lawn-ghosh*) to be different than **placinte** (*plah-cheent-eh*), they are essentially the same, although the first comes etymologically via the Hungarian language and the second via Latin.

In both cases they are a large piece of round dough that is fried. Usually for **langoşi** the bread is fried first and then the toppings added afterwards while **placinte** have the filling added first and then they are fried.

---

[40] Although quite rare in Bucharest and in most of the larger cities, which have their own delivery vehicles.

By far, the most common topping/filling for this food is cheese and sour cream, referred to as **brânză şi smântănă** (*bruhn-zah she smunt-uh-nah*).

Another common topping is **mujdei de usturoi** (see page 48), an extremely garlicky sauce.

## Desserts

Much of Romanian cuisine is quite sour and overly sweet dishes are the exception rather than the rule.

That being said, there are some wonderful sweet treats to eat in Romania.

## Clătite

Although generally referred to as Romanian "pancakes", these are much thinner creations, often served with a very sweet topping and eaten as a dessert. The **clătite** (*cluh-teet-eh*) are made from a thin batter of flour and eggs, most similar to a French crêpe. Since the Romanian word **clătite** is plural, usually an order will get you 2-3 pancakes.

While sweet toppings such as chocolate or caramel are popular (sometimes with ice cream as well), other common choices include cheeses and/or sour cream.

**Clătite** are often made and eaten at home but most sit-down "proper" restaurants will have them on the menu. Additionally, in some cities you will find fast-food restaurants that specialize in them.

## Papanaşi

Known sometimes as "donuts", **papanaşi** (*poppa-nosh*) are little fried rounds of dough, usually sprinkled with powdered sugar and/or jam before serving.

Quite delicious!

## Gogoşi

While technically these are often referred to as "donuts", they're actually much closer to a **placinta** (page 54), a fried piece of large dough that's been folded around a filling.

While many flavors (fillings) are available and these are quite tasty treats, they are nothing like a standard American "donut" in any way. Some variants are largely just a slightly sweetened dinner roll.

**Romanian Food For Special Occasions**

Christmas (page 121) and Easter (see page 118) are universally occasions for great feasting and it is quite traditional to prepare a lot of foods.

Especially in rural areas, an entire pig is slaughtered before Christmas to provide a wide variety of meats.

Also, the national dish **sarmale** (see page 49) is often made for Christmas.

A lot of desserts are prepared for the Christmas and Easter seasons, the most ubiquitous of which is **cozonac** (*co-zo-knock*), a loaf of mildly sweet bread, similar to "fruit cake" in other countries.

The biggest feast of the year for most Romanians occurs during Easter, and is the occasion for eating a lot of meat prepared from lamb (**miel** – *me-el*).

One of the most famous Easter dishes is known as **drob** (rhymes with *lobe*) **de miel**, and is perhaps most similar to the Scottish dish *haggis*. **Drob** is a combination of organ meats, minced and spiced and then roasted in the oven.

There is also a strong tradition of coloring and eating boiled eggs for Easter but in Romania these are almost always dyed red.

For food served primarily at funerals, see page 236.

For food served at weddings, see page 235.

**Fast Food**

A few years ago, my verrah own mother came to visit me here in Romania. And despite trying and eating homemade foods here as well as at "proper" sit-down restaurants, she kept returning over and over again to the **fast food**.

It's easy to understand why, even if the food isn't of the highest quality nor is really cheaper than other places to eat. It is, however, convenient and tasty.

Although a few major, international fast-food chain restaurants (like McDonald's and KFC) exist here in Romania, the vast majority of fast-food is sold at corner "mom and pop" operations with no corporate name, image, logo or marketing involved whatsoever.

Note: A meal eaten from an international chain is actually quite expensive. Un-named Romanian fast-foods are much cheaper (and better, in my opinion) by far.

56

<u>Most workers at international fast-food chains (McDonald's, etc) do not speak English</u>. I know it's disconcerting but so it is.

Since Romanians use the English word (*fast-food* not *mâncare repede*) on all signage, a **fast-food** is really easy to spot for the foreign traveler. Most **fast-foods** consist solely of a sidewalk, walk-up window. Occasionally some have an interior restaurant where you can sit down, but the menu is roughly the same either way.

What's for sale varies slightly by city and by region, but below is the core menu:

**Shawarma** (*shah-warm-ah* but often just *shwarm-ah*) – Because this is an Arabic word (and Arab food), it has a wide variety of spellings, especially ones which more phonetically resemble the pronunciation, such as **shaoarma**, etc.

This is a large hunk of mixed meat that sits on a thin, metal spike that rotates in front of a heat source. As the outer layers get cooked, the restaurant worker shaves them off with a knife into strips, which are piled together in a sandwich.

Technically the meat can be anything (including blends of different meats) but in Romania it is often pork. If it made of chicken it is sometimes differentiated as **shawarma de pui**.

**(Doner) Kebab** (*keh-pop*) – Essentially exactly the same as shawarma except it may be of higher quality meat. Sometimes can even be composed partially or entirely of lamb meat, which is considered "more authentic".

**Schnitzel** (*shneet-zell*) – Again because this is a foreign word (it's an Austrian dish), it has variable spellings to more accurately reflect Romanian pronunciation, such as **șnițel**.

In all cases, this means some kind of meat that's been dipped in egg, breaded and fried. Usually this means pork in a Romanian fast-food as well. If it is solely comprised of chicken, once again it is sometimes differentiated as **schnitzel de pui**.

**Cașcaval Pane** (*cawsh-ka-vol pon-eh*) – Similar to *snitzel* above, this is a thick slice of cheese that's been dipped in egg, breaded and fried. Since this is a name derived entirely from Latin, the spelling is thankfully always the same.

**Hamburger** (*hum-boo-ghare*) – Again, a foreign word so occasionally spelled in various ways.

Theoretically this should always be a slice of beef but it isn't always so. Beef in Romania is generally of fairly low quality throughout and so your expectations of what this should be might be contrary to what a *hamburger* is in Romania.

If it helps, think of it more as a slice of beef SPAM rather than a juicy, All-American "God Bless Texas" burger.

**Cheeseburger** (*cheece-boo-ghare*) – This is sometimes written as *Hamburger cu Caşcaval* meaning of course, a hamburger with cheese.

Same as hamburger above except with a slice of low-quality individually wrapped cheese added, sometimes not even melted, added to the sandwich.

**Gordon Bleu** (*gore-dawn blue*) – This one always makes me smile because in English it's known as *Cordon Bleu*, both languages of course butchering the original French.

In Romania however, this is a **şnitzel** sandwich (see above) that's been filled or wrapped with cheese and a slice of ham.

All of the items listed above are sandwiches, that is to say, they consist of a bun holding the "filling" and some condiments.

In Romania the word for sandwich is spelled in several different ways but it is always pronounced *send-veesh*.

All sandwiches also are available in a "platter" variety, which is called **la farfurie** (*lah far-foor-ee-eh*), literally meaning "for the plate".

Before I explain what all that means, let's go through the process of ordering a sandwich.

**You**: *O shawarma, vă rog* (one shawarma, please).

Quite often, there is a choice of bread to be made and if there is, the worker will quiz you. Here are a few common ones:

**La chiflă?** (*lah kee-fluh*) – This means in a "regular", round sandwich bun.

**La lipie?** (*lah lee-pee-eh*) – This means the filling is placed into a kind of flat bread and rolled into a kind of cylinder, sometimes called a "wrap" in English.

**Pâine araba** – The same thing as **lipie** and pronounced *pwee-nay ah-rob-ah*, although occasionally it may be closer to true Middle Eastern "pita" or flatbread.

**Prajit(a)?** (*prah-zheet ah*) – This means "toasted", as in the sandwich is put in a kind of two-sided grill and squashed but the entire sandwich gets quite crispy and crunchy.

This grilling/toasting process may also sometimes be referred to as *la toast* or *toastat*. I've also occasionally seen it referred to as *presat*.

---

After you choose your bread style, the worker will start getting busy making your sandwich and then tell you the price and you pay, using *Standard Romanian Money Touching Rules*, i.e. don't touch their hands ever, if possible (see page 40).

It's very important to understand that, in almost all sandwiches, the worker will add the filling you ordered (i.e., shnitzel) **and** some french fries (UK: chips) automatically to the sandwich.

For some reason, this irritates some foreigners so if you do *not* want french fries added to the meat/filling inside your sandwich, you have to speak up and stop them. The phrase for this: **fără cartofi** (*furrah car-toaf* literally "without potatoes").

Then you get to choose your toppings. Often the worker will prompt you by saying **de toate** (*day-twat-tay*)?

This means "with everything" and can often mean a ton of different condiments, so unless you're sure what all of the "*toate*" are just pass on this option.

The most common:

**Ketchup** – Pronounced the same as English more or less, this is far sweeter and yummier and "thinner" than mainstream American ketchup.

Normally just saying "ketchup" will get you what's sometimes specified as **ketchup dulce** or sweet ketchup.

The other kind of ketchup, **ketchup iute** (*yoo-tay*) means "spicy" or hot ketchup, although the truth is that this is often extremely mild and only slightly hotter than regular, "dulce" ketchup.

For more information on Romanian ketchup, see page 53.

**Maioneză** (*my own eza*) – Obviously mayonnaise. If you can see the receptacle holding the mayonnaise and notice it has a more "custardy" look to it, perhaps with a slightly yellow tint, you've hit the jackpot because this means it is homemade.

**(Salată de) Varză** (*sah-lotta day var-zah*) – Usually means a kind of "salad" of finely shredded cabbage that's been dressed with oil or pickled.

**Castraveți (Murați)** (*cah-strah-vet-eh moo-rots*) – What in English would be called pickles, as in cucumbers that have been pickled.

However there can be a few other exotic choices as well:

**Muştar** (moosh-tar) – Regular, yellow mustard. Romanians rarely eat mustard on anything but **mici** (page 43) and sausages.

**Tzatziki** (*sot-seeky*) – A thin, white sauce made with cucumbers, garlic and yog(h)urt. Because this is from a Greek word, there are other more phonetic spellings used as well.

**Sos cu usturoi** (*soze koo 'ooster-oy*) – Garlic sauce. See page 53.

**Porumb** (*poe-roombh*) – Kernels of corn, quite sweet.

**Roşii** (*roh-shee*) – Slices of raw tomato.

**Sfeclă Roşie** – (*sfeck-lah ro-shi-eh*) – Beets, quite often pickled.

In nearly all cases, at a "mom and pop" Romanian fast-food, whatever toppings/condiments you see offered are included with the price of the sandwich. Very rarely do you have to pay for any normal topping, even if you want a little extra.

However, in all international mega-chains like McDonald's, etc, those operations make you pay for *every deviation* from the menu as an extra charge. That means every packet of ketchup (or other condiment) is sold separately.

---

Once you've communicated (or pointed your finger at) your toppings order, the worker will slop each of these on your sandwich in progressive layers.

If you're at a walk-up window, you must next communicate how you wish to have your sandwich packaged.

**La mână?** (*lah muh-nuh*) – Literally "at the hand" this means you plan on eating the sandwich immediately. It will be put in some kind of paper envelope or outer layer and <u>exactly two napkins</u> will be wrapped around that as the outside layer.

-OR-

**La pachet?** (*lah-pock-ette*) – Literally "at the package", meaning wrapped up as a "to go" or "take away" sandwich. Or in simpler terms, if you're not going to eat the sandwich immediately, ask them to give it to you *la pachet.*

Amazingly, shockingly, astoundingly difficult as it is to believe, *in almost all cases "la pachet" does not cost you any extra money*! Surprising, isn't it? I know.

At this point, the worker hands you your **sendviş** and off you go on your merry way, plowing your mouth into a tremendously large serving of hot, steamy goodness on a bun. Clearly none of the these foods are in any way low in fat or calories but they can be quite tasty.

Another quite surprising thing is that most fast-foods in Romania serve a *very* generously sized sandwich, sometimes freakishly huge.

But wait a second, remember all that **la farfurie** stuff I mentioned above? Well, I had to tell you about how to order a sandwich in order to explain what "at the plate" means.

**Sendviş** = Bun/Wrap that is filled with main filling then topped with condiments.

**La farfurie** = A plate where the bun/wrap is separate from the main filling which is separate from the condiments, which tend to be solely the big four listed above (ketchup, mayo, pickles, cabbage).

Usually the portion of the filling is larger and so the price for the **la farfurie** variant is therefore higher.

Not every single fast-food has both variants but if they do, it should be written on the menu somewhere. Occasionally they'll ask you from the outset if you want it **un sendviş** or **la farfurie**.

A few other things you can get at most Romanian fast-foods that aren't sandwiches or *la farfurie*.

First though, it's good to know **o porție de** (*oh portsy a day*) meaning "one portion of…"

**Aripi de pui** (*ah-reap day pwee*) – Fried chicken wings, just like your sweet old granny made ever' Sunday after church!

**Cartofi pai** (*car-TOAF pie*) – French fries or, in UKEnglish, "chips".

Unfortunately, it is considered normal practice to serve french fries at room temperature. The only way to get hot fries/chips is to be there fortuitously when they make a fresh batch.

Note: Usually the price listed is per 100 grams so you can order as much as you want (by specifying how many grams you want).

**Cartofi prajiți** (*car-TOAF pra-zheets*) – Exactly the same as above. *Pai* simply means (in the shape of a) straw and *prajiti* means "fried."

**Salată de varză** – Exactly the same as above in the list of toppings.

What about the drink?

In the Romanian language, all soft drinks are generically called **suc** (*sook*). In all fast food situations of the "mom and pop" variety, all items are sold separately, including the drink.

If soft drinks are served, they will be listed on the menu with their price. In every local fast-food, these will always be <u>bottled drinks</u>, consisting of your standard hyper-galactic corporation's choices, namely a cola, a diet/light cola, a fizzy orange drink, a fizzy lemon one, a tea-flavored non-carbonated one and both "flat" and "sparkling" water.

Due to the Romanian Iron Law of Cold Drinks (see page 75), be aware that these bottled drinks may or may not be any colder than room temperature and are only rarely likely to be quite cold indeed. Ice, in all "mom and pop" operations, does not exist.

Your standard international fast-food chains (McDonald's etc) serves their normal "menus" or "combo meals" that do include a fountain drink.

**Hotel/Hostel Breakfast**

If you are staying in a luxury hotel and breakfast is included in the price, by all means go for it. It will usually consist of coffee, some kind of bread, slices of meat, slices of cheese and some raw vegetables, especially tomatoes and cucumbers.

Incidentally, this is just about what an average Romanian would be eating at home for breakfast.

If breakfast is offered as a separate option that you have to pay for, particularly if it is priced in euros (page 41), it's probably far more expensive than it needs to be.

In almost every case, it is cheaper and easier to simply buy your breakfast on the street, as Romanians quite often do as well.

**The Piața**

This is absolutely the best (and cheapest) place to get food in Romania. If you want an authentic experience *and* save money then understanding the **piața** is of vital importance.

Not to be confused with the Romanian word for town square/plaza (page 31), the word **piața** (*pee-AHTza)* in Romanian also means "market" and refers to a location where fruits, vegetables, meats and dairy products are sold, often directly from the farmer him/herself.

The correct long form is **piața agroalimentara** meaning "market of agricultural foodstuffs". Every Romanian city will have one or more **piețe** (*pee-EHT-zay*) that are open seven days a week.

Due to what the nature of the **piața** is, all of the food being sold there is fresh and in season. There are some obvious imports (bananas, pineapples, etc) but a good part of what's being sold is fresh local produce.

Not only that but because it is essentially being sold at wholesale, the prices are lower than absolutely anywhere else. So you're paying the *least* amount of money for the *best* food.

Note: It is rare to non-existent to find sellers who speak a foreign language.

Depending on where you are, you're going to find one of two different versions in your neck of the woods.

- **Open Air, Rough and Rowdy**, or
- **Semi-Indoors and Stuffy**

The mayor of Cluj-Napoca went hog wild in the past few years and therefore pretty much all these "markets" in town are of the second variety. In other cities it's hit or miss.

Whether it's out in the open and treading over muddy paths or inside a large barn-type structure, the **piața** is going to be a warren of plastic tables with a wide gamut of people behind them, hawking various fruits, vegetables, dairy products and meat.

If possible, always go to the BIGGEST **piața** in the city as it usually will be the best as well.

Orienting Yourself

Due to refrigeration laws, the meats (and if you love meat, they got it here from snout to tail) are always going to be in a separate area along the sides. Likewise the dairy products are usually sold in separate areas along the side. Usually you can smell the cheese from about 50 meters[41] distance.

Other small stores you might see on the sides: eggs, honey and bee products, pickled vegetables.

At the direct main entrance there should be a public scale (Rom: **cântar** – cun-tar**)** provided by the government for verification of sales. Also scan around and see if you see any publicly-accessible wash basins (especially for **backpackers** on the go).

In the center and dominating most of the action is a maze of plastic tables piled high with fruits and vegetables (and honey/bee products). Behind each table is the seller. In front of each product is written the price (always in **lei**) per kilo (or per bundle).

Most sellers in _Indoor, Semi-Stuffy_ **piețe** have digital scales.  However be on the look out for manual ones, especially in outdoor markets.

Equipment Necessary

Some kind of bag, carrier, backpack or holdall or something with which to lug all your purchases out with you. You can buy one inside if you like for between **1-5 lei** (depending on size and strength).

Small bills of cash. This is not the place for credit cards or plastic of any kind. This is a cash wheel and deal situation and you don't need large bills. It might be very hard to change them so don't bring anything into play larger than a 50 lei note. It's also good to have coins to make/pay change with as well.

---

[41] 164 feet

Phrases to Know

**_Poftiți_** (*pofe-teets*). This is what all the sellers will yell at you as you pass. It can mean a lot of things depending on the usage but here it means something along the lines of "how may I take your order, sir/madam?"

**_Un kilogram_** (*oon keelogrom*) – Ordering one kilogram (2.2 lbs) of whatever item.

**_O jumatate de kilo_** (*oh jew-mah-tah-tay day keelo*) – Ordering one half of a kilogram of something.

How to Get a Good Deal on Fruits/Vegetables

The first thing to do is take a walk throughout the entire **piața** or through the sections with the kind of foods you might be interested in buying.

Compare the prices with one another. As well, compare which ones look the freshest or the most wholesome or appealing. Also you need just to get a feel for what's in there and what looks like a good purchase for your needs/financial ability.

Let's say you've got your eye on some apples and you've done your walk-through and found a couple of semi-appealing stalls, each selling what looks like the same kind of apples for the same price.

First, the price you see is per kilogram. Do you want a kilo (2.2 lbs) or just a single apple? If you only want a few/little of any item, check and see if the seller has a digital scale. If they do, this operation is a lot easier.

Following the correct market protocol (see below), select the items you want and hand them to the seller. She (rarely he) will tell you the price in Romanian. If they're reading off a digital scale, you might be able to see the price yourself but be aware a lot of scales still use the old money denominations so everything has a bunch of extra zeroes on it.

Dirt Market Protocol

Despite the fact that *you're* the buyer, the sellers in outdoor **piețe** are all quite surly and grumpy. You are allowed to eyeball their produce but as soon as you start touching it, you'll get yelled at.

Should you want something, you simply tell the seller what you want (3 apples or 1 kilogram of apples) and she will brutally scoop it up into a bag for you. Often she will try to upsell you to a slightly better deal if you buy a little bit more.

It's always better if you have your own plastic bag because otherwise you might be forced to buy one off the seller.

Whenever you're doing haggling, you put the money and lay it on the fruit/vegetables itself and never hand it to her directly. Unless perhaps it's a single bill and you make sure your fingers don't touch (see page 40 for more about this).

Stuffy Indoor Barn Protocol

Sellers are a lot less surly but some of them may be quite country and mumbly and difficult to understand.

Paw through the items and hand what you want to the seller. She will then weigh it and tell you the price. Or just order a kilogram and let her do the picking and sorting. If the seller is handling the produce, watch out that they don't slip a few bruised/rotting items into the bag.

Many sellers have digital scales which makes buying just a handful of fruit/vegetables a lot easier. This results in prices often ending with the need for someone to exchange coins and so if you have the ability to pay in coins, the seller is much happier.

Usually the bag comes for "free".

Once again, always lay your money down on the produce and not in the person's hand (see page 40).

Crowd

There is a good chance that throngs of people will be milling around alongside you, making shopping in the market a bad idea for anyone who is claustrophobic.

See also page 129 for more on this.

## What Grows in Romania

Local food is the best and this is some of the best (for a complete list of Romanian fruits and vegetables, see page 265). When these are in season, they are incredibly delicious. I think 50% of the reason I live here is because of how delicious the tomatoes are in the summer. It's indescribable. You just have to taste them.

Oh yeah and the strawberries! Whew, I could wrote sonnets about them.

In additional you'll find a couple of local vegetables that aren't commonly found elsewhere:

**Dovlecei** – (*dove-lay-chey*) a kind of squash or zucchini, usually immense in size.

**Gogoşari** – (*go-go-shar*) a variant of a (bell) pepper that has a unique taste. It is also the critical ingredient in **zacuscă** (page 72).

## Meat Buying

I don't really eat meat anymore but I can tell you the set up is that Romanians generally eat a lot of chicken (**pui** – *pwee*) and pork (**porc**) so you're going to find lots of this.    For a full list of vocabulary words concerning meat, see page 262.

Beef (**carne de vită** – *car-nay day vee-tah*) is to be had but at a high price and maybe not the cut you were looking for.

Especially around Easter time, a lot of lamb is sold (**miel** – *mee-el*).

A good indoor **piața** may also have *live* fish and usually you can get pretty fresh or frozen fish of a few types, where available.

## Eggs

When eggs (**ouă** – *oh-ah*) are sold, they can usually be bought individually, as in one at a time.  Other times they also come in small plastic bags or containers of 3, 6 or 12 apiece, for the price marked.

During Easter, Romanians like to hardboil and dye eggs red (page 56).

Dairy

You can get a fresh liter of milk (**lapte** – *lop-tay*) at a good price but for everything else, you need to know your dairy on sight or else know the Romanian names for what you want. Especially the cheeses, many of which exist only here and therefore have no true translation. The good news is that the sellers will always let you taste a bite of each kind before you buy it.

Note: the soggy looking white wet cheese is incredibly delicious, known as **telemea** (*teh-lay-may-ah*), a cousin to the more well-known feta cheese.

Honey/Bee Products

Romania has a thriving bee-keeping industry and produces honey and other natural bee products that are usually of extremely high quality.

Many **piețe** have vendors selling honey (**miere** – *me-air-eh*) of various sorts, including **miere de salcâm** (*day sull-come*) or honey made from the blossoms of acacia trees, considered to have restorative properties (it's also quite tasty).

Other apiary products such as honeycomb (**ceară** – *chah-rah*), pollen (**polen**) and **propolis** (which is used to treat certain ailments) are available for a very good price.

**Hungarian Food**

Wherever Hungarians still live today, you can find many of their traditional foods for sale and these can be quite delicious.

Romanian food is very "bland" so if you like spicy food, try out a Hungarian restaurant for some truly fiery food – I've tasted some sauces that would melt the paint off the walls, which isn't something you'd normally expect from such a calm people.

Hungarian cuisine is also famous for its use of **paprika** and huge sacks of the spice are sold in the markets where they congregate.

The most famous of all Hungarian foods is **goulash** (Hun: *gulyás*, pronounced roughly the same as English), a kind of thick and hearty stew, often referred to by the longer name of *gulyásleves*.

Another super tasty treat is **kürtős kalács** (*kurt-osh ka-latch*), which is popular for a good reason. It's a kind of hollowed out tube of pastry with a sugar or cinnamon topping and is quite delicious.

## Vegetarian, Vegan and Raw Foods

### Vegetarian

This means not eating meat but still consuming dairy and eggs (or perhaps even fish).

At just about any **fast food** (see page 56 for a complete guide to fast-food restaurants), there are a number of vegetarian options.

One is known as **caşcaval pane**, which literally means "breaded cheese". It's a thick slice of cheese, breaded (which includes eggs) and fried and served on bread, often with homemade mayonnaise (made from eggs), although the toppings are chosen by the customer (you).

Other fast foods have different sandwiches with the word "vegetal" in their title, meaning "vegetarian". Examples include **"hamburger vegetal"** and sometimes just **"sandwich vegetal"** and refers to a slice of processed vegetarian material on bread with the toppings of your choice, which again may include mayonnaise made with eggs. Without the mayonnaise, these sandwiches are usually vegan.

**Mămăligă** (page 46) is usually served with cheese and/or sour cream. Very rarely it does include meat but this will be listed on the menu if that's the case.

Romanians are avid consumers of pizza (which varies in quality from utter crap to fantastically delicious) and most restaurants have a "*vegetariană*" option, usually the contents of an entire garden's worth of vegetables on top (including peas and corn).

The plain version of pizza, i.e. sauce, cheese and nothing else is known as a **pizza margherita**. Technically speaking, a "margherita" should include basil on top as the third ingredient but it rarely does.

Most pizza places also have a mushroom (**ciuperci** (*choo-pear-ch*) or often the Italian word *funghi*) choice which is vegetarian. Beware though that another common pizza is **şunca şi ciuperci** (ham and mushroom) so avoid that one.

Another vegetarian pizza is **quattro formaggi** (*kwah-tro for-mah-jee*) from the Italian meaning "four cheeses". Unless you're eating at a quality place, avoid this as often this is an overpriced rip-off and not worth it compared to the **margherita** option.

For the complete guide on pizzas, see page 50.

**Cartofi** (*kar-toaf*) – Romanians grow a lot of potatoes and serve them in a variety of ways, almost always vegetarian. That being said, watch out for some of the baked varieties (i.e. **cartofi ţaraneşti** or "country style") as cooks here have a tendency to add lots of MSG (known in Romanian as **vegeta**).

Stuffed mushrooms (**ciuperci umplute** – *choo-pear-ch oom-plew-tay*), a common and much-beloved side dish, usually filled with cheese and baked. Delicious!

**Orez şi ciuperci** (*or-ez she choo-pear-ch)*, a common side dish meaning "rice and mushrooms", this too is often flavored with MSG.

**Pilaf de orez** (*pee-laugh day or-ez)*, another common side dish meaning just a portion of plain (but savory) rice, often commonly flavored with MSG.

Salads (**salate**) – With a few exceptions, most salads here in Romania are made with mayonnaise and meat so you've got to read through the ingredients carefully before ordering.

That being said, two very famous (and delicious) Romanian salads are always vegetarian – **salată de vinete** (*sah-lah-tah day veen-eh-tay* - eggplant salad) and **salată de ciuperci** (*sah-lah-tah day choo-pear-ch* - mushroom salad), both made with mayonnaise.

I hated eggplant my entire life until I tried some **salată de vinete**, which is usually eaten as a spread on a single slice of bread. As for the "mushroom salad", it is extraordinarily tasty and I've never known anyone, foreign or Romanian, who didn't rave about it.

Some vegetables are served **pane** (*pon-eh* - breaded), especially **dovlecei** (a local squash – page 67) and **conopide** (*cone-oh-pee-day* - cauliflower). Sliced and breaded and fried and quite tasty. Otherwise vegan except that eggs are usually used to stick the breaded coating to the vegetables in question.

Note: the Romanian word for lettuce is **salată verde** and simply means the vegetable alone rather than a mixture of vegetables.

Honey in Romania is absolutely the best I've ever tasted, cultivated in the "old ways" and sold freshly harvested in the **piaţa** or market (page 63). Other bee products include the honeycomb, wax, pollen and royal jelly.

If you do eat fish, there are a wide variety of grilled fish dishes usually available as well as **salată de icre** (*sah-lah-tah day eek-ray*), a form of spreadable caviar often eaten with bread. That being said, other forms of seafood are rare except at the seaside.

## Vegan

This means that you neither eat meat nor any products coming from an animal (dairy, eggs, etc).

If you are vegan, you have hit the jackpot when it comes to Romania. This is because the Romanian Orthodox church encourages a twice-yearly dietary change known as the **post** (literally: "fasting"). If you're Catholic, think of giving up chocolate for Lent and it's roughly the same thing.

In the period before Christmas and Easter, all of the faithful are encouraged to eat **de post** (*day post*), which is 100% vegan with the sole exception that fish is allowed. Therefore, whether at a restaurant, fast food or grocery store, anything that is labeled as **de post** is 100% vegan (unless it has fish, which is easy to spot).

The rest of the year it's a little harder to get **de post** products but they can be found. Some examples:

**Maioneză de post** – Largely a chemical compound, it looks, smells and tastes almost exactly like regular mayonnaise but is 100% vegan. On the other hand, a number of Romanian cooks at home can make a much tastier and healthier version.

**Cașcaval vegetal** – A solid slice of faux "cheese" that is completely vegan, often used to make sandwiches. Some pizza places offer some or all of their pizzas to be made with **caș vegetal**, rendering them completely **de post**.

In any **fast food**, especially during the two fasting seasons, it is possible to get a completely vegan sandwich (anything labeled "vegetal") if mayonnaise is skipped or else is of the **de post** variety.

Not to be missed is **sarmale** (page 49), one of Romania's signature dishes, stuffed rolls made with cabbage leaves. The standard variety is made with meat but it's usually easy to get the vegetarian version, filled with rice and mushrooms instead (**orez și ciuperci**).

**Iahnie (de fasole)** (*yawn-ee-eh day fah-soul-lay*) – If you're American, think "pork and beans" but it is easy to find (especially at grocery stores) a vegan version, again labeled **de post**. In fact, most large grocery stories have a whole section of shelving with **de post** products. In Romania the beans are generally blended together to make a paste.

Not to be missed is **zacuscă**[42] (*zah-koo-skah*) which is about 500 times tastier when made at home than the varieties you can find at the store. This is always, always vegan and very popular even with the most ardent meat eaters in this country for a simple reason – it's freaking incredibly delicious. It derives its unique taste from **gogoşari**, a domestic variant of the "bell" pepper (page 67).

**Salată de ardei copţi** (*sah-lah-tah day ar-day copes*) – Meaning "roasted red bell pepper salad" it is the divine result of roasting peppers and them steeping them in oil and vinegar. Not to be missed!

### Raw Food

Meaning people who do not eat food that is cooked in any way. And yes, I do know raw foodists in Romania.

For the best choices, you want to visit the **piaţa** (open-air market, see page 63) and save money and load up on fresh fruits and vegetables. Selections are a lot fewer in the dead of winter but these days plenty of fresh fruit and vegetables are imported from warmer countries, including bananas, oranges, tomatoes and lemons.

**Salată de cruditaţi** (*sah-lah-tah day crew-dee-tots*) – Literally meaning "raw salad" it is a combination of raw vegetables, sometimes dressed with oil. The ingredients are usually listed on the menu.

**Salată de varză** (cabbage salad) – Easily my all-time favorite Romanian food, it is usually just shredded cabbage that is salted and (usually) either lemon or vinegar has been added. This too can easily be found in the **piaţa** and bought by weight.

**Salată de varză murata** – Same as above except the cabbage was pickled (*murata*) first. Quite sour for some tongues, it is an absolutely delicious side dish.

**Muraturi** (*moo-rah-tour*) – Just meaning "pickled vegetables", most commonly cauliflower, **gogoşari** (page 67), carrots and sometimes beets. This is a very common side dish and can be found homemade (at the **piaţa** or someone's home) as well as on the menu at restaurants.

For unpasteurized juice drinks, see "The Fresh" on page 79.

---

[42] from the Russian *закуска*

Raw (unpasteurized) milk and cheeses can be found for sale, usually only at the **piața** where they are called either *cruda* or *naturala* (both words meaning "raw").

# Drinks and Beverages
## Țuica, Palincă and Horincă

I grew up in cities and to me, alcohol was something other people made in some far-off place and then bottled and shipped to a store for me to buy. How alcohol was made was a mysterious enigma. In Romania, however, making your own alcohol is virtually a national right. Therefore over time I began to understand how it was done.

There are two kinds of alcoholic drinks, those that are *fermented* and those that are *fermented and then distilled*.

"Fermented" means yeast was added to something (grain, fruit, etc) which then converted some of the sugars into alcohol. Roughly speaking, drinks that are (only) fermented are wine and beer.

The problem with fermenting a big batch of plums is that you get a barrel of stinking, rotting fruit mixed in with the alcohol. Therefore this mess has to be distilled, which can be done in a number of ways, but always means a process by which the alcohol is *separated* from the other components of the liquid.

The most common distillation process is to heat the liquid and then capture the alcohol vapors in a (usually) copper tube, which then drip down into a container.

Almost all Romanian traditional strong drinks are made from fruit, which technically makes them a brandy. The term "brandy" simply refers to any alcohol made by fermenting and distilling fruit.

The fruit used to make strong liquors in Romania is almost always the plum, confusingly called **prune** in Romanian (*proo-neh*), referring to the fresh fruit. The dried version, **prune uscate** refers to what in English are known as prunes.

Therefore fermenting and distilling plums is how the nationally famous drink **țuica** (*tswee-ka*) is made. In fact, it is estimated that over 75% of all the plums harvested in Romania are used to make **țuica**.

In Romania the term **rachiu** (*rocky-you*) just means that it is the same drink but made with a different kind of fruit (such as pears).

The very best **țuica** is made with nothing but plums and yeast and has no sugar added. It usually comes out crystal clear, looking identical as water and having little to no taste in the mouth. It is only when it hits the stomach that you truly feel its gut-warming power.

**Palincă** is simply a term people use to refer to **țuica** that's been distilled a second (or third) time, meaning it is much stronger and has more alcohol per volume.

In general, for some reason, Hungarians often prefer **palincă** (i.e. the stronger stuff) over "regular" **țuica**.

**Horincă**, **Jinars** and **Fătăta** are other terms that generally mean "very strong" **țuica**.

The drink **slivovitz** however is slightly different, as the ground-up pits or stones from the plums are added in the fermentation process, which gives it a slightly nutty overtone. This drink is less common in Romania than it is elsewhere in this region of Europe.

In all cases, these drinks are usually consumed as just a shot (or two) right before digging into the big meal of the day, i.e. about 10-20 ml in metric.

Although a few store brands of these drinks are palatable, for the truly good stuff, (including wine), it is best to find a person who made them in their home. In fact, the only alcohol regularly made better by factories in Romania is beer.

**Țuica** and these other strong drinks are rarely, if ever, served at bars or nightspots.

Once you've sampled (and presumably enjoyed) a few glasses of **țuica**, you can learn to determine its characteristics simply by sight and smell alone. If you see a little old lady on the sidewalk peddling Fanta bottles filled with **țuica**, simply remove the cap and inhale to see if you've hit the jackpot.

**Wine and other Alcoholic Drinks**

Romania (and Moldova) are rightly renowned for their wines, which are both delicious and affordable. There is a wide variety of choices to suit any palate, from very tart and crisp chardonnays to dizzingly sweet dessert wines.

Romanians consume a tremendous amount of beer, much of it locally produced even if the brewery is owned or operated by a trans-national chain. These are generally pilsners.

Beer is sold just about everywhere from (some) fast food restaurants to kiosks to movie theaters to grocery stores and comes in various sizes, including 500 ml (about 16 oz) and 1 and 2-liter plastic bottles.

Bars, clubs and nightspots will usually serve a fairly standard panoply of beer, wine and mixed drinks. Be aware however a **martini** in Romania generally refers to the *brand* of vermouth known as Martini rather than the mixed drink (gin and vermouth).

Sadly, a great number of strong drinks (usually cheap grain alcohol) are sold in small plastic flasks and individual shots at some kiosks and corner stores, catering to the many chronic alcoholics in this country.

### Cheers

The tradition when "toasting" alcoholic beverages is to clink your glass with every single other person's and then say "**noroc**" (*no-roke*), literally meaning "luck", the equivalent to saying "cheers" in English.

Another common variant when clinking glasses is to say **sănătate** (*sah-nah-tah-tay*), literally meaning "(to your) health".

It is considered bad luck to clink glasses with someone who is drinking a *non-alcoholic* drink, so don't do it! Only say "**noroc**" or "**sănătate**" and bump glasses with people consuming alcoholic drinks with you.

### Cold Beverages and Ice

In general, Romanians believe that drinking a liquid that is quite cold is bad for your health.

I did an informal survey with some people I know, including one who is a bartender (here in Romania) and my amateur research found that while a small, select minority of people *do* drink cold beer, the vast majority of drinks consumed (alcoholic or not) are either hot or at room temperature.

This means ice is often a rare commodity and consumed quite infrequently, making it hard to get and potentially expensive (i.e. you pay extra for it).

While certainly Americans are prolific consumers of ice and cold drinks, interestingly enough ayurvedic medicine also recommends only the consumption of warm or hot liquids. Deepak Chopra in particular thinks it's an issue of health to not drink cold liquids[43].

## Soup

There are essentially two kinds of soup in Romania, **ciorbă** (*chore-buh*) and **supă** (*soup-ah*), both of which are extremely nutrient-rich, "thin" mostly liquid broths with only a small percentage of solid ingredients.

The main difference between them is that a **ciorbă** is usually going to have a sour component while a **supă** doesn't.

In Romanian culture, it is extremely traditional to eat a small bowl of soup right before digging into the main course of the day (usually lunch). In fact, almost all full-spread dinners at a Romanian restaurant come with a soup course first.

In western countries, modern medicine is only now discovering that there are many health benefits to eating a thin, hot soup before a large meal.

Traditionally in Romania, you drink one shot of **țuica** neat (page 73) as an aperitif and then eat a bowl of soup and then begin feasting on a large, home-cooked meal.

I can tell you from long personal experience that **aperitif + bowl of soup + full meal = delicious** and have "converted" many people to this style of dining, which is of course meant to be a lengthy and languorous affair, not "grabbing a bite" on your hurried way out the door.

A thicker, heartier soup, often referred to as a "stew" in English, is called **tocană** (*toe-con-ah*) in Romanian.

## Ciorbă de Burtă

It's time to talk about **ciorbă de burtă** (*chore-buh day boor-tah*), which is a mainstay of Romanian cuisine.

Literally it is tripe soup, which the name alone scares off a lot of people. Since tripe is something of a mystery meat to a lot of people, let's get into what it is (especially in Romania).

Every cow has four stomachs or to be more precise, four chambers of one large digestive system. Tripe is the stomach lining of the first three of these stomachs (or chambers).

---

[43] http://tatvagyan.blogspot.com/2008/10/summary-on-deepak-chopras-book.html

It is carefully washed to remove all undigested plant matter and then is cooked in this soup to provide a unique taste. Despite the fact that some people consider "cooked stomach material" to be unpleasant, it really isn't fundamentally different from cooking and consuming other parts of the cow for meat (assuming you eat meat).

This soup is a direct descendant of a similar Turkish soup and Romanians kept this recipe for a good reason – it's delicious. It is a **ciorbă**, which is a very "thin" soup, mostly all broth. It has a high fat content mixed in with a delicately balanced sour component.

It is served hot with a dollop of (cold) sour cream mixed in. With every other spoonful, one takes a bite of a hot pepper (**ardei iute**). Although I do not consume meat products anymore, I can tell you from previous experience that this soup is delicious.

Coming from an American perspective, I often think of Jewish tradition and how a bowl of homemade chicken soup can cure almost all minor ailments. Think of **ciorbă de burtă** in the same way, if you will.

Its most famous use however is as a cure for hangovers. Apparently this recipe truly does have a powerful effect on hangovers because it is rich in electrolytes. Plus because it's a "thin" soup, you're ingesting a lot of liquids to combat dehydration.

All in all, unless you're a strict vegetarian, don't pass up a hot bowl of this soup, particularly if you've overdone it the night before.

**Water**

In Romanian there are two kinds of bottled water consumed everywhere: **apă minerală** (*ah-pah me-knee-rahl-ah*) or mineral/fizzy water, and **apă plata** (*ah-pah plah-tah*) or "flat" slash "regular" water.

I think the global brand-name most associated with "mineral water" is Perrier, which many people don't like because it has a "bitter" taste they're not used to.

In Romania, the terms are a little confusing because there are actually four kinds of water with two different names.

Technically speaking, "mineral water" refers to water that has certain minerals dissolved into it. However, what's less clear is that it can be carbonated (with bubbles) or also non-carbonated.

Similarly, "flat" water or "regular" water without any dissolved solids can similarly be carbonated and made "fizzy", although this is less common in Romania.

In general however, **apă minerală** is going to be carbonated mineral water, while **apă plata** is both "flat" and without trace minerals.

Every bottle has an informative label on the side where you can see the composition of the dissolved solids, which are easy to parse out even if you don't speak a word of Romanian.

This country is blessed to have many springs of unbelievably delicious spring water, both "flat" and carbonated mineral waters. These are sold all over Romania under different names. Some of the most well-known brands are:

- **Borsec** – Considered the "gold standard" in Romania, this water has a harsher "bite" to it than many foreigners prefer. Often purchased by Romanians purely for prestige purposes.
- **Dorna** – A mediocre but acceptable water. The company is owned by the regional Coca-Cola firm so it is found everywhere that Sprite and Coke are sold.
- **Rouă Munţilor** – Literally meaning "Mountain Dew", this water has a light, refreshing finish to it.
- **Harghita** – Since most of Romania's best springs are found in Harghita County, this is one of the sweetest, most refreshing brands out there.
- **Izvorul Minunilor** – Or "The Spring of Wonders", this water is largely unpopular with Romanians but personally my all-time favorite. To me it tastes exactly like 7-Up if you add a slice of lemon to your glass.

What's interesting about all mineral water, carbonated or not, is that it is an excellent source of a lot of key minerals, especially calcium. One glass of ordinary mineral water can give you roughly half the calcium equivalent of a glass of cow's milk and mineral water is also an excellent source of magnesium and iron.

If you go to a hipermarket (see page 132) or perhaps a "natura" or healthfood store, you can often find a "medical" version of mineral water where the dissolved contents are far higher, with quite large doses of calcium and other minerals. This is often sold as a kind of health tonic to treat a number of ailments.

With so many varieties of mineral water available in Romania and knowing all of the health benefits, I definitely recommend trying different brands until you find one you like.

That being said, conventional folk wisdom in Romania (especially amongst women) is that drinking carbonated water makes you fat.

**The "Fresh"** – It's usually easy to find restaurants in Romania (including at the malls) that sell the "fresh" (literally that's the term, written in English), meaning fresh-squeezed and unprocessed juices.

"*Un fresh de portocale*", for instance, means a glass of fresh-squeezed orange (*poor-toe-call-eh*) juice as opposed to the bottled, pasteurized variety.

### Soft Drinks/Sodas

The vast majority of soft drinks come from the standard international corporations, Coca-Cola and Pepsi, with Coca-Cola holding the lion's share of the market in Romania.

The generic term for any non-alcoholic drink is **suc** (*suke*), literally meaning "juice". If you truly want a juice (as opposed to a carbonated, fizzy soft drink or soda), order a **suc de...** where the kind of fruit is specified.

**O cola** (*oh cola*) is the generic way of ordering a Coca-Cola specifically, whereas if you want a Pepsi instead, you have to say it (i.e. *un Pepsi, vă rog*).

These are almost always served in bottles, rarely very cold and/or with ice.

Note: both kinds of water (page 77) are sold everywhere soft drinks are sold.

### Drinking Liquids While Eating

I did some scanning around and it seems most western health experts think that drinking water (or other liquids) while you eat your meal is good for you. I've seen many people talk about it specifically as a dieting aid, to wit that you will feel more full and eat less if you drink water with your meal.

Romanians in general rarely consume any liquids with their meal at all. It's not that it's forbidden on the table or something but the average Romanian will not drink anything while he/she is eating.

Personally I was raised to always have a large glass full of some kind of drink and to consume it with almost every bite. I saw on the internet that I'm not the only person who used to find it almost impossible to eat at all without some kind of drink.

After doing it "both ways", I can say that I highly recommend the Romanian style of abstaining from liquids while eating. I found out, to my surprise (although it seems self-evident now) that it was hard to eat a lot of "junk" food without a drink at hand because the food was far too salty, over-flavored or otherwise hard to consume on its own.

You can also taste your food a heck of a lot better without diluting it by drinking and you truly know when you've hit your "pleasure spot".

And last but not least, it's hard to overeat almost anything without chugging down liquids simultaneously. Sweet foods become cloyingly sweet and salty foods become unbearably sharp once you've eaten your fill and not flushed down bite after bite with your drink.

Give it a try and see what you think!

## Tea

In general, hot teas are considered a kind of remedy for colds and other common ailments more so than a daily drink. There will always be a "nature" store in any town that not only sells a wide variety of herbal teas but can "prescribe" one for you if you tell them what illnesses you are suffering from.

In a restaurant it is likely that the only tea on hand will be a fruity, sweet herbal tea that is not caffeinated. In posher or fancier places you might be given the choices of either green or black tea as well.

In the very largest cities, there are places called **ceainărie** (*chy-nah-ree-eh*) that have a full spread of teas.

During summer especially, a lot of women in Romania consume chilled, pre-made tea "drinks", especially by Nestle or Lipton. These are actually tea-flavored, sickeningly sweet beverages but they're quite popular here, especially with Hungarians, primarily because they're not carbonated.

Note: It is nearly impossible to buy "iced tea" almost anywhere made from actual brewed tea leaves.

## Coffee

Romanians drink a heck of a lot of coffee (**cafea** – *cough-eh-ah*) and you can find it for sale nearly everywhere. With a few exceptions like Starbucks, coffee in Romania generally is one of three kinds:

- **Ness** – This means "instant" and is made by mixing hot water with a powder. It is extremely cheap and usually served in a small, plastic cup, heavily laced with sugar.
- **Filtru** (*feel-true*) – This means "brewed" and is the middling level for coffee, more akin to a typical American style than a heavier, more intense European style. It is made by allowing unpressurized hot water to drip or flow over the ground beans. A cup of *cafea filtru* will rarely cost more than $1 USD.
- **Espresso** – Although the name is Italian, in Romania an espresso is actually comprised of a lot more water, which would technically make it a *doppio* but it is never referred to as such. A common variant in Romanian is the *espresso lung* (or sometimes *cafea lungă*) meaning "long" and has more water mixed into it. Even at the most expensive places, it is unlikely to cost you more than $3 USD for a cup of coffee.

If you're at a walk-up window selling coffee at the train station, it's most likely going to be **ness**.

If you're at a sit down restaurant (or café) however, simply ordering a coffee will get you an *espresso*. Please be aware that there is no "x" in this word and is pronounced *es-press-oh* ;)

Note: Some restaurants actually have an item called an "American coffee", which is a larger cup of coffee that's much more diluted due to the amount of water added to it.

There are also two pseudo-coffee drinks worth mentioning:

- **Frappe** (*frap-pay*) – Generally speaking, a blended concoction of instant coffee, milk, sugar and other flavors to make a kind of weak coffee "milkshake". Almost never homemade.
- **Cappuccino** – Nowhere near to what a proper "cappuccino" should be, in general in Romania these drinks are nothing more than a regular cup of coffee with some cream dolloped on top and perhaps a sprinkling of cinnamon. Only at higher-end places can you find a true cappuccino.

Note: While you will always be served hot coffee in a restaurant or café, many Romanians habitually brew coffee at home (or at the office) and let it sit and grow cold. They will rarely, if ever, re-heat coffee and will drink it "cold" or room temperature.

Beware of being offered a cup of coffee in someone's home or office that's cold and not fresh!

**Drinking Vessels**

Romanians and Europeans in general have a preference for using a "proper" glass, i.e. coffee in a mug, wine in a wineglass, beer in a stein, etc. That being said, there is almost no use of *plastic* drinking cups, except for small children.

Depending on where you go, you might see some traditional Romanian glasses, made to look like little brown, wooden barrels. A larger, similar version of the barrels are usually used as a carafe for wine.

More rarely, you may be given ceramic vessels for drinking in certain traditional settings as well.

**Milk and Drinkable Dairy**

Romanians in general, and women especially, drink a tremendous amount of dairy. While UHT milk can be found, most milk sold in Romania is fresh, either whole milk (3.5% fat) or skim milk (1.5% fat).

Milk is almost always sold in 1-liter containers, usually a kind of waxy, stiff cardboard box but sometimes in a bag. Yes, I know it's weird to buy a "bag of milk" but it exists here, so hush.

A kind of "drinkable yogurt", often sold under the brand-name *Activia* is marketed as a cure for "digestive troubles" and is mostly consumed by women.

There are other more common dairy drinks such as **lapte bătut** (literally "beaten milk" but in English known as buttermilk) and **sana**, both of which are essentially higher-fat drinkable yogurts (*sana* usually being sweeter than *lapte bătut*).

# Alcohol, Smoking and Drugs
**Drinking For Men**

The law states that only people older than 18 may buy alcohol but this is often winked at by some merchants. Rarely, if ever at all (it's never happened to me once in over 10 years), will you be required to show identification at the time of purchase, yet another good reason to leave your passport at home (see page 22).

Literally my first day ever on Romanian soil, a Romanian couple whom I'd never met and who spoke zero English met me. For a few hours I was all alone with them and we were completely unable to communicate.

They fed me lots of nice food (which was great) but they also kept pouring me shot after shot of țuica (page 73), which is a very strong kind of liquor. In fact, every single time a neighbor or friend would come over my hosts would say "Aha! Let's celebrate the arrival of our newest and bestest American friend!" and they'd pour one shot for me and one for the guest. Well, the guests all had exactly one shot apiece, so they were fine. I, on the other hand, got completely plowed and was drunker than I'd ever (probably) been in my life at around 3:00 in the afternoon.

If I had any inclination, genetically or otherwise, to be an alcoholic then living here in Romania I really *would* be an alcoholic. That much is true. But the truth is that drinking in Romania is completely different than drinking in America and other places so let me back up and start there.

In America, I'd say about 80% of the population is extremely prudent and prudish about alcohol, rarely touching it, perhaps a beer or glass of wine with dinner and would consider slamming shots of hard liquor at 3:00 in the afternoon to be some kind of abysmally shameful behavior so you're probably also a pedophile, rapist and bank robber to boot.

The other 20% of the population pretty much *lives* for alcohol, drinks it all the time, are bona fide alcoholics and quite often consume "drugs" along with the alcohol. You wake up at 6:00 am and crack open your "breakfast" and go to work just long enough so you don't get fired and then race home so you can indulge in your one and only passion in life – drinking some more.

In Romania however (for men), drinking is essentially a "code of manliness". It also is something that is done, more or less, without shame.

Except for perhaps your old nagging wife yelling at you, nobody frowns at you for drinking or being drunk, not even if you're in line at the local store at 7:00 am to be there right when it opens to buy a cheap plastic bottle of the local rotgut. That's considered mostly a "so what?" kind of activity here.

In fact, making your *own* alcohol aka "moonshine" is not only (still quasi) legal here but extremely common, both wine as well as hard liquor. So men not only drink a lot but many of them are quite proud to be involved with the making of their own drink so it's a big part of the culture (see page 73).

There are also some pretty standard "rules" about when drinking is "necessary", one of which is that when a valued guest comes over to your house for the first time and you're welcoming him with open arms, etc, etc, as what happened to me. It isn't like anyone's going to spit on you or cast you out if you DON'T drink but pretty much they're going to assume your manliness is in serious doubt so generally it's better to say yes.

Drinking is also how men "bond" and pretty much all sins are forgiven (amongst men) if you're one of their drinking buddies. I've gotten a lot of flack before for some of my lifestyle choices (such as the fact that I don't eat meat – see page 71) and drinking has been a very useful and powerful way to win friends and influence people.

Here's a sample of what's happened many *ahem* times in my life in Romania.

**Me**: Yep, that's right. I don't eat meat.

**Girlfriend's Dad**: What? Not even fish?

**Me**: Not even fish.

**GD**: What about slănină[44]? Come on, nothing's better than some slănină!

**Me**: Nope, not even slănină.

**GD**: What about chicken? Come on, it's not fattening.

**Me**: Nope, not even chicken.

**GD**: (Incredulous). What? I'm surprised you're even alive with this crazy diet. It doesn't sound too healthy. What about pork? Surely you eat pork.

**Me**: Look, I'll keep it real simple. If it has eyes, I don't eat it.

**GD**: Nothing with eyes, eh? Hmm… (strokes chin while thinking deeply).

(LONG PAUSE)

**GD**: Well beer doesn't have eyes, does it? You like to drink beer, don't you?

**Me**: Yep. Alcohol is fine.

**GD**: Well all right! (hearty pat on the back). You're all right, son. You're a real man. I had my doubts about you but now we're super cool buddies for life. Come on, let me pour you a drink. Welcome to the family! I love you forever.

**Girlfriend's Mom**: (big frown) Oh don't you get him sloppy drunk, you're

---

[44] See page 51.

*always a pain in the ass when you drink.*

**GD**: *(whispers aside) Ah women, always bitching about a man having a*

*teeny, tiny sip, am I right or am I right?*

**Girlfriend**: *(super big frown). What are you doing?*

**Me**: *What, honey? I'm bonding with your dad! (evil naughty grin)*

During big parties, such weddings or on New Year's Eve (see page 123), Romanians take their drinking very seriously and do it similar to Russian style, which means a round of food/snacks in between rounds of drinking so the party can last a long, long time.

Unlike in America and many other prudish countries, clubs and bars stay open until whenever (see page 32), so there's no need to slam 50 drinks in the two hours before "last call" so please pace yourself.

If you're a man, be aware that drinking is something pretty much everyone will expect you to do on numerous occasions and it's kind of hard to get out of without looking like a total pantywaist and effeminate girl[45].

If you absolutely must beg off and don't want to offend someone, say that you just spoke to your doctor for a severe medical condition and tragically he (the doctor) has forbidden you to consume alcohol.

**Drinking For Women**

If you're a woman in Romania, you won't be expected to drink so if that's not your thing, it won't be any problem for you at all.

In this country, drinking is pretty much a *males-only* activity. Yes, women do drink here a little and yes occasionally young women out at the club do drink too much wine or champagne but there's *very, very* little of the old "whee it's girl's night out and "oh my god I'm so wasted" going on here.

Women drink here but rarely ever get plastered or pee in their pants or flash their boobies in public and all that sort of "used to be shameful but now it's ho hum" stuff that goes on in USA or Britain.

That's not to say that women don't go out to clubs and bars and consume alcohol because of course they do. Yet a much higher sense of decorum is expected of women and drinking to a point of losing control is rarely done.

---

[45] No offense is meant by this phrase, I'm simply reflecting here the mentality involved.

**Drugs**

In Romania, "drugs" as in illicit or illegal narcotics are basically non-existent, rarely used even by bums and/or university age young adults. By far and away, the most common recreational drug in Romania is alcohol.

Of course other drugs are consumed but this is exceedingly rare and far less common than in western Europe or the United States.

The "drug of choice" for the absolutely most bereft people in Romania are chemicals (including gasoline/petrol) sprayed into a bag and then inhaled, sometimes known as *huffing*.

**Smoking**

Like many countries in this region, smoking (cigarettes) in public areas and is widespread and a very common practice.

In the past, many restaurants and bars were separated into smoking and non-smoking sections. Due to a recent change in the law, however, all bars and restaurants under a certain size[46] must be entirely smoke free or permit smoking throughout. Since most establishments in Romania are fairly small, this means that just about every place will be either one or the other.

The law states that each establishment must declare what they are (smoking or non) and so you will often see signs, including the red circle with a line through it over an image of a cigarette (indicating non-smoking):

**Pentru fumatori** – For smokers

**Aici se fumeaza** – For smokers

**Nu se fumeaza** – Non-smoking

**Fumatul interzis** – Non-smoking

I'd say roughly 90% of the businesses that had to choose between one or the other chose to allow smoking, so if this is a concern for you, choose your venue carefully.

A few places that will <u>never</u> permit smoking:

- Interior of hospital or clinic
- Mass transportation (bus, plane, train, etc)
- Inside a church

---

[46] 100 square meters.

- Theaters and opera houses

Just about everywhere else is usually smoker-friendly, including some taxis, shopping malls, bars, clubs, airports, train stations and even some retail locations. I buy cat food from a guy who smokes openly right in his little store.

Be aware that some places, especially bars and night spots (see page 31) may be incredibly smoky, difficult to handle even for some smokers.

A few years ago, smoking *was* permitted on Romanian trains although it isn't anymore and therefore you may regularly encounter people still sneaking a smoke. There is now a *de facto* compromise between the rules and smokers that it is generally permissible to open the train car doors and smoke while the train is at a station.

By law, all cigarettes have a government mandated maximum price. This means that regardless of where you buy cigarettes, they will be the same price and no one place is better than another.

The law states that only people older than 18 may buy tobacco products but some merchants often wink at this. Rarely, if ever at all, will you be required to show identification at the time of purchase, yet another good reason to leave your passport at home (see page 22).

In some larger cities you can find a bar that specializes in *narghila*, sometimes also called "*shisha*" (spelled multiple ways) or a hookah, an Arab-style water pipe used to smoke flavored tobaccos.

Note: In rural areas and even in some urban areas, it is considered "unladylike" for women to smoke while outdoors in public.

# Transportation – Getting Around

### Bus/Tramvai/Troleibuz

If you ever find yourself in a Romanian city of a decent size, sooner or later you're going to see a lot of buses trundling about and you may begin to wonder how you too can climb aboard and enjoy the adventure as you are whisked on your way by the reliable and earth-friendly scions of public transportation.

**Autobuz** (*auto-booze*) – A city bus that normally runs a loop pattern.

**Tramvai** (*trom-vye)* – Known as either a "tram" or "trolley" in English, this is a kind of light rail train that runs on a fixed track inside a city, similar to a bus route.

**Troleibuz** (*trolley-booze*) – Exactly the same as an ordinary city bus except that it is powered via overhead electrical cables.

The first thing you need to know is that all city buses (i.e. buses that circulate within the same city versus buses that go between different cities) are often marked with a logo that starts with **RAT**[47].

For example in Cluj it is known as **RATUC** while in both Braşov and Bucharest it is known as **RATB**. The **RAT** stands for *Regia Autonoma de Transport*, a delightfully Communist-era phrase which literally means "Autonomous Transportation Regime".

This being the modern age, most **RAT**s have their own websites but sadly, as in the case of **Cluj** and **Bucharest**, finding a decent route map still remains pretty much useless. Therefore I have prepared this handy guide on how to ride a city bus in Romania!

**Step 1** – *The ticket.*

Before you board any Romanian bus (or tram), you must have your ticket ahead of time.

Some cities (like **Timişoara**) have a very liberal policy on who can sell tickets. Just look for any corner store or kiosk with the little RAT(x) sign on it and you can buy your ticket there. Other cities (like **Cluj**) only sell tickets via official RAT(x) kiosks and these are located only at major bus stops and sometimes the kiosk is closed so good luck finding one that's open!

The odd thing is that in almost every city they will only sell you a bus ticket for "two rides" (or more). This is bad if you only need one single bus ride but the good news is that the tickets are generally affordable[48].

**Step 2** – *Which bus to take?*

So now you've got your ticket (good for two rides or more) but you're in one part of town and how do you get to the other part of town? Usually the front of the bus will show you the destination but generally it's pretty useless as it will just say "So-and-so Neighborhood", which is pretty general and not specific (for more on neighborhoods, see page 30).

---

[47] Although not in all cases, as in Oradea, where it's known as OTL-RA.
[48] For instance, in **Cluj** a "two ride" bus ticket is 4 lei or slightly more than 1 US dollar. Interestingly enough, **Bucharest** seems to have the cheapest public transportation fares.

To begin with, there are no maps. Even if you find a map, it is useless. Therefore you MUST ask another human being which bus to take. Every long-term resident of the city has an entire bus map route in his/her head and can tell you exactly which bus to take and where to catch it.

Although it is true that the ticket vendors often do know the routes and schedules, it can be next to impossible to hear them behind the window and they rarely speak English.

**Step 3** – *Waiting for the bus.*

First of all, make sure there are other people waiting around with you. Romanian bus stops don't follow the logic of "well there's a stop on this side of the street so there's also one on the other side". No! Sometimes one bus stop is miles away from another one, depending on which direction you're traveling.

What you want to do at this point is cast your eye slyly over the crowd of fellow people waiting on the bus. See any old ladies? These are your "markers". They've got arthritis and bad hips so they know exactly where to stand to be as close to the doors as possible when the bus stops. Teenagers who are goofing around and men fiddling with their phones are less knowledgeable about these sorts of things. So find some old ladies and stand directly to the left of them.

**Step 4** – *The bus arrives.*

Immediately there's going to be a scrum. First, the passengers disembarking the bus will exit down the open doors. Remember how you were staked out just to the left of the old ladies? Before the doors open but after the bus stops, slide directly in front of the old ladies. DO NOT GET BEHIND THEM or you will rue the day!

Your mission, should you choose to accept it, is to cut directly in front of the old ladies so you can pop through the open doors the exact second the last passenger disembarks.

**Step 5** – *Validating the ticket.*

You never deal with or interact with the driver. Instead, scattered throughout the bus are devices mounted to poles which you will use to validate your ticket. Some cities (like **Timişoara**) have fancy, modern devices which print a time code stamp on your ticket or simply detect it magnetically.

Other cities (like **Cluj**) have an old-fashioned mechanical "punch" that you slide your ticket into and then pop out a coded set of holes. Either way, your first mission must be to validate your ticket as quickly as possible.

If you possess one of the ubiquitous "valid for 2 rides" tickets then only validate/punch ONE side of the ticket! Save your ticket and then at a later time you can use the other side of the ticket for another ride. Things like "transfers" do not exist in Romania so every time you switch buses you must validate another (half) ticket.

If there are two of you traveling together, validate both sides of ONE ticket as each side is good for one person for one ride.

**Step 6** – *Finding a seat.*

You've got to be super quick about validating your ticket because a lot of your fellow passengers have "passes"[49] and don't need to punch a ticket. And they're all scrummed up right behind you and scrambling to get a good seat so this isn't time to daydream and dilly-dally around.

Cast your eye over the length of the bus and figure out where an elderly person might like to sit and do not choose those seats, if possible, because later on they're going to board the bus and then you'll feel guilty and want to stand up and give them your seat just because they're aged and tired and put in 80 plus years of hard work and perhaps remind you of your sweet grandma, the sneaky devils.

Otherwise, anything is fair game but watch out for the rearward facing seats as they can induce a sense of nausea in all but the hardiest of bus passengers.

**Step 6** – *The ticket inspector.*

In Romania, the driver just drives the bus and nothing else. It's up to a separate guy (and it's ALWAYS a man) to covertly board the bus and then after it's in motion, unzip his jacket and whip out his RAT(x) ID badge and begin inspecting tickets.

Since you're an honest and upstanding person, you've got your ticket handy and already validated so you just hand it to him and you're done. If for some inexcusable reason you either don't have a ticket or haven't validated it yet, you can get in a world of trouble and have to pay a large fine.

---

[49] Outside of **Bucharest**, it is difficult for non-residents to get passes that allow for multiple rides at a reduced rate.

If you're a foreigner and have some "genuine" (snort) excuse not to have a ticket, begin shouting and waving your hands and making a scene and you can probably get away without paying the fine as most ticket inspectors don't speak English. It's still rather unpleasant though so don't do it.

**Step 7** – *Your stop.*

Where the bus stops is always fixed and immutable and so you don't need to worry about ringing a bell or otherwise signaling the driver you want to get off. The bus just stops where it stops and each stop is often QUITE a ways away from the next one, so you aren't likely to get confused.

Your goal, however, is to get up close to the door *before* the bus stops because you don't want to get caught in the surge of boarding passengers. If you're sitting in an inside seat or otherwise caught behind some passengers and want them to move, the phrase to know is **cobariți?** (*coba-roots* literally "*You go down?*") which means "Are you getting off at the next stop?" and they'll move to let you get by.

Tada! Congratulations, you did it! You successfully rode a Romanian city bus or tram!

A couple of notes: sometimes the number on the bus is flat out wrong. It doesn't happen often but it happens so be aware of it. Also, half the bus passengers are blind so they can't even read the bus number so be sure to ask someone (with good eyesight) if you're not 100% sure which bus it is you want/are taking.

Also: your ticket is good for all forms of public transportation in the city equally, i.e. either bus or tram or in the case of **Bucharest**, a ride on the subway. One ride is one ride is one ride regardless of distance or type.

The good news however is that just about all Romanian buses run extremely frequently so you don't need to worry too much about timetables and schedules. They also run 365 days a year, including holidays, and in just about every kind of weather so whenever it is you need to avail yourself of public transportation, you're in luck!

Generally all forms of public transportation run from very early in the morning (around 5:30 am) to around 11:00 pm or midnight.

**Bucharest Bus/Tram System**

Unlike every other city in Romania, Bucharest has different tariffs for some of their bus/tram system.

Anyone can buy an electronic travel pass (called ACTIV) which can be pre-loaded from between a minimum of 3.7 lei (good for two rides on everything but the Express buses) to a maximum of 50 lei. This card can be used equally in buses/trams as well as the subway (see next section).

It is still possible however to buy the older style paper tickets at some locations, valid for a minimum of two rides (again, costing 3.7 lei).

There is also a second type of card called MULTIPLU which is good for unlimited travel during a single day on all Bucharest urban transportation types (including Express buses). At the time of this writing these cost 9.6 lei.

There are two Express buses with special (higher) fares, a two-ride ticket costing 7 lei if purchased individually or 2.7 per ride if one is using a pre-loaded ACTIV card. These two buses are the **780** and **783**, which serve the airport (see page 103).

## Bucharest Metro/Subway

Romania's capital has a surprisingly extensive and efficient underground system, called the "metro" in the local language.

**RATB** (page 87) tickets work equally well on the metro as on buses or trams.

There are four subway lines (M1 through M4) but sadly, the markings and signage inside most **Bucharest** metro stations are quite inadequate and confusing. The easiest thing to do (assuming you know which stop you want to go to) is simply ask someone which way to go.

Some metro stops share two different lines and transferring between them is free. Signage however is often inadequate and you may be required to walk a convoluted path up and over the tracks to get to another subway line (or switch directions).

Because much of the metro system was designed and built during the Communist era, **Bucharest** actually has a greater number of stations than it truly needs, so don't be surprised to exit to grassy fields and wandering livestock at some stations.

## Inter-City Buses And "Maxi Taxis"

Today this industry is dominated by a plethora of private companies.

Although it can be confusing sometimes how to *find* the right transportation, the good news is that you can get just about anywhere you want to go without needing a car, even to very rural areas.

I have to be quite frank – the inter-city bus system in Romania is pretty awful.

The only bright spot is that there is a rather comprehensive website[50] that details just about every bus in the country and what the various schedules are. Sadly, it's a little clunky but it does have the option of choosing between nine (!) languages, including both Russian and Bulgarian (click on the little flag in the upper right-hand corner).

After that I'm afraid that things get steadily worse. While the posted schedules and destinations seem to be fairly accurate, what actually happens on the road is a gamble.

The Autogara

In every city of any decent size, there is an *autogara* or main bus terminal. In several cities, like **Brasov** and **Sibiu**, these are literally next door to the *gara* (*de tren*) or the main train station. In other cities, like **Timisoara** and **Cluj**, the *autogara* is close by but not in direct sight of the train station. **Bucharest**, as you would expect, has an entire constellation of bus stations.

Some *autogari* in mid-size towns, such as **Alba Iulia** or **Medias** are woeful outposts of humanity. The one in **Pitesti** looks like a bomb went off in the parking lot. Some of the *autogari* in larger cities will have a modicum of stores to serve the needs of the traveler, such as food shops, a place to buy a coffee or other drinks, and a bathroom. Sometimes these *autogari* have fairly decent facilities and seem more or less tolerable in terms of spooky people hanging around, stray dogs and scowling gypsies. Sometimes however you feel like you've reached a way station in Outer Mongolia.

In all cases, as far as I am aware, be advised that there will always be someone "manning" the entrance to the bathrooms to charge you a fee. The posted fee in the **Medias** *autogara* was something like 2 lei, which I felt was ridiculous and so I negotiated the price down to 1 leu but you will **always pay** to use the restroom.

Finding where your bus is, however, and boarding it and knowing where it will arrive at is an onerous undertaking. Sometimes there is a helpful dispatcher slash information office with perhaps the (accurate) information posted on a board or sheet of paper. Other times you have to scout around

---

[50] www.autogari.ro

for your particular company's logo and ask their own specific staff members. Still other times, you just have to walk around and pester people until you find your bus.

Note: it is **extremely** difficult to find information in English or someone who speaks anything but Romanian.

The Ticket

Sadly, there is no uniform method of acquiring a ticket. The majority of buses require you to queue up for the bus when it arrives in the station, board the bus and if there are seats still available, you buy your ticket directly from the driver.

Still others require you to make a phone reservation ahead of time and then buy the ticket from the driver when you board. The only advantage to this is that you're "guaranteed" a spot on the bus, something that might not happen if it is a popular route. Some companies now allow you to reserve (but not buy) your ticket online directly from the website.

Still others require you to buy a ticket from a separate office in the bus station and then present it to the driver when you board. In these cases, the driver will absolutely refuse to sell you a ticket unless you board the bus at a very small town or location (see below).

Assuming you acquire a seat and a ticket, you're basically set. Or are you?

Note: on some rare occasions, the driver will assign you a seat on the bus but the norm is just everyone sits where they want to.

The Vehicle

There is absolutely **no way to know** what kind of vehicle you will be riding in. I have ridden in two vastly different vehicles on separate occasions on exactly the same route with exactly the same company. You just never know.

Sometimes it will be a large, full-size coach with over 50 passengers and full amenities, including air conditioning and a movie to watch. Other times you will be riding an oversized van that is in terrible condition and barely roadworthy. Sometimes the vehicle will have a spacious capacity under the bus for you to stow your larger bags. Other times you'll have to cram your bags either in the (sometimes pitifully undersized) overhead racks or else any which way you can in the aisle between the seats. I've seen people have to perform Olympic-level hurdles to get to an open seat as they cross over mountains of luggage.

Sadly, in just about every case, be aware that even on the modern, large coaches there will **rarely, if ever** be onboard restroom facilities. This means you better be able to hold yourself high and dry for several long hours of jolting and bumping over Romania's patchy network of roads.

Note: regardless of whether you are riding the world's rustiest rattletrap of a van or a sleek, modern coach, it is mandatory that the radio will be on the entire way. A Romanian driver cannot operate his vehicle without the radio playing! This is the law! (see page 176).

Theoretically the major stops that the bus is taking will be posted on a sign in the vehicle's front windshield. But not always! Sometimes you just have to ask.

On The Road

Theoretically your bus will only stop at certain cities (usually mid to large ones for longer trips) and only at the official *autogara* or bus station. In practice however, the bus can and will stop just about *anywhere*. Savvy passengers will rise as their desired location approaches and pester the driver to drop them off at unmarked locations. Furthermore, in larger cities the driver will always stop at completely unmarked locations to pick up or drop off passengers.

In some cases, including at the posted last stop of your route, the driver will not stop at the *autogara* at all. This happened to me one time when the driver unceremoniously threw us all out in the rain instead of going to the **Cluj** *autogara*, where we had someone waiting to pick us up. Nice!

Despite all the stopping at strange places to pick people up or drop them off, usually the bus will only make one stop that's long enough for people to get off the bus, stretch their legs, buy a snack or use the restroom. Where will this stop be and for how long will it last? There is no way of knowing!

I speak Romanian just fine but what happens every time is the driver will suddenly kill the engine (your clue if you don't speak the language) and mutter something. I've sat two seats behind him and barely understood him but it's something like *pauza de X minute* (break of X minutes). Again, you have no idea where this will be or when and you had better hustle to the crappy (paid) bathrooms if that's what you need to do on your sole break. Only on extremely long trips (over 6-8 hours) will there be more than one break.

Therefore I have been on a four-hour trip on a bus full with more than 50 passengers and had exactly one rest stop of about 5 minutes, meaning there was a tremendous scrum for the bathrooms. Not very nice but hey, that's how it goes.

During the trip, aside from the radio, you have no idea what will happen. Sometimes the air conditioning (or conversely, the heat) will work and sometimes just barely and sometimes not at all. Sometimes you'll be swung all over the road as the driver hot dogs his way to the next stop. Sometimes you'll get burned alive as the sun scorches through the windows. Sometimes it'll rain and water will blow through the driver's window onto your face. Sometimes the driver will light up a smoke and you get to enjoy it second-hand. You just never know.

Note: they are cracking down on this now but it still exists for shorter routes – the existence of the paying passenger who has no seat and so is forced to stand up in the already crowded aisle. This could be you!

Illegal/Weird Stuff

I've seen everything under the sun, including the driver stopping at his girlfriend's apartment, the driver sleeping during the 10-minute break, the driver picking up weird packages at unannounced spots in tiny villages, the driver smoking continuously while driving, the driver helping some old peasant woman board the bus in a tiny village, the driver going over twice the posted speed limit to the driver jamming on the brakes as he failed to notice a road obstruction until the last minute, pitching all of the passengers into the seat in front of them.

I've seen drivers transport nearly everything except for live animals and I've often seen people slip the driver cash to take their packages. I've seen buddies of the driver board and ride around for free. I've seen just about everything and if you ride the inter-city bus in Romania long enough, you will too.

Your Destination

The driver will never, ever announce where you are. I've heard even Romanian passengers shout out to the driver to ask where we are because it is often difficult to determine unless you are going to a very large city. Many times the *autogara* is located in the outskirts of a city or town and signage is nearly non-existent so if you're not sure where you are, ask someone.

Furthermore, be aware that not all bus routes even go to the *autogara* at all. Check the website to see where the bus picks up passengers as a lot of shorter routes skip going to the official *autogara* altogether.

Note: do not count on the driver to stop at smaller destinations even if you've told him that's where you want to go. I saw one poor Romanian lady break into tears as she realized too late that the driver had just barreled past her stop, leaving her no choice but to get off at the next city and take another bus or taxi back to where she wanted to go.

Conclusion

Between unmarked buses, decrepit vehicles, unscheduled stops, unannounced and surprise breaks, lack of adequate climate control and a raft of surly drivers making bizarre unplanned stops to the lack of English (or other language) information from just about anybody, riding an inter-city bus in Romania remains quite an adventure and is not recommended for the timid or the cautious.

So why do people ride the bus? Well frankly, it is far cheaper than the train for comparable routes. Not only that, but in just about every case, the bus route takes far less time than the comparable train route. Sometimes riding an intercity bus is faster, more economical and a better choice.

If you've got a choice and prefer your comfort to saving a little time or money, always choose Romanian railways. But if speed and economy are your driving factors, roll the dice and hop aboard an intercity bus. The inter-city bus companies also do a thriving business in transporting cargo both domestically and internationally and are far more popular (and cheaper) than international delivery firms such as DHL or FedEx.

If you are traveling around Europe and want to ship goods efficiently and cheaply, usually one of the **autocar** companies are going to be your best bet.

With the advent of low-cost airlines however, transporting *yourself* around Europe by plane is usually going to be cheaper than (or on par with) bus routes and much, much faster.

For a list of the best ways to get (yourself) to nearby international destinations, see page 113.

**Train**

Romania has an extensive network of trains that can get you almost anywhere you want to go, domestically or internationally.

Rail passes, either regional or pan-European, can be purchased ahead of time and used on Romanian railways. If you are coming from outside the

European Union, these are called **Eurail** passes and can be purchased ahead of time from your home country.

If you are coming from inside the European Union, you can buy a pass before you leave, usually called an **InterRail** pass.

Romanian railways are called **CFR** (*chay-fay-ray*) and generally most routes are run on a timely manner but occasionally there are maddening delays.

Schedules and Buying Tickets

Every train station will have a large board somewhere, listing the schedule of all trains stopping in that station. All larger cities will always have an information booth with someone working there who should speak at least a little English.

Note: Most Romanian trains run on the same schedule all 365 days a year regardless of holidays.

There is also a great website online showing all train schedules[51] (click on the British flag for English). Be aware that **CFR** uses the "old" spellings[52] for some cities so **Târgu Mureş** can only be found under **Tîrgu Mureş**.

Many cities now have electronic information kiosks in **centru** where you can find train schedules.

In all larger cities, **CFR** will have a separate ticket and reservation office somewhere in town (away from the train station) called **Agenţia Voiaj CFR**.

Once you are in Romania, you can buy tickets online (with a discount, see below) but there is no difference (in price) between buying them at a train station or at an **Agenţia Voiaj**.

Tickets can be bought as little as 10 minutes before the train departs or months ahead of time.

Most of the time, you can easily find a seat on any train by buying your ticket a half hour before it leaves. Be aware, however, that on some holidays and other busy days it truly is wise to buy your ticket ahead of time.

Tickets are sold from pretty much any ticket window[53] at the train station but the clerks are often behind thick panes of glass and impossible to hear or

---

[51] http://www.infofer.ro
[52] For more on Romanian orthography, see page 303.
[53] Each window has a bizarre and bewildering array of signs on it but don't be confused – any ticket window will do in most cases.

understand. It may be helpful to write down which train you want and know the price ahead of time.

On the contrary, the clerks at an **Agenția Voiaj** are rarely behind panes of glass and therefore you can both hear and understand what they are saying.

Types of Trains

**CFR** operates three types of trains, arranged in ascending order.

Note: These trains used to have different names and are still referred to by some people as well as in signage by their old names.

**Regio:**           The slowest, oldest (and cheapest) trains, often stopping at villages and remote locations (formerly called **Personal**).

**Inter-Regio:**    These trains stop at both smaller towns as well as larger cities (formerly divided into **Rapid** and **Acelerat**).

**Inter-City:**      The cream of the crop, usually only stopping at larger cities and international destinations.  Some **Inter-City** trains have on-board restaurant and/or internet services available.

These are abbreviated online and on printed signage **R, IR and I-C** respectively (formerly written as **P, R, A** and **I-C**).

Accommodations

Trains have a number of compartments divided into first class (Rom: **clasă întâi** – *class-ah untie*) and second class (Rom: ***clasă a două*** – *class-ah dough-ah*).  If you don't specify when buying tickets, they'll assume you just want a second-class ticket.  Frankly there's not much point in riding first class[54] unless you want a little more space and privacy.

Most **Regio** trains have just one kind of compartment and seats are not differentiated by classes.

For overnight and international trains, you can get a berth in a sleeping car, which is always more expensive than a regular seat.

---

[54] The one exception is the first-class sleeping car, which is quite nice and far better than second class.

One kind is called **cuşetă** (*coo-shet-ah*) that is a fold-down bunk that you can sleep on[55]. In 2nd class compartments there are 6 of these beds and in 1st class compartments there are just four.

The other kind is called **vagon dormitor** (*vah-goan dormy-tore*), an entire train car full of 1st class (only) sleeping compartments, each one having two beds and one functional sink. There is also a communal shower at the end of the train car.

Saving Money

Generally speaking, **Regio** trains are going to be the cheapest and shabbiest trains while **Inter-City** trains will be very high-quality and more expensive.

**CFR** offers several discounts on tickets available to non-citizens:

- *Round-trip* – Buying a round-trip ticket (Rom: **dus-intors** – *deuce-in-torse*) instead of two separate tickets will save you 10% on the total price for adults and 50% for children.
- *Online* – Buying tickets online with a credit card will save you 5% on the cost of any ticket.
- *Advance tickets* – If you buy your ticket 21 days (or more) in advance you'll save 13% on the total price. If you buy the ticket 11 (or more) days in advance, you save 10%. And for 6 (or more) days in advance, you save 5%.
- *University Student tickets* – Only those people who are a student at a *Romanian* university can get these discounts, which can be as high as 50%. You have to get a document from your university (ahead of time) to be eligible.
- *"Mini Group" tickets* – For 2-5 adults traveling together, you can save anywhere from 10-25% if you buy your tickets at the same time. To get this though, you have to get a document called **legitimaţia de "mini-grup"** from a CFR station/voiaj agency at least one day *before* you buy any tickets. You only need to get this document once however to be able to keep using it for the discount.
- *Larger group tickets* – For groups of adults (or mixed adults/children) of 30 people or more you can save up to 30% on the cost of all tickets.

There are other discounts available but only for Romanian citizens.

---

[55] CFR will provide the linens and pillow for these.

Understanding Your Ticket

Once you buy a ticket, you'll be handled a computer-printed piece of green paper with a lot of information on it. This will be the ticket you will need to show to the conductor once you're on your way.

The printed ticket has a number of contractions on it:

**Ple**: When the train is leaving.

**Sos:** When the train is arriving at your destination.

**Vag:** The number of the train car.

**Loc:** Your seat number.

Train Protocol

Although smoking is forbidden by law on all trains, sometimes people still do it (see page 86). Consuming food and drinks (of all types) is permitted and commonplace.

On crowded trains, people might insist on sitting in their "correct", assigned seats but you are free to move around anywhere you want to, as long as you remain in a 2nd class compartment (if you bought a 2nd class ticket).

Luggage can be stowed almost anywhere and thefts are very rare beyond a few opportunistic snatch and grabs. In all my years, I've never seen or heard about anyone's luggage ever being tampered with on board a train. For more on dangers on trains and elsewhere, see page 18.

The bathrooms are generally unpleasant and poorly stocked, so bring your own supplies. Surprisingly though, the water in the sink usually works as does the electrical outlet.

The toilet is (usually) nothing more than a hole in the floor of the carriage so using it while the train is in a station is forbidden.

**Plane**

Flying in Romania is quite affordable, especially domestically and definitely worth looking into if you are planning on traversing this very large country.

There are five major cities with airports, **Bucharest, Cluj, Constanţa, Iaşi** and **Timişoara** with regular domestic and international flights.

The only airline with a regular schedule of domestic flights in Romania is the national carrier TAROM[56], which has ticket offices in the downtown section of all cities they fly to.

Low-cost airlines are increasingly flying (from outside the country) into **Sibiu** and **Tîrgu Mureş** as well but the volume at these airports is still relatively low although it is growing every year.

Except for **Otopeni** airport in **Bucharest** (see below), all of these airports are extremely small and easy to negotiate. Security screenings and check-ins usually operate very quickly and efficiently. There are usually a few gift stores and duty-free shops.

## Otopeni and Băneasa Airports

Bucharest is served by two airports, a smaller one called **Băneasa**[57] and a larger one called **Otopeni** (*oh-toe-pen*) where most international flights take off and land from.

**Otopeni**, being Romania's busiest and biggest airport, is actually officially called *Henri Coanda*[58] Airport.

The airport is not inside the city limits of Bucharest but is near a tiny village named **Otopeni** in the next judet ("county") so for years and years and years the airport was called **Otopeni** as well.

Even today, the airport's international three-digit code is still **OTP** because of this. And absolutely everybody and their brother still *calls* it Otopeni. In fact, printed on my last TAROM ticket it actually said "Otopeni" so only in official reports and on maps is the airport called "Henri Coanda" Airport.

Getting There

Obviously you can fly in from outside the country as **Otopeni** is the main international airport. More on that below.

If you have a personal car, it's super simple to find **Otopeni** as it's right off the main road (north of **Bucharest**) with clear signage. There's a ton of parking, whether short term or long. It's been a while since I've traveled to **Otopeni** that way so I can't give you the details but I believe the parking (at least short-term) is based on the "park your car then go buy a ticket from an automated machine for how long you're going to stay" system.

---

[56] http://www.tarom.ro
[57] Officially called Aurel Vlaicu Airport. For more on who he was, see page 278.
[58] For more on who Henri Coanda (the person) was, see page 278.

Taking a taxi from downtown **Bucharest** is insanely cheap, especially using fully licensed, metered taxis at only 1.39 lei a kilometer (for more on taxis, see page 109). I'd say even from somewhere super central like **Piața Romana** the total to **Otopeni** shouldn't run you more than 20 or 25 lei.

There are two city buses that terminate at the airport and the folks in **Bucharest** went out of their way to make sure only the nice, new modern buses[59] are on these two lines, so at least your ride will be comfortable.

**Bus 780** connects from the main railroad station (Gara de Nord/Bucharest North) and makes only a few stops before arriving at the airport.

**Bus 783** meanders through all of the main downtown squares in Bucharest and makes quite a few stops before eventually arriving at the airport.

There's also a well-advertised new service with some kind of local train running from the main railroad station (Gara de Nord) directly to the airport and costing only **6 lei**[60].

At the moment there is no metro (subway) stop going to the airport.

Airport Layout

There are two buildings that compose **Otopeni** Airport and neither one of them has a name. They're built on two different levels as well. Years ago there was no way to get from one to the other except via a perilous journey on foot or else riding a bus that had to weave around acres of parking to get to the other terminal.

The good news is that now there is a pedestrian-friendly "bridge" between these two buildings.

Again, there are no official names or identifying marks for these two terminal buildings so I'm going to make up my own name and call one **Right Terminal** and one the **Left Terminal** based on which direction they'd be in if you were in the parking lot and facing them.

At the moment, all arrivals (domestic and international) come in the upper level of the **Right Terminal**. By the time you clear security you'll be in a long, thin hall with not much more than a couple of cafes. If you want a

---

[59] For more on riding city buses, see page 100.
[60] Honestly I've never taken it so I couldn't tell you much about it but there are literally signs for it everywhere. Apparently it drops you off just close enough to the airport that you can see it but it's too far to walk so they use a bus to shuttle you over the rest of the way. How this is simpler than just taking the 780 bus is beyond my capability to understand.

taxi[61], just walk right outside and take one from the queue, bypassing anyone "helpfully" offering to give you a ride by saying the word "taxi".

Downstairs in the same building is where you can find the buses. There's a nice, very clear and easy to understand map and a kiosk that sells the tickets you need. The buses seem to run every 10 minutes or so all throughout the day so scheduling isn't really much of an issue. The ticket seller also usually speaks English.

Downstairs in the **Right Terminal** is a store called "Billa" which is essentially a very well-stocked grocery store and a great place to load up on snacks and drinks rather than pay the far, far higher prices at the airport restaurants and cafes. Literally every single airport worker goes in there to shop so you'll get a chance to meet the people who make things happen.

The lower level of the **Left Terminal** is for all international departures. There's an enormous board showing the status of flights, check-in desks and all the standard things you'd expect. There's not much to do there but sit around and wait for your flight.

Upstairs in the **Left Terminal** is the connecting walkway over to the **Right Terminal** as well as various offices and the like. But if you want to see something interesting, wander around there until you find a completely sealed-in "bridge" that goes *over* the security area. It's super cool to stand there, peer down and watch people's luggage being scanned and the like.

On the other side of that short "bridge" is the best restaurant in the airport. Not only do they serve full, hot meals but there's a wonderful set of windows that look out over the tarmac and you can watch planes land and take off. If you've got lots of time to kill at **Otopeni**, this is the place to do it.

Now here's where it gets confusing. At the moment, all check-ins for all flights are done in the lower level of the **Left Terminal**, that is to say, the board announces your flight, you walk over to the little man or woman behind the counter, present your ticket, get your boarding pass, etc.

BUT.... all domestic flights actually take off from the **Right Terminal**. Fun, eh? You go to the **Left Terminal** to check in and then haul all your gear to the **Right Terminal** (lower level) and then pass through security, etc, there. That's a fairly new development so who knows how long it'll stay that way but I had to have a fairly long conversation (in Romanian) before I even understood that kooky system. Be aware that due to sheer stupidity in planning there is no way to take a cart from one building to another.

---

[61] For the complete guide on taxis, see page 120.

All international flights check-in and have their boarding right in the same area though, the lower level of the **Left Terminal**, extremely well marked and easy to find.

Other than that though, things are pretty basic and simple. Security is pretty normal and moves along quite quickly without much hassle.

**Otopeni** airport is ten thousand times more modern than when I first came so you really shouldn't have any difficulties.

## Boats

Generally there are only three situations in which you are going to travel by boat in Romania.

### Black Sea International Travel

Likely this means you will be leaving **Constanța** (page 159), Romania's largest port on the Black Sea (Romanian: **Marea Neagră**).

Various private companies (including cruise operators) operate routes between Romania and various destinations reached via Turkey and the Bosporus Strait.

### Danube River Cruise

There are many private companies offering boat trips starting (or ending) in one of the many European capitals and cities that lie along the length of the Danube River (Romanian: **Dunarea**), including Budapest, Bratislava and Vienna, Austria.

These tours are popular because as you enter (or leave) Romania, you pass through the **Porţile de Fier** (Iron Gates[62]), a very impressive gorge that now connects to a modern dam (for more on this, see page 166).

Once you enter Romania, the Danube River snakes through various rural areas along Romania's southern border until it fans out into the world-renowned **Danube Delta** (see page 167).

### Exploring the Danube Delta

The entire area between **Constanța** and **Tulcea** is a very large river delta area, quite similar in many ways to the bayou of Louisiana.

---

[62] In German this is called *Kataraktenstrecke*.

Much of this area can be more easily (or only) explored via boat, including the region that is home to the **Lipoveni** people (page 209).

It is also the home to an incredible amount of wildlife, especially birds, which migrate to this region in the millions.

Guided tours, regularly scheduled trips and private-hire watercraft are available from a number of operators. If you're unable to search for something suitable online, try a tourist agency, especially one in either **Constanța** or **Tulcea** or elsewhere within the delta region itself.

### Hitchhiking

If you want to save even more money, hitchhiking (called **auto-stop** in Romanian) is a common, legal, ordinary and safe practice done by thousands of Romanians every day. I've known young women traveling by themselves who have hitchhiked with no problems.

The ordinary custom is to stand on the outskirts of the city with a placard or sign held up, stating where you want to go. Otherwise you can stick your arm out straight from your body[63] at oncoming traffic.

You will be expected to chip in a few **lei** for whoever stops and picks you up. Whatever the cost, it will be cheaper than other forms of transportation.

Obviously never get in a car with someone you don't feel comfortable with. For more on dangers in Romania, see page 18.

### Private Automobile

I've driven a bit in Romania and I know a lot of (foreign) people who have, both with their own personal cars as well as cars rented while here.

Having your own vehicle in Romania can be extremely useful if you're going to be doing a lot of traveling, especially outside of the larger cities. On this issue, there is no question.

Please be aware though that maintaining, operating, parking, driving and actually using a private vehicle in Romania can be quite an adventure.

Some people, especially those who enjoy a good thrill, who can be said to have an "adventurous spirit", really enjoy driving and operating a vehicle in Romania. In fact, one of the most challenging and beautiful roads in the entire world is in Romania (see page 166). But people who enjoy an

---

[63] The "thumbs up" gesture isn't as common as simply holding your arm out straight. Some people do flap their outstretched arm though.

orderly, systematic and predictable driving experience often find Romania very frustrating, scary and sometimes even downright terrifying.

Literal obstacles will impede or deflect your path of travel at all times, whether that's flocks of animals crossing the road, unmarked holes or construction work, lanes that disappear or are unmarked, suddenly swerving and erratically moving vehicles, people standing with mouths agape in the middle of the road, wandering loose animals, unexpected rock or mudslides, extremely slow moving vehicles like horses and wagons or ancient cars, huge, threatening trucks (lorries), weaving bicyclists, zooming scooter drivers, children playing and trees fallen across the road are just a few of the common encounters you will meet.

If you consider it to be a kind of "real life" video game and therefore a very fun adventure, then I recommend driving a personal vehicle in Romania.

Otherwise, there is a very easy to use (and affordable) system of public transportation in Romania and in extremely rural areas, hitchhiking is also an option (page 106).

If you do decide to drive a personal vehicle, please be aware that driving at nighttime, especially between cities or in rural areas is <u>extremely dangerous</u> and should be avoided whenever possible.

Besides all of the hazards listed above, you also have vehicles operating without lights, much lower visibility (including due to adverse weather conditions) and sometimes very tired and/or inebriated drivers sharing the road with you.

Gasoline/petrol is sold in Romania at about **6 lei** (or more) per liter at various gradations according to European Union standards. In Romanian this is known as **benzină** (*ben-zeen-uh*).

Diesel is sold almost everywhere that **benzină** is sold (at roughly the same price) as many vehicles in Romania operate on this fuel. In Romanian this is known as **motorină** (*motor-een-uh*).

Note: A gas/petrol station is known as a **benzinerie** (*ben-zeen-eh-ree-eh*).

Vehicles entering Romania that are licensed and registered elsewhere usually do not require any special paperwork or any fees.

Generally speaking, your driver's license from your home country (assuming it's valid) is all you need to operate a vehicle in Romania unless you stay here longer than 30 days[64].

Using your home country driver's license (and your passport) and a credit card, it is possible to rent automobiles usually for between 30 euros and 60 euros a day. If you're traveling in Romania, this might be a very economical option, although I highly recommend using a GPS device (see page 7) as well.

Road signs all use the standard European markings, which generally are easy to understand but may confuse some non-European drivers.

Drinking nearly any amount of alcohol and driving is illegal in Romania and can lead to severe penalties[65] so don't do it. Taxis (see page 109) are cheap and plentiful and are your best choice for a night out on the town.

Parking can be a haphazard affair, with cars partially blocking streets or partially (or wholly) on sidewalks and often the only places available are technically illegal. The rule of thumb to go by is do as the Romanians do, so do whatever they do and you should be okay.

Although in no way do I wish to encourage criminality, parking tickets and fees are rarely enforced, even on Romanians, and many times it may be a more rational choice to park somewhere (technically) illegally. Certainly never pay a fine to anyone, including a police officer, if you think you are being scammed (see page 18).

That being said, larger cities now have tow trucks that pick up obstructing vehicles (sometimes in a haphazard way).

Use common sense and don't leave valuables in plain sight when parking your vehicle. Be aware that many hotels that offer "parking" leave your vehicle out in a public area that's under no surveillance or vigilance – the "parking" simply means that they will make sure you *get* a space to park your vehicle. If this is an important issue to you, ask ahead.

If you do get into a crash or a collision, remember that the number for all emergencies is **112**.

If there are serious injuries to anyone or serious damage to the vehicles, call the police and wait. If the crash, however, was minor, the standard

---

[64] If you're interested in what to do for longer term stays, see page 255.
[65] Unless of course you're an American with diplomatic immunity and then you can just run over people and kill them with impunity.

procedure is for all parties involved to drive to the local Traffic Police station and file a report there.

The police can become quite irascible if summoned for minor incidents but always be conscious of your safety and call them if you feel it is a necessary safety precaution.

**Taxi**

Cars are expensive in Romania and gasoline/diesel is as well. Therefore a lot of the population takes taxis, which are numerous and plentiful just about everywhere. Unless you're visiting Romania and driving your own car, chances are likely you're going to take a taxi at some point.

Before I say anything else on the subject I want to make one thing abundantly clear – the vast majority of taxi rides are safe, economical ways of getting around town when it's either too far to walk or else you're tired or have been drinking. The drivers are professionals and get you where you want to go at a set rate and all goes well in the vast majority of cases.

That being said, I have had a few bad experiences in all my years of living and visiting here and I've certainly heard a few horror stories. Therefore I present to you my guide for taking a taxi in Romania so that your visit is unmarred by any unpleasantness.

Understanding Taxi Markings

First of all, all genuine taxis are marked in a clear way with the word taxi on top in a lightbar as well as a car number. They're not all necessarily yellow but a lot of them are (requirements vary depending on the city).

If you look at the front quarter panel of the taxi vehicle, you will see the various rates. There are always four lines, starting from the top:

- Pick-up fee
- Rate per kilometer (day)
- Rate per minute while standing
- Night rate

In **Cluj** the "pick-up fee" is **1.79 lei**[66] that I owe just for getting inside the taxi. Then I pay the rate per kilometer for the distance that the driver took me.

If we're stuck at a red light, the "Rate per minute while standing" kicks in, which is ten times the normal rate *per hour*, which sounds confusing.  For

---

[66] Roughly 60 cents USD at the moment of writing this.

example if the "pick-up" fee is **1.79 lei** per kilometer, the "standing rate" is **17.9 lei** per hour, making it just **30 bani** per minute of waiting (such as at a red light).

Nighttime fares are higher, although not much, and run from about 10pm to 6am.

In some cities, like **Cluj**, all taxi companies charge exactly the same rate. In other cities, each company has a different rate per kilometer.

**Before getting in any taxi, check out the rates** listed on the front quarter panel (on both sides of the vehicle).

Note: In some cities, particularly **Timişoara** comes to mind, there are companies with insanely high rates, often parked outside the train station and other popular tourist destinations. It's all completely legal but if you ignore the rate before getting on board you might be in for a nasty surprise.

"Gypsy Cabs" – Although rare, there are people operating "gypsy" or illegal, unmarked taxis. These can be a major rip-off so be sure to never get into a vehicle that's not clearly marked and identified as a taxi.

How to Get a Taxi

Assuming you don't speak Romanian, there are various good ways of getting a taxi.

**Taxi Stand** – There are usually several spots around town in key locations where taxis queue up and wait for passengers. Just pick whichever taxi looks best to you (keeping in mind the rates) and get in and off you go. You do not have to take the very first one in line. Couldn't be easier!

**Calling a taxi (by phone)** – Many vehicles are marked with a three-digit phone number. If you have a working phone in Romania and dial that number, nothing will happen. Say what? These 3-number codes are actually shorthand as Romanians know it *actually means* "dial the city's prefix code first then the 3-digit taxi number". For example in **Cluj** the city prefix is "0264" so to call a cab showing the "short" number 941 I'd have to dial 0264-941.

Other numbers have a * or # symbol in front of them. If you have a Romanian mobile phone you can call these short codes (i.e. #944) and be connected directly to the taxi company's dispatcher.

For more information on telephones and telephone numbers, see page 26.

Most dispatchers don't speak English so I wouldn't recommend this option. However a far easier way to do it is to walk into the nearest (and fanciest) business, whether a hotel, restaurant or even gas/petrol station and ask the workers there to call one *for you*. I don't think I've ever had a Romanian turn down an offer to help me in this regard.

If you do insist on calling one yourself, say **"o maşina la....vă rog"** (*oh masheena la.... vah rawg*) which means "one car to (address) please". The dispatcher (always a surly woman for some reason) will then ask for your name (*numele*) and tell you how many minutes it will be until the driver arrives.

Note: For a culture that's not exactly keen on punctuality, Romanian taxi companies rather bizarrely always tell you the exact number of minutes it will be until they arrive. I never did quite understand that!

**Flagging down a taxi** – As in seeing one drive by and making a motion and it pulls over. This is usually not necessary but if you ever need to do it, the correct motion is to extend your arm out and then flap your hand *down* like you are trying to imitate a bird in flight (with one hand).

The Ride Itself

Whether or not the driver will understand anything but Romanian is a gamble but usually if you can communicate the address (or landmark or hotel), they'll either figure it out or get on their radio and find out where it is with no problems.

You can sit in either the front or back with no worries and while some drivers are quite chatty, the norm seems to be complete silence during the ride with a preference to listening to the radio over talking.

Note: If you are a smoker and want to smoke in your cab, have the company dispatch a "smoking car" (aka a driver who doesn't care if you smoke). Or conversely if the thought of someone else smoking in the car previously disturbs you, have a non-smoking car dispatched. Usually though the majority of Romanian taxis are non-smoking (and it's usually a short ride anyway).

Up in the front however, either mounted on the dash or between the seats is a black metal box with a green, digital readout. This is the fare meter known as the **ceas** (literally: "clock" and pronounced *choss*).

Make sure this meter is running as you drive!

As long as the meter is running, you should have no unpleasantness or unexpected surprises in terms of the fare.

Also, the name and ID badge of the driver should be displayed somewhere prominently, although this doesn't always happen. If for some unexpected reason you encounter a real problem, at least note down the number of the car (behind rear windows on the outside usually) and the company's name.

Tipping

When you get to your destination, the driver will push a button on the fare meter and a total will pop up. Tipping is appreciated in Romania but it is not necessary beyond rounding up to the nearest whole leu, i.e. if the total fare is **7.20 lei**, go ahead and give the driver **8 lei** and all is well.

If the fare is just **7.10 lei** however usually the driver will just expect **7 lei** and "eat" the overage of **10 bani** ("cents"). It all depends on the driver of course but generally just rounding up will be sufficient unless you've received unbelievably outstanding service.

A Few Things To Be Aware Of

By law, all Romanian taxi vehicles must be fairly new and in good condition. If you see some old rusty, broken down vehicle that's supposed to be a "taxi", avoid it.

Make sure the meter is running unless you know what you're doing (and speak Romanian). Sometimes the driver might ask you at the *beginning* if you want a receipt (Romanian: **bon fiscal**). When in doubt, always say yes that you want the receipt. Not giving you a receipt means not turning the meter on. Some drivers do this to avoid paying taxes and for other reasons but never say "no" to the receipt.

At airports and train stations (especially in **Bucharest**) there will always be guys trolling the crowds, saying "taxi?" and trying to persuade you to go with them. Avoid these guys and go outside where there is always a line/queue of genuine, safe, metered taxis available.

Sometimes the drivers will try to "upsell" you and offer to take you somewhere (such as a nearby city) for a negotiated fare. In almost every case, the standard bus and train lines are cheaper so avoid this.

During very "bad" weather, such as heavy snow or rainfall, it can be hard to get a taxi. Just hang in there and breathe as they will come around to you soon!

## A Few Useful Phrases

| English | Romanian | Pronunciation |
|---|---|---|
| Is this taxi free/ available (to take me somewhere)? | E liber? | *Eh lee-BEAR?* |
| Is the meter running? | E pornit ceasul? | *Eh porneet CHASS-ool?* |
| To "X" destination, please | La "X", vă rog | *Lah... vah rawg* |
| Keep the change | Vă rog, pastrați restul | *Vah rawg, pah-strets rest-ool* |
| Step on it! | Conduceți mai repede! | *con-DOOTCH-ets my reh-peh-day* |
| Follow that car! | Urmariți mașina asta! | *oorm-ah-reets mah-sheena ah-stah* |
| Good lord, you're driving fast as hell | Doamne, e ca in filme cum conduceți | *dwam-nee eh ka in film-eh koom con-doo-chets* |
| Turn right | Dreapta | *Drop-tah* |
| Turn left | Stânga | *Stung-uh* |
| Keep going straight | Tot înainte | *Tote in-a-een-tay* |
| (Stop) Here | Aici | *Ah-eetch* |

## Getting to International Destinations

Generally speaking, it is often easier and more affordable to get to other destinations in Europe by flying out of one of the five major airports in Romania (**Bucharest, Cluj, Constanța, Iași** and **Timișoara**).

Note:    *You are not required to pay any kind of fee to leave (or enter) Romania.*

## USA and Canada

Since there are no direct flights to the United States or Canada, you're going to have to first fly to a large city in western Europe and then take a second flight.

Almost all USA and Canadian bound flights start extremely early in the morning. Therefore you will have to get to the airport quite early, which can pose some challenges.

## Hungary

From either the Banat or most places in Transylvania (page 248) and northwest Romania, getting to Hungary is often easier and faster with a **minibuz** (page 92).

Since the Budapest airport is extremely popular for USA and Canada-bound flights, getting to the airport at 5:00 or 6:00 am is often most easily accomplished by taking a **minibuz** directly to the airport.

There are many daily flights from several Romanian airports to Budapest. Additionally, there are multiple train connections to Hungary.

## Western Europe

There are numerous, daily flights (including on low-cost airlines) at good prices from most Romanian airports to Britain, Spain, France, Italy and Germany.

Taking an overland bus route is still the absolute cheapest option but not generally recommended.

## Eastern Europe

Very, very few flights can be found from Romania directly linking any other Eastern Europe countries (besides Hungary) and the ones that do exist fly almost exclusively from **Bucharest**'s **Otopeni** airport (see page 102).

Getting to Ukraine, Poland, Serbia or Russia is usually twice as difficult and expensive as getting to France, Germany or Britain.

## Serbia

Despite how close Belgrade is to **Timişoara** (page 163), getting in and out of Serbia remains extremely difficult. At the moment there is only one train per day that moves extremely slowly.

By far the easiest way is to either fly into Serbia directly or else into Budapest, Hungary as the transportation connections in that direction are in much better shape.

I haven't heard of anyone having difficulties entering Serbia by private car aside from terrain obstacles (roads in poor conditions, etc).

Ukraine

In just about every case, you will have to first make your way to **Iaşi** (page 149) and then you can either take a train or **minibuz** to most larger cities.

There are also **minibuze** that leave from **Suceava** (page 163) that run directly into northern Bukovina (Chernivtsi oblast). There is also a crossing from the Romanian city of **Sighetu Marmaţiei** in Maramures that leads into western Ukraine.

Republic of Moldova

Again, all major land transportation routes run through **Iaşi**, as the city lies just a few kilometers from **Moldova**'s borders. There is also a crossing near the Romanian city of **Galaţi** that leads into the extreme southern portion of the Republic of Moldova.

Bulgaria and Turkey

Train and other inter-city bus routes operate out of either **Bucharest** or **Constanţa** as part of a network that runs through Sofia, Bulgaria and terminates in Istanbul, Turkey.

Due to a number of factors, the part of **Bulgaria**'s coast on the Black Sea (especially the city of Varna) is more popular with tourists (including Romanians) than the sections in Romania near **Constanţa**. Therefore there is a lot of vehicular traffic in this area during the summertime and you may be able to catch a **minibuz** going there as well.

Furthermore, some boat traffic leaving **Constanţa** will make stops along Bulgaria's Black Sea coast en route to Turkey.

# Major Holidays

### Marţişor – March 1

Pronounced *martsy-shore*, this is one of the very oldest holidays in Romania, with some experts thinking that it can be traced back to Dacian or pre-Roman times (for more on the history of Romania, see page 240).

Whenever its origin, this is a day with a long and storied history, being the official beginning of spring.

There are a great number of regional variations in how to honor this spring festival (such as foods to eat, etc) but by far the most common is the wearing of lucky amulets.

The talismanic amulets are called by the same word as the holiday itself, i.e. **marţişori**, and are usually a small brooch designed to be pinned to one's blouse, with a small tassle hanging down made of intertwined red and white thread.[67]

Women predominantly wear the amulets and it is the custom for males (of nearly all ages) to purchase them for the women in their lives, whether family, friend or romantic partner.

About a week prior to March 1, sidewalk vendors will pop up to start selling these talismans, which range from the very simple[68] to the elaborate and expensive.

Primarily in Transylvania but also occurring elsewhere, there is a custom called the **udat** (*ooh-dot*), literally meaning "the wetting". Males of all ages purchase (relatively cheap) perfume and then give each female in their life a healthy dose of spray when they meet her on **marţişor**.

In practice, this means some women can be thoroughly doused with a wild medley of conflicting scents by the end of the day.

Note: *This is not a "bank holiday" and all retail stores and government offices will be operating on their normal schedules.*

---

[67] There are a few regional variants in tassle color but generally speaking red and white is the most common.

[68] Costing about **1 leu** or about 25 euro cents at the moment.

## Women's Day – March 8

A holdover from the Communist days, this is an international holiday given a lot of attention still to this day in Romania.

It is customary to give flowers and/or a small gift to any woman you are close to in your life whether family, friend or romantic partner.

Note: *This is not a "bank holiday" and all retail stores and government offices will be operating on their normal schedule.*

## May 1

Ah yes, the sun is shining, the birds are singing, winter is over and so begins one of Romania's great holidays – **First May**.

Everywhere around the world, except in the United States (anymore – a long time ago it was), the first day of May is known as International Workers' Day, the kind of a day where everybody gets off of work and sometimes holds marches or protests or generally those sorts of things.

Back in the Communist days in Romania, **May 1** was a huge holiday – not only did everyone get off work but there were lots of long-winded speeches and rallying cries rallied and slogans sloganeered and motivational posters plastered everywhere and that sort of thing. Communism was all (allegedly) about *the proletariat* aka the workers, so ideologically **May 1** was the most important day of the year.

Nowadays in Romania it's an entirely "secular" sort of holiday. The stores are almost all closed, there are no school or government offices open and everyone and their brother heads to the beach. The water is still far too cold to go swimming but the beaches will be crammed from one end to the other with people drinking, dancing, grilling **slănină** (page 45) and **mici** (page 43) and listening to music.

The people who don't go to the beach head for somewhere in a rural outdoor setting to conduct similar merry-making.

The winters in Romania can be kind of long but pretty much every year by the time **May 1** rolls around the days are warm and summer is just around the corner so it really works out well to have a nice day off, head out to somewhere in the country or at the seaside, hang out with friends and grill some food.

For anyone coming to Romania as a tourist, **May 1** is really when the "good weather" season kicks off so head on over!

Note: Romanians use a very unique way of saying dates, especially for the FIRST day of the month, which in Romanian is **întâi**, literally meaning "first". They don't say second, third, fourth, etcetera (aka ordinal numbers) but they always say "first".

Therefore, in Romanian, this holiday is known as **Întâi Mai** (*untie my*), literally "First May", which is how you'll often hear Romanians translate the name of this holiday into English.

For more on Romanian numbers, see page 277.

## Easter

By far the central holiday in both Orthodox and Catholic forms of Christianity, Easter (Rom: **Paște** – *posh-tay*, Hun: **Húsvét** – *hush-vet*) is easily the most important day in Romania.

The Orthodox and Catholic calendars use a different calculation to determine when Easter occurs, so in many years they are celebrated at different times, although in some years they do overlap.

This is of critical importance because it is generally Hungarians who celebrate Easter on the Catholic date (which is always the the same date as when Easter is celebrated in the United States and most of western Europe) and Romanians on the Orthodox date, so the impact of Easter will vary depending on where you are.

Religious services, bell ringing and a great number of participatory rituals are performed[69], almost always of significant duration. Be aware that most Romanian churches do not contain seating of any kind and therefore the congregation might be left standing three hours or even more with no respite.

Easter is entirely a friends and family affair and the custom is to spend a tremendous amount of money[70] (and/or effort) to cook up an enormous feast, including some special foods (page 56) and quite often lots of alcohol as well.

The only commercial activities in operation on Orthodox Easter Sunday[71] are public transportation, including trains as well as city bus lines[72]. It is

---

[69] Such as lighting candles, walking around the church x number of times, etc

[70] If you can even find a store open after Easter, it will generally be deserted. That's because everyone spent literally all their money on the Easter food and is too broke to buy anything for a while.

[71] As noted, in majority Hungarian areas, observance would be far lower.

extremely rare to even find a restaurant open, with the single except of McDonald's[73], the international chain.

On the Monday after Easter, many stores may remain closed or only be open for a limited number of hours during the middle of the day. All government buildings and banks will likewise be closed.

Especially in the Orthodox tradition there is a season of fasting leading up to Easter known as **de post** or not eating meat and therefore a wider range of vegan food options are sold (for more on this, see page 71).

Starting on Easter Sunday and continuing for a week (or sometimes more) afterwards, there is a custom in many parts of Romania to greet everyone you know[74] in a ritualized way in lieu of the normal "hello" and it requires a ritualized response:

**Person 1:** *Hristos a inviat! – (hreestoze ah envy-ott)*

**You:** *Adeverat ca a inviat! – (ah Davy rot convee-ott)*

This literally means "Christ has risen" with the response being "It is true that he has risen indeed".

### Ziua Copilor – June 1

Originating in the Communist era, this is still a popular holiday today, literally translated as "Children's Day".

Games, festivals, activities, magic shows and all kinds of entertainment, learning and fun activities are planned for the children on this day. Many of these are public events and have no admission or entry cost.

Candies and other sweet treats can be a common gift for any young children you know on this day.

Most Romanian cities of any size have a **Palatul Copilor** (literally: Children's Palace), a kind of local recreational center dedicated primarily to children's needs.

---

[72] The buses will run on their "weekend" or reduced schedules but oddly enough, the train schedules in Romania almost never vary.
[73] Who are scrupulously open bright and early on every religious holiday, thus getting all the business since their competitors are all closed.
[74] Including sometimes store clerks or even a neighbor in your *bloc* that you literally only know in passing.

## August

Like most of the rest of Europe, practically the entire nation is on vacation/holiday for most of the month of August.

Many, many tourist sites, including along the Black Sea, will be extremely crowded during this period. If you are planning on spending any time in popular destinations during August, it is wise to plan ahead!

Note: Surprisingly, many government offices remain open during this period, albeit with fewer staff (who are rotating through their vacations). Sometimes you can actually get paperwork processed a lot faster during August.

## November 1 – Ziua Morților

In many areas of the country, it is traditional on November 1 (the day after Halloween – see below) to visit and clean the graves of loved ones and family members.

As with all Romanian holidays, a great number of special foods are prepared, most of them identical with funeral foods (see page 236).

Candles and other lights are often lit at nightfall, giving the entire cemetery an ethereal beauty.

Note: this holiday is much more commonly observed in areas with a significant Hungarian population as it has origins in the Catholic faith.

## December 1

Now known in Romanian as **Ziua Națională a României** or Romania's National Day, this holiday commemorates the signing of a declaration stating that Transylvania, the Banat, Bessarabia (page 245) and Bucovina (page 165) were, for the first time, now unified with all the majority Romanian lands – Wallachia and Moldova.

The declaration was signed on December 1, 1918 in the city of **Alba Iulia**[75] and every year all Romanian politicians and bigwigs of every stripe go there to give speeches to commemorate this day of unification.

Note: In many cities, you will see a **Piața Unirii**, which means "square/plaza of the unification" and refers to this date.

---

[75] I've been to Alba Iulia many times and it is a relatively small city with warm, friendly inhabitants but not much to see otherwise any time of the year.

In other cities besides **Alba Iulia** there will be other patriotic speeches, parades and demonstrations but nationwide the weather is usually extremely uncooperative, often with heavy snowfalls and bitterly cold winds, dampening the patriotic fires of all but the most ardent of Romanians.

Historically this brief union was the high water mark of Romanian political fortunes as all of Bessarabia was wrested away by the Soviet Union just a few decades later, now known as the sovereign nation of the **Republic of Moldova**.

Likewise the top 2/3rds of Bucovina were mandated to the Soviets, forming what is southern **Ukraine** today, still containing a significant portion of ethnic Romanian people.

Transylvania was wrested away twice and returned to Hungarian control before Romania finally solidified its governance of the territory at the end of World War 2.  To this day, there is a small but steady rumbling of instability and friction between the Romanian and Hungarian population with rare but sometimes violent results.

All banks and government offices will be closed on this day but retail stores should generally remain open.

### St. Nicholas Day – December 6

December 6 is the feast day for Saint Nicholas (Rom: **Sfântul Nicolae**) an important saint in both the Catholic and Orthodox religion.

Similar to "Santa Claus" or "Father Christmas" in other traditions, on this day he "brings" children gifts.

A common tradition is for children to leave their shoes or boots out in a conspicuous place (especially on a windowsill) for them to be filled with candies and small presents.

Note: if you are buying presents for small children for the Christmas season, December 6 is the day to give them.

### Christmas

While this is important as a religious holiday, it comes in second behind Easter.

The good news is that Romanians and Hungarians alike celebrate Christmas on December 25 so there is never any confusion on what day it falls.  Only in neighboring **Republic of Moldova** is the Orthodox calendar

Christmas observed, which generally speaking occurs some time in the first week of January.

Note: This can lead to certain winter resorts and tourist destinations being especially full or busy in this period.

The name of this holiday in Romanian, **crăciun** (*crah-choon*), has a long history, first referring to an ancient Slavic pagan holiday called *korochun*, borrowed into Hungarian to mean Christmas (Hun: **Karácsony**) then flattened into Romanian as **crăciun**.

The name of Santa Claus or Father Christmas in Romanian is **Moş Crăciun**, literally "Old Man Crăciun".

It is a nationwide holiday and almost no one goes to work or conducts commercial transactions besides public transportation employees[76].

Many, many workers often have the entire week (or even two weeks) off with paid holiday stretching directly into New Year's and sometimes beyond. Therefore almost all retail stores and government offices will have a shortened schedule with many dates completely closed.

Most popular tourist destinations will also be busy during this season, especially those involving winter sports such as skiing and snowboarding.

The custom of a Christmas tree (Romanian: **brad crăciun**), as in a large, full-sized fir or pine tree of some sort, is fairly rare although many Romanians do like to at least have a branch or a wreath from a live tree in their homes.

Giving gifts is usually reserved for only your closest friends and loved ones, although small tokens of your affection are always appreciated. Extravagant and numerous gifts are rarely given as the emphasis is more on having a large meal with your family.

More gifts are usually given (especially to children) on December 6 or **St. Nicholas' Day** (page 121).

For a list of some Christmas foods, see page 56.

---

[76] With the exception of McDonald's of course, as noted on page 64.

## New Year's Eve and New Year's Day

It is considered nearly mandatory for Romanians to have an organized, formal party on the last day of the year, known as **Revelion** (*revel-yawn*).

This party is usually held at a restaurant, hotel, bar or other public spot rather than at someone's home. These establishments do a brisk business as **Revelion** parties are usually reserved months ahead of time, each guest paying a set cost.

The actual party usually involves lots of music, drinking and several rounds of food, lasting late into the night.

Many cities have public (free) concerts and other festivities on the evening of December 31.

At midnight there is usually a large fireworks display, especially in main downtown squares in larger cities.

Note: The first few days of January are generally a holiday for most people as well, so almost all businesses will be closed, including many grocery and food stores.

## Halloween, Valentine's Day and St. Patrick's Day

Generally speaking, these three holidays are imports from the Western world and are not officially celebrated here in Romania. Nonetheless, it makes good gist for theme parties at bars and the like.

Romania has an ancient local holiday called **Dragobete** which falls on February 24, roughly analogous[77] to Valentine's Day in other countries. As it falls *after* Valentine's Day, every year **Dragobete** gets more and more neglected in favor of its more commercial, imported cousin on February 14.

The holiday **St. Patrick's Day** is usually only limited to a few bars holding themed parties.

As for **Halloween**, this is barely commemorated or marked in any way, although pumpkins are grown here and quite often *eaten* around this time of year, if not actually carved.

Some bars of course will hold themed parties, probably your best chance to see people in costumes.

---

[77] Historically, Dragobete was the official kick-off to "marriage season" in Romania, wherein several festivals were held in order to introduce rural men to prospective future wives.

In a few places around Romania on October 31, a number of **Vampire Porn Lovers** (see page 214) gather to do those things that they do, including visit **Bran Castle** (page 169) which is open all night during this night only and which hosts a popular party for foreigners.

# Romanian Cultural Basics

Understanding a few, basic cultural norms will greatly smooth your visit to Romania and make social interactions a lot easier.

### Shaking Hands

Although the following seems complicated, it's actually not. Shaking hands is an important social act in many cultures so learn it and do it right!

Most important of all: **always shake with your right hand**.

Always. I don't care if you're left-handed or your right hand is wet, always shake with the right hand. If your hand is irreversibly dirty or otherwise unshakeable, proffer your right arm to be grasped above the wrist. Also, always remove any gloves you are wearing to shake hands, especially if the other person isn't wearing any.

Secondly, if you're not sure whether to shake hands, just wait for the Romanian in question to initiate it.

If you're a woman – quite frankly you don't need to shake anyone's hands at all. Certainly never initiate a handshake.

If you do get in a situation to shake someone's hand, simply hold yours out loose and unmoving. You really don't have to do much more than just barely grasp the other person's hand and certainly do not give it a *squeeze*.

If you're a man – first off, in many situations it's considered a kind of flirtatious move to shake a woman's hand so rarely, if ever, do this (unless that's your intent).

In a few business situations (or innocent goofs) you will raise your hand to shake a woman's hand. If so, do it lightly and quickly and don't expect her to squeeze you back in any way.

A much better idea is simply to turn to face the woman in question and give her a very short bow.

If it's a man on the other hand (whose hand you're shaking), a mild grip is quite fine. Trying to show how you are quite a fine masculine fellow and demonstrating it with an iron grip isn't really done in Romania.

Again, it's usually best to wait for Romanians in question to begin the hand shaking because it really isn't *de rigeur* outside of some strictly professional situations.

Since handshakes often accompany introductions, here is how to properly introduce yourself:

Whether shaking hands or just a courtesy bow to the person in question, you say *your name* and they will say their name to you. You don't even say "my name is so-and-so", all you do is just shake hands/bow and say, "Sam" and they say their name.

**The "Euro Kiss"**

Although this form of greeting is common throughout Europe, in Romania it is performed slightly differently.

How it's done:

Put your cheeks squarely together and then curve your lips toward their face and give them a "sideways" kiss. Aim right at the extreme outside corner of their lips. Make sure it is a solid kiss though, as in definite lip to cheek contact.

Then switch sides and do the exact same thing on the other side.

If you're a woman – first off, you always give the Euro kiss to any female relatives.

Secondly, concerning other women, you'll be doing it primarily with your female friends as a sign of closeness and friendship. Basically you Euro kiss your BFFs[78].

As a woman Euro kissing a guy, you only kiss either extremely close relatives or else about a handful of guys whom you count as friends as well.

If you're a guy – well you won't be Euro kissing any other guys except perhaps your very closest male relatives.

---

[78] Best friends ("forever")

Concerning women however it is mostly a sign that you're good friends with them, so probably someone you've known for a while. It really does *not* have a sexual component to it and doesn't mean that she's "into you".

The frequency of whom you kiss also determines how close you are to the person in question as it is never mandatory to kiss the same people every time or on every occasion (both coming and going).

It is much more common to Euro kiss people on "special occasions" such as their birthday or after you haven't seen them for a while.

Since this is generally a kind of "friendship" kiss, it is usually reserved for non-professional situations (i.e. not at work).

Note: In very rural and conservative areas, the "Euro Kiss" is reserved for close family members only.

All of the above being true, sometimes you'll get involved in a Euro kiss unexpectedly. Enjoy it, it's quite fun!

**Holding Hands**

If you're a "romantic" couple in any way, holding hands anywhere is absolutely fine. No one will give you the slightest trouble over it.

Two females, whether little children or young adults, holding hands is very common and means nothing more than friendship.

Males holding hands on the other hand is quite rare and usually only seen when it's involving a father (or male adult relative) holding the hand of a small child.

**Romantic Kissing**

Again, absolutely fine just about anywhere so long as it is heterosexual, i.e. a male and a female.

In fact, I almost punched out an American traveler I met in **Otopeni**[79] one time I was there because he passed a couple kissing their last goodbyes and tossed off the sardonic remark, "Get a room!". No. As long as you're heterosexual, kissing someone romantically in public is both tolerated and welcomed as a good thing because duh, it is.

---

[79] The main international airport in Bucharest. For more information, see page 112.

That being said, homosexual romantic kissing in public, especially between two guys, would probably start an incident that would end up on the nightly news.

## Hugging

Hugging is extremely rare in Romania, even in cases of close family members or romantic couples. It's not something "natural" to the ordinary way of life for most Romanians.

Never, ever initiate a hug with a Romanian! There are a few huggers out there but wait for them to reveal themselves to you first. Furthermore, the "bear hug" is almost never welcomed so if you do hug, hug gently.

The last thing you want to do if you're flirting with a girl is to give her a surprise hug.

## Public Displays of Affection (PDA)

Again, like the romantic kissing above, it's understood that two people feeling good about each other are going to like to touch their partner in intimate ways. And yes sometimes that happens in public, particularly if you're young and don't have a place of your own to go to.

I find it all quite natural now but if you're unused to seeing young people dry humping on a park bench, then steel your jangled nerves before coming here.

## Doors

If you have to open a door, always close it behind you. This isn't a "maybe sometimes" kind of situation, but mandatory.

If you are approaching a closed door in some kind of business setting (government office, medical clinic, etc) then the correct procedure is to knock first and wait to be summoned.

## Gypsies

In general, Romanians loathe gypsies and strongly discourage any fraternization with them, other than to (quickly) conduct business.

For more information on gypsies as a people, see page 200.

The main thing to understand here is that almost no one in Romania likes gypsies or wants to hear about them in any way. Although by law they are

Romanian citizens, very few people consider them *Romanians*, as in ethnically or culturally.

## Moving Air – Bringer of Sickness

Romanians have a worldview on illness and health that is a blend of modern medicine and traditional beliefs.

Where this most impacts the visitor is that Romanians believe that moving or drafty[80] air can lead to illness, called the **curent** in Romanian.

Therefore on train cars, it is customary for Romanians to lock up windows very tightly in all but the most sweltering conditions. Travel on buses and **minibuze** (page 92) can also reach sauna-like conditions due to Romanians wanting to avoid drafty air.

It is also common to get into a taxi (page 109 for the full guide on taxis) in summertime and find that the windows are down but that the driver will raise them as the car begins to drive without asking for your permission (the driver assuming you wish to avoid the **curent**).

While you can insist on rolling your own window down, this may cause the driver to become ornery. Lowering a window on a bus or train may also provoke hostile comments from your fellow passengers.

## Religion

The vast majority of the citizens of Romania are at least nominally Christian, some fanatically devout and others who easily approach being secular in outlook and lifestyle.

That being said, while mocking and insulting religious customs is often practiced by some here, outright atheism is strongly offensive to almost all people.

In Romania it is generally considered rude to be overly inquisitive about one's religious views, so if you do hold an atheist or contrarian viewpoint, the best course is to keep it to yourself unless you want to open a confrontational dialogue.

Because being pro-Christian is about as uncontroversial as wearing blue jeans, the culture here is extremely tolerant and benign concerning Christian

---

[80] Or "draughty" to use the older spelling

missionaries of every possible flavor[81], who flock to this country in great numbers (see page 211), especially in the summertime.

Other religions, such as Buddhism, Judaism and Islam are so rare that they are generally regarded as harmless curiosities.  Also, there are a plethora of small cults and non-denominational spiritual societies operating in Romania.

## Crowding/Claustrophobia

If you're from a culture that highly values a lot of personal space, Romania is often going to seem quite crowded and even claustrophobic to you. There are a lot of daily situations where you're going to be in very tight quarters with a lot of people around you.

Furthermore, Romanians quite often have the tendency to bunch up very close together in situations like lines (queues) and it can be disconcerting to have someone right behind you "breathing on your neck", sometimes literally.

While there is no physical danger involved in being jostled around a very crowded bus or subway car, it can be quite a stressful experience for people not used to such situations.

It must be said here that the vast majority of Romanians severely dislike being in cramped quarters but it's just a fact of life that they've all gotten used to.

Places likely to be crowded:

- Bus, tram, subway car or any other form of mass transportation, including "minibuses" or "maxitaxis"
- government offices (post offices, etc)
- train stations
- sidewalks in major thoroughfares in big cities
- the **piața** (page 63) or marketplace

Additionally, many elevators (lifts) in Romania are extremely small and sometimes of dubious safety and reliability.

## The Beep

If you befriend a single Romanian, sooner or later you're going to run into "the beep", which is written in Romanian as **bip**.

---

[81] Not trying to be offensive here but this seemed to be a convenient metaphor.

What is this?

It is when one person calls you (or you call them) and the receiving party *does not answer.*

What is this for?

The **bip** in Romania is a way to communicate something to someone. Since the call was never completed, there is no charge (cost) to either party but information has been communicated.

A few uses of the **bip**:

- Hi, I'm thinking about you
- I'm outside your *bloc* so come downstairs
- I'm at specified point X
- I made it home okay, goodnight, I kiss you
- I'm out of credit so call me back

And many more...

### Iarbă Verde

The phrase **iarbă verde** (*yar-buh ver-day*) literally means "green grass" but is used as a catch-all phrase for when urban dwellers are craving some time spent in a natural, unspoiled, rural environment.

Especially when the weather is nice, Romanians will pack up their cars and head out somewhere, anywhere, an "official" spot or not, just as long as there's some green grass, fresh air and unspoiled nature.

During a trip to the **iarbă verde**, Romanians usually grill out some food (especially **slănină** – page 45 and **mici** – page 43) and have a picnic and listen to music.

The most traditional time to head into the countryside for a weekend of fresh food and air is **May 1** (page 117).

### Phone Etiquette

Answering a phone: **alo?** (*ah-low*)

Saying goodbye to a friend: **pa, ciao, szia** (*see-ah*) or **servus**.

Saying goodbye formally (to everyone else): **la revedere** (lah ray-vay-day-ray). This is <u>mandatory</u>.

If someone calls you by accident (wrong number):

**Îmi pare rău dar aţi greşit numarul** (*eem porry reuw dar ots gresheet numar-ool*).

## Public Conduct

In general, a high sense of decorum is expected of you while in public.

Farting, belching and burping are never permissible in public or in the company of others and considered extremely rude.

Spitting, especially by men, is however quite commonplace even though it is considered somewhat rude and low class.

In addition, most people in Romania dress as well as they can afford to. Raggedy, dirty and/or unkempt clothes or appearance is highly frowned upon as it makes people think you are a gypsy or a beggar.

## Public Dress

How you dress largely determines your social status here and will definitely affect the way you are treated. Clean, pressed, appropriately fitting clothes are considered the bare minimum.

Ragged, stained and excessively baggy or slovenly clothes will essentially be signalling others that you are a low-status person.

Romania is also one of those countries where Shoes Matter.

## Pajamas

You may be somewhat surprised to see ordinary adult Romanians wandering around town dressed in their pajamas (and slippers).

For some reason, if you are ever interned in a Romanian hospital, they make you wear pajamas at all times (which you provide yourself). Therefore even if you walk out of the hospital to go down to the corner store, you must remain dressed in your pajamas.

It is only when you are formally discharged that you are allowed to dress in your ordinary "street clothes".

## Astrology and Magic

As a culture, Romanians (especially women) have a high level of interest in the zodiac and astrology. It is common practice to see horoscopes in most daily papers as well as on television news broadcasts.

Additionally, there is a strong cultural tradition of wearing lucky talismanic amulets (page 116) that continues to this day.

Furthermore, there is always a strong emphasis on *magical, supernatural* and/or *(religiously) divine* actions in the news and other informative media[82].

Even in mainstream political speech it is common to see some elements of the magical or divine, including the belief that people can cast spells, witches exist and are real and that curses can have powerful effects.

## Names

Both for Hungarians and Romanians, it is common to choose first names for children from a rather limited pool. Many children are given the first name of the saint whose birthday they share.

Hungarians, using the Asian custom, always write the last (or family) name first and the first (or personal) name last. Therefore the world-famous composer Bela Bartok would be written "Bartok Bela" in Hungarian.

Romanians, when talking, tend to use "first name, last name" but any time names are listed "officially", whether on documents, contracts, legal papers, school records and the like, the Hungarian format is used – last name, first name.

First (personal) name – **nume** (*new-meh*)

Last (sur)name – **nume de familia** (*new-meh day famil-ee-uh*)

Be very, very attentive to this when dealing with contracts, bank transfers and the like where having names in the correct order is critically important.

## Shopping In Romania

For a list of common types of stores in Romania and their names, see page 266.

Shopping in Romania requires a certain etiquette for a smooth transaction.

---

[82] Including about the undead. For more on this, see page 16.

There are two kinds of retail environments in Romania:

## You tell the clerk what you want to buy

This is most common in small shops, especially stores selling food or snacks. The clerk(s) will be behind a counter and you have to tell them what you want.

You can certainly get away with pointing and gesturing alone but it is extremely helpful to know the Romanian names of what you want.

## You yourself select items to pay for at a cash register

To begin with, if you have to open a door to enter a shop, always close it behind you (see page 127).

Inside near the door should be a stack of plastic baskets with a handle, generally known as a **coş (de mână)** - (*koash de muh-nuh*). If the store is larger, there may be large metal shopping carts/trolleys, each known as a **cărucior** (*karoo-chore*).

The custom is that it is <u>mandatory</u> to pick up a basket or cart even if you're going to just wander around and look at the merchandise. All items you want to buy must be put in the basket/cart and taken to the cash register. If you don't buy anything, you just drop off the empty basket when you leave.

Most hypermarkets (page 268) have shopping carts that can only be liberated by the insertion of a **50 bani** coin (that's given back to you when you return the cart) but if you're patient, usually you can corral a loose one.

If you enter the shop with a product you purchased elsewhere (like a bottled drink) and they see you with it, they may pressure you to pay for it (twice). Also, be aware that if you inadvertently break something, many shops will force you to pay for it.

You may be prohibited from entering the store with large bags or have them searched.

If this is the case, most of the time you will see a little locker area or shelf of cubicles for you to store your bag or outside purchases in while you shop. Generally these are free although sometimes do not come with a key and are thus not lockable.

Generally, you will <u>not</u> be given any bags for your purchases. If you want one you have to buy one from the cashier at the register when you pay for everything else, and it'll usually cost you **1 leu** or so.

The most common Romanian word for this shopping/carrier bag is **pungă** (*poon-guh*).

**Rudeness**

In all the years I've been here in Romania, traveling everywhere from **Bucharest** to living in a remote mountain village, I've been treated incredibly well. Yet I often hear many stories of visitors who come here and are frustrated or dismayed when they receive (unexpected) rude behavior.

There are two simple things to understand to ensure that you receive good treatment in Romania.

    1.   This is still a communist country.

Yes, although Romania is both a member of the European Union and NATO and the government might be superficially democratic, many, many of the *people* who live here are communists.

When I say "communist" I am referring more to a *mentality* rather than some kind of adherence to dogmatic Marxist literature. The way this mentality most commonly impacts the visitor from a capitalist country is when they find out that *not everyone cares about profits above all else.*

Sometimes people whom you may think are supposed to do your bidding just because you're paying them will ignore you or refuse you. Maybe an obviously empty restaurant won't let you in. Perhaps a taxi driver takes one look at you (or your luggage) and says, "No way." Maybe someone brushes you off when you try to ask for directions, even if they're uniformed police.

    2.   Blondes prefer diamonds and Romanians prefer Romanian

A great number of the inhabitants of Romania do not speak English or other foreign languages. Knowing a few basic phrases (which you can find at the end of this book) will be incredibly useful.

Furthermore, most Romanians who speak English (or other foreign languages) find it extremely stressful to speak it. They are often very hesitant to even *admit* they speak it.

Therefore, if you stop someone on the street and you're speaking *English*, often times it's the equivalent of asking them to take a quick math quiz, a stressful mental task that may not be all that enjoyable.

It is far better to at least initiate the conversation in Romanian and then bumble your phrases because then the person you're talking to will feel confident in their own ability to respond to you and feel much more at ease.

Solution

First:

**Să nu vă suparați** (*sah new vah super-ots*) – Excuse me

There are several variants of how to greet a total stranger but this is the easiest one to pronounce for English speakers.

Every time you initiate a non-commercial conversation, you must beg the pardon of the person whose life you are interrupting. This opening phrase is therefore critical in situations like asking for directions.

**Nu vorbesc româneşte foarte bine dar stiți...** (*new vore-besk row-moo-nesh-tay fwart-ay bee-neigh dar shteets*)

This means "I don't speak Romanian very well but do you know..." and is a great way to set the other person at ease. It also alerts them (hopefully) to the need for them not to talk back to you at high speed.

**...unde** (*oon-day*) – where is/are?

> **gară** (*gah-rah*) – the train station
>
> **autogară** – the inter-city bus station
>
> **centru** (*chen-true*) – downtown/city center
>
> **un hotel** – a hotel
>
> **un restaurant** – a restaurant
>
> **un bancomat** – an ATM/cash point

**...când** (*kund*) – when?

> **vine autobuzul** (*vee-neigh auto-booze-ool*) – does the bus come
>
> **pleaca trenul** (*plockah train-ool*) – does the train leave
>
> **deschide** (*desky-day*) – does it open
>
> **inchide** (*een-key-day*) – does it close

**...cât costă** (*cut coast-uh*) – how much does it cost?

> **un bilet** (*oon bee-let*) – a ticket

> **doua bilete** – (*dough-ah bee-let-tay*) – two tickets

> **pe noapte** – (*pay nwop-tay*) – per night

Even if that's literally all the Romanian you can speak, it'll be of incredible use to you, assuming you know your numbers.[83]

**dreapta** (*drop-tuh*) – right

**stânga** (*stunguh*) – left

**tot înainte** (*tote un-a-intay*) – straight ahead

Note: Some of the above is not prestige dialect "100% correct" Romanian but has been compressed for ease in saying and using it. Although slightly butchered, Romanians can understand it.

Far and away the most important thing to remember is that regardless of which language you're speaking, politeness counts for a great deal in Romania and is widely respected.

Furthermore, be sure to use the proper greetings (see page 258) whenever engaging in a commercial transaction (when you're the paying customer).

No Over Smiling!

I'm making that its own separate heading because of how important it is. For a Romanian walking down the street and then suddenly being stopped by a total stranger with a big grin on their face it is a somewhat frightening experience.

Imagine a fully costumed clown with a rainbow wig and oversized red shoes suddenly stopping you on the street, wanting to ask you questions in super rapid Spanish about how to get to some museum and you'll start to get the gist of how this comes across to Romanians.

Smiling is only for people you know. It doesn't mean you frown or scowl at other people, simply just be fairly neutral and dignified in your carriage. I know in many Western countries it's hard to be polite without smiling on all occasions.

---

[83] See page 305.

The easiest way I can say this in English is to be a *gentleman* or a *lady* and you'll generally be treated as one. Stand up straight, comport yourself with dignity and treat others with courteous respect and accept nothing but the same from others.

Romania has been a deeply hierarchical nation for generations and how you portray your status will have a dramatic difference on how you are treated.

And last but not least, this country is an incredibly old land, steeped with powerful forces that sometimes combine in WTF moments, little pockets of chaos. You just have to learn to shrug them off. Sometimes it's not *you* and no it doesn't make sense to anyone else either. It's just Romania.

### The Scolding Of Righteousness

I think it is fair to say that Romanian society is guided by two principles – adherence to social customs (be polite and decorous) and making sure everyone else around you does too.

It is this second part that I call the "Scolding of Righteousness", which is my own term[84], and understanding it and using it can make your visit or stay in Romania go a lot more smoothly.

In Romania there is exactly one way to do everything. I've been traveling around Europe since I was a kid but Romania is easily the most *homogenous* country I've ever been to, culturally speaking. If you walk into a school in one city and look around, it's a carbon copy of any other school in any other town. Everyone is taught exactly the same and individuality is NOT a strong suit of the Romanian people.

It's so ingrained in the culture here that Romanians are rarely consciously aware that there is Only One Way to do everything, known as *să fi corect*[85]. In English, "correct" just means "accurate" or "the right answer" but in Romanian it means something along the lines of being "proper" or "adhering to the One Way".

Romanians are never happier than when their house looks *corect*, they dress *corect*, they speak *corect* and in all ways generally conduct themselves in the *corect* manner.

It's a little eerie sometimes (the lack of individuality) but it has a tremendous advantage when you understand it. Why? Because Romanians are all brought up from birth to submit to Higher Authorities on how to be *corect*.

---

[84] In Romanian this would be *Muştruluială Justificata*.
[85] Literally "being proper".

Their parents, their neighbors, their teachers, the police, the conductor on the train, whomever – they've all spent years being chided (scolded) on how to be *corect*.

The way this scolding is done is always the same. First, the one doing the scolding (known as the Scolder) has to adopt an indignant and slightly pissed off tone. It's not yelling exactly as in foaming at the mouth and overly loud volume (which is definitely NOT *corect*) but it is more forceful than normal conversation.

The Scolder must employ the most *righteous* tone possible, as if the Scolder were a very strict and morally upright preacher and the receiver of the scolding (known as the Scoldee) were nothing but a low down, filthy sinner who is in the verrah danger of going straight to hell.

And last but not least, the Scolder must adopt a sort of sad, regretful look to his/her face, as if they really, truly did NOT want to resort to the scolding but gosh darn it, the Scoldee forced the Scolder to do it and don't you know deep down it hurts the Scolder more than it does the Scoldee to even do this? So quit being so silly and intentionally mischievous and naughty and save ourselves both the embarrassment of this situation already!

An example from my past of how I learned the technique of the Scolding of Righteousness:

> After years of the trains in Romania being a safari on rails[86], CFR (Romanian railways) scored some sweet European Union money and bought a brand-new series of Inter-City trains known as the "Blue Arrow" (Romanian: **săgeată albastră**).
>
> Just super nice, modern trains, top of the line, very clean, spacious and modern with little digital scrolling signs inside and music piped in through overhead speakers, the works. And yes, the bathroom itself was quite modern, new and most importantly, CLEAN.
>
> One morning I was riding the 6:00 am <u>Blue Arrow</u> train to **Timişoara** when I realized I had to use the restroom quite badly. I went to the bathroom but saw the little red indicator was turned, meaning it was occupied. The (female) conductor was standing right outside so I realized she too had to go so I settled in for a bit of a wait.

---

[86] See my website www.kingofromania.com for some anecdotes from these days.

The toilet flushed, the door indicator went from green to red, and a young man stepped out, evidently finished with his "business". The conductor went inside. A moment later she came out and marched right up to the young man who had just exited the bathroom.

**Conductor**: Hey you, what is this?
**Young Man**: What?
**Conductor**: The bathroom. Look at this. You were just in here and now there's pee on the seat. You did this.
**Young Man**: (hangdog look)
**Conductor**: This is a nice train and it must be kept nice! This is not how you use the bathroom! I realize you did not have 7 years at home[87] but when you make a mess like this, you must clean it up. Now GO back in there, take some paper towels and clean it up.
**Young Man**: Yes ma'am (still hangdog look)

And yes, I had to wait a little bit longer but it was totally worth it.

And THAT is how a Scolding of Righteousness is done. Romanians are so well-trained to respond to Scoldings of Righteousness that they immediately become like the young man in the example above: adopting a sort of hangdog, guilty, submissive attitude and then they hop to it and immediately begin trying to redress the problem.

This is of vital importance for the visitor to understand because sometimes Romanians goof around and don't act professionally, giving you poor service, etc., because they *expect* to be scolded when they cross the line.

Often times the visitor is shy or cautious, not wanting to make trouble, and this gives a mixed signal to Romanians, essentially condoning their "bad behavior". In fact, I often see bad behavior rewarded in a misguided attempt to appease the offending person, which ends up having the opposite effect.

When in doubt, always rely on politeness and tact to resolve problems and issues. If this strategy fails, however, stand up for yourself and insist on decent and fair treatment.

**Money**

In terms of using, handling and spending money yourself, see page 37.

---

[87] See page 252

Romanians often have a stilted, repressed sort of love/hate affair with money and find it a difficult topic to discuss. It is important to be extremely sensitive when discussing financial topics with Romanians, particularly personal questions concerning income and the like.

That being said, the *flaunting* of wealth or the ostentatious display of expensive cars, clothes and other accoutrements is widely practiced and rarely, if ever, considered crass or unrefined.

Romanians tend to put a lot of stock in *appearances* and will spend a significant portion of their paychecks on looking good, even regrettably when this is a largely unwise financial move.

## Snitching/Tattling

Although it sometimes comes across as craven or cowardly, Romanians in general prefer to avoid face-to-face confrontations and so will often attempt to resolve problems by "snitching" or going to some authority to criticize you instead of doing it directly to your face.

This is rarely much of a concern for the temporary visitor but can have long-term ramifications for people living here.

Likewise, direct face-to-face confrontations, especially done in a very blunt manner, are to be reserved only for the most urgent circumstances. Resolving problems in a calm, firm and respectful tone is easily the best attitude to adopt here in Romania.

## Showers/Baths

Romanians are a very clean people and will always have facilities for washing up in their homes.

However, be aware that both in hotels and in people's homes, it is very common to use a hand-held shower hose/wand as opposed to one that is permanently mounted to the wall above your head.

Some visitors are used to shower facilities that feature an overhead mounted shower only and find a hand-held device to be uncomfortable and clumsy to use because essentially you must do some tasks one-handed.

## Toilets

Romanian toilets are almost universally the standard "Western" sit-down style with either a cord or a handle to activate the flush.

That being said, it's important to understand that many toilets are designed to use very little water, which may lead to two delicate situations that are important to understand.

1. If you are in someone's home and using their facilities, there may be undesired "remains" in the toilet after a flushing. There will always be a brush (near the bowl) provided precisely for you to leave the toilet (visually) in the same condition in which you found it.

2. Especially in some rural situations, the toilet itself may be connected to a sewage system that cannot handle toilet paper. If this is the case, you will usually be informed to discard your toilet paper in a trash can/rubbish bin for this purpose.

Public toilets, especially those in train stations, are to be avoided at all times as often you have to pay for the "privilege" of using very filthy and unsanitary facilities.

If you are in public and in need of a restroom, the best strategy by far is to find a nice café and simply ask to use their facilities. If they balk and say that the restrooms are for customers only, simply inform them that you want to wash your hands (and make a hand gesture to match) and usually they'll relent.

For the sake of others, please keep yourself clean at all times in this country!

# Top Recommended 5 Cities To See

It must be remembered that over half of Romania's population lives in rural or agricultural areas.

Of the urban dwellers in this country, 1 in 5 live in **Bucharest**, a gigantic, sprawling metropolis.

Therefore cities in Romania (besides **Bucharest**) tend to be small, not heavily populated and with a lot of country and rural areas in between them. Romania is also a very large country and it can take a significant amount of time to travel between cities (or regions).

Most of the cities in Romania were heavily industrialized in the Communist era and are often polluted, ugly shells of their former glory and not very attractive places to visit.

Yet many visitors from around the world, whether for tourist or business purposes, tend to spend a lot of time in the cities. Some of these are absolutely gorgeous and definitely worth seeing.

**Braşov**

Easily my favorite over-all city in Romania and a perennial top pick of tourists for a very good reason – the downtown (city centre) is an absolute gem.

**Braşov** (*bra-shove*) is at the very southernmost portion of Transylvania and the city itself directly abuts the Carpathian Mountains. All around **Braşov** are many wonderful mountainous areas to hike, ride horses, ski and explore.

As you head south from Braşov and cross over the last of the mountains, you enter the smoothly rolling plains of Wallachia (page 244) and in just about 3 hours you are in **Bucharest**, so it's very easy to make **Braşov** (and the surrounding areas) a quick day trip from the capital.

**Braşov** was largely settled and fortified by Germans (page 206) and today the city is still known by its German name – *Kronstadt*. Most of the medieval charm, the churches, the old city walls and the surviving historical elements are German. Many German tourists come to visit this area every year but almost all of today's residents are ethnic Romanians.

Although a relatively minor incident at the time, the up and coming prince of **Wallachia**, Vlad "Ţepeş" Dracul, got involved in a dispute with the German merchants in this city, leading stories about what a dastardly villain he was that have endured for centuries (page 10).

Getting There

The main highway north of **Bucharest** (DN1) runs right to **Braşov** and it takes between 2-3 hours, depending on conditions, to drive the 170 kilometers.

There is currently no airport or other nearby air services.

There are regular Inter-City trains (page 97) running between **Bucharest** and **Braşov** and between **Braşov** and many other Transylvanian cities.

The **autogară** (page 93) where you can find inter-city buses is located directly adjacent to the main train station (**gară**). These are often cheaper and quicker to use for travel to **Bucharest** and other cities (relatively) close by.

Note: The buses running to nearby areas, including **Poiana Braşov**, tend to depart from the medieval city walls near downtown in an area called **Livada Postei**, which is very easy to find.

**Braşov** has a reliable network[88] of city buses and trams although the city is so small you can pretty easily get around on foot or by use of the occasional taxi.

On foot, walking from the train station to the historic downtown should not take more than 30 minutes.  A taxi ride in town shouldn't cost you more than **6-8 lei.**

Attractions

Everything you will want to see is nicely nestled in the historic downtown and if you are staying overnight, you should definitely find lodgings as close to **centru** as possible.  Since **Braşov** is annually visited by millions of people, there are a wide variety of hotels, hostels and *pensiuni* to choose from.

The outskirts of the city and many other neighborhoods are heavily industrialized, grey and not worth visiting with the exception of the *Şchei* neighborhood (page 30) on the northern end of town, which is quite lovely although built on a steep incline.

Most of the western edge of the historic downtown area abuts directly against **Mt. Tâmpa** (*tum-puh*), which is a gorgeous, tree-covered slope about 1000 meters high, abounding in wildlife including bears.  There are several (marked) hiking trails to the summit but there is also a cable car service that ascends to the top, revealing a gorgeous, panoramic view of both **Braşov** as well as the surrounding areas.

At the top of **Mt. Tâmpa** is a large, illuminated sign with white letters spelling out "**Braşov**" extremely similar to the iconic "Hollywood" sign that many people are familiar with.

Downtown is dominated by **Piaţa Sfatului** (*sfot-ool-wee*), literally meaning "Councillor's Square"[89], a large open area with a gorgeous fountain and a clear view of **Mt. Tâmpa** just a few hundred meters away.

On the northern end of **Piaţa Sfatului** is the famous **Black Church** (Romanian: *Biserica Neagră* – German: *Schwarze Kirche*), 65 meters tall

---

[88] http://www.ratbv.ro
[89] If you're truly interested in Romanian grammar, this parses out to "Square of the Advice" due to noun declensions.  This is where the "city elders" or town council used to meet.

and the largest Lutheran house of worship in the country. Although it is called "black", it is actually largely grey with a red tiled roof (almost every building in **Braşov** has a similar roof) and there are numerous impressive sculptures in the niches that surround the outside of the building.

On the southern end of **Piaţa Sfatului** is an entirely pedestrian street, filled with shops, cafes and wonderful places to linger and enjoy the view or perhaps to tasty treat from one of the many restaurants.

Just a few meters southwest of **Piaţa Sfatului** on an adjacent street is the famous *Strada Sforii*, (Rope Street), the narrowest street in the country.

On the slope just east of **Piaţa Sfatului** are two historic towers, one called the White Tower (Romanian: **Turul Alb**) and the other the Black Tower (Romanian: **Turul Negru**). Despite the names, physically both towers are actually white/grey in color.

Although there's not much to see in the towers *per se*, they do allow the visitor to climb to a height to see a wonderful panoramic view, especially of downtown **Braşov** and the Black Church.

Wandering around this quaint, homey and extremely lovely town is an attraction unto itself, as many of the original medieval walls and gates still exist. That plus the pedestrian-only zone can be so pleasurable that often an entire day has flown by before you even realize it.

**Braşov** also has a wonderful central park (Romanian: **Parcul Central**) with gorgeous flowerbeds, abundant flowers and even tables with inlaid chess boards.

Special Notes

Braşov can be *exceedingly* cold in the wintertime, especially with wintry winds blowing into town off of **Mt. Tâmpa** and the surrounding mountains. This is why **Braşov** (and the surrounding region) is the skiing and winter sports capital of Romania.

The lovely, cool, fir-scented breezes in summertime are heavenly, especially during the sweltering hot weeks at the end of summer when just about everywhere else in the country is unbearably hot.

Due to the large volume of tourists, finding a good place to swim in **Braşov** is probably better than anywhere else in the country. There is also an aquatic resort located on the southern edge of the city[90], complete with water slides.

If you're interested in "foreign" foods, especially American, Chinese, Serbian, British and German, **Braşov** probably has more choices than just about any other city in Romania.

Again, because of the high volume of tourists and visitors, just about everyone in the historic downtown area is extremely confortable in speaking and understanding English. Locals are almost universally friendly and welcoming to foreign visitors.

What's Nearby

One of the most popular destinations in Romania, the castle at **Bran** (page 169) is just a short car/bus ride away and makes for an easy day trip for those staying in **Braşov**.

The nearby city of **Poiana Braşov**[91] is also the epicenter for the country's wintersports industry, including skiing, snowboarding, ATV and even horseback riding. Lodging in **Poiana Braşov** can be incredibly expensive and generally it is more affordable to stay in **Braşov** and make visiting **Poiana Braşov** a day trip.

Similarly, the hiking, skiing and wilderness mountainous areas of **Sinaia** (including **Peleş** – see page 170), **Predeal, Buşteni** and others are just a short car/bus/train ride to the south.

There are frequent and affordable bus routes running between **Braşov** to all of these areas departing from *Livada Postei* in the historic downtown area.

There are multiple train/**autobuz** connections to **Bucharest**, taking about 2-3 hours to reach.

The city of **Sighişoara** (page 155) is about one hour away to the north by car, train or **autobuz**.

**Sibiu** (page 152) is about four hours away by train/car to the west.

**Cluj-Napoca** (page 158) is about 5-6 hours away to the north by train/car/**autobuz.**

---

[90] This would be very difficult to get to without a taxi/car.
[91] "Poiana Braşov" means "The Glade of Braşov" and is a separate city or area from **Braşov** proper.

Other regions, such as (Romanian) Moldova, Maramureş, the Banat and Crişana are further away.

## BUCHAREST

As the capital and largest city, Bucharest (Romanian: **Bucureşti**) is almost a second nation unto itself.

The combined metropolitan area has about 2 million residents, comprising roughly one fifth of all urban dwellers in the country. Millions of visitors come here every year from every nation on Earth and it is a bustling, thriving, modern metropolis.

It is home to a large, vibrant community of foreigners and it seems that the population in **Bucharest** is amongst the most cosmopolitan, sophisticated and friendly in the entire country.

<u>Getting There</u>

The main international airport is **Otopeni**, now officially called **Henri Coanda** (page 102). This airport is located a few kilometers outside of **Bucharest** proper. A secondary airport, **Băneasa**, is only used for a few flights and should be avoided whenever possible.

The main train station is called **Gara de Nord**, critical to know because there are actually several secondary train stations. I am not aware of any reason why you will ever need to go to these other train stations. For general information on trains, see page 97.

The train station at **Gara de Nord** itself has several restaurants, cafes and newsstands, all at standard prices. Be aware however, restroom usage is restricted to customers only. There is a public restroom facility at the end of the terminal but it is only to be used as a last resort in case of the worst emergency of your entire life.

There is a subway/metro stop[92] (also called **Gara de Nord**) one level directly under the train station, easily discoverable via signage. Be aware that you will have to switch lines somewhere later in order to reach most of the downtown stops.

An adventuresome traveler can easily walk from **Gara de Nord** to the main downtown area but if you want to take a taxi, be sure to follow the safe procedure (page 109) and select one out of the main queue.

---

[92] For more information on the **Bucharest** metro, see page **Error! Bookmark not defined.**.

<u>Attractions</u>

Because **Bucharest** is so large, it would be impossible to list every attraction. Suffice it to say that it has a thriving entertainment calendar, complete with concerts, performances, operas, ballets, rock festivals and everything else you could ever want.

Because **Bucharest** underwent so much renovation and redevelopment during the Communist era, there are, in essence, two "centers" of the city.

The modern center of the city is **Piața Universitații**, which today is marked with a large compass and the distances listed from **Bucharest** to other cities in Romania. This is referred to as the "Zero Kilometer Monument".

Once you can align yourself to this square, finding just about everything else of interest in **Bucharest** is incredibly easy.

Right near this square and up and down the main road are several markers, commemorating those who were killed during the 1989 Revolution and where they fell.

It is easy to walk around **centru** but there is also a subway line paralleling the main north/south road called Bulevardul General Gheorghe Magheru during this stretch.

The street parallel to Bulevard Gheorghe Magheru directly to the west is Calea Victorei, considered by many to be **Bucharest's** most charming street, lined with gracefully historic houses and **Cantacuzino Palace**, which now houses the **George Enescu Museum**, dedicated to one of Romania's most famous classical music composers.

Heading north on Bulevardul Gheorge Magheru from **Piața Universitații** the next main square is **Piața Romana** and then **Piața Victoriei**. Just north of this is a former royal palace that is now home to Romania's **National Museum of Art**.

About two kilometers north of this (passing through the fantastic **Kiseleff Park**) is the "Arcul de Triumf", a very close copy of Paris' Arc de Triomfe. Farther to the northeast begins the enormous and lovely **Herestrau Park** (over 400 acres in size), complete with multiple lakes.

Heading south from **Piața Universitații** the next main square is the absolutely enormous **Piața Unirii**, which is unmistakable as it is festooned with advertisements of every kind, very similar to Times Square in New York City or Piccadilly Circus in London.

Just west of **Piața Unirii** is the gargantuan "People's House", sometimes called the "House of the Parliament" (Rom: **Casa Poporului/Casa Parlamentului**), one of the largest buildings on Earth.

Visitors can explore many of the over 1,000 rooms and marvel at this gigantic feat of egotism built by the late Nicolae Ceausescu.

Just a little further southeast of this monstrous building is the idyllic and beautiful **Carol Park**, which often hosts concerts in the summertime.

Just northwest of **Piața Unirii** is the only historic remnant of **Bucharest**'s old center and is now zoned only for pedestrians. This quaint little neighborhood of small shops and strolling grandmothers is referred to as **Lipscani** (*leaps gone*). There are also many old historic churches in this area, including one first built in 1559.

Just west of **Piața Universitații**, following **Bulevardul Regina Elisabeta** is one of the finest city parks in all of Europe, known as **Cismigiu** (*chee-smee-jew*), which has a wide variety of lakes and tree-lined footpaths and is home to a flock of black swans.

There are dozens of other museums and historical sights to see but your main needs will be found along this route, which can probably be walked in no more than 60 minutes each way by an unencumbered visitor. Again, there is a main subway/metro line also running up and down this route.

Special Notes

Most of what you might want such as shopping, eating out (including traditional Romanian food) and entertainment are also to be found in this zone ranging from **Piața Romana** to **Piața Unirii**, or close enough by that you can easily find it once you are oriented.

Although **Bucharest** is a very large city, many of the outlying areas are largely residential or industrial and you won't have much reason to travel there. Be aware that some zones of **Bucharest** are partially or somewhat agricultural and it may be normal to see livestock and other animals, even in the heart of the city.

Driving in **Bucharest** can be an enormous challenge and is recommended only for the most adventuresome drivers. Walking, public transportation and taxis are inexpensive and efficient ways to get around.

Public transportation in **Bucharest** is now moving away from the use of paper tickets (like in other cities) and relying exclusively on magnetic-stripe cards, which can be "refilled" and used over and over again.

<u>What's Nearby</u>

**Braşov** and the beginning of Transylvania are only about 2.5-3 hours away to the north and make an easy trip, with a national highway and multiple high-speed train and bus connections.

There is a high-speed highway directly connecting **Bucharest** to **Piteşti**.

**Constanţa** and the Black Sea areas are only 4-5 hours away by train with multiple connections.

There are multiple daily domestic flights to **Timişoara, Cluj-Napoca** and **Iaşi**. It is far quicker (and may even be cheaper) to reach these cities by air than in any other way from **Bucharest**.

For international connections, see page 113. Be aware that all major trains will depart from **Gara de Nord**.

About 30 km north of the city of **Bucharest** is **Snagov Monastery**, which lies on an island in the middle of a lake. Although it is difficult to find this area, there is now a footbridge which you can walk over to the monastery on the island to see a tomb that holds the purported remains of Vlad "Dracula" Ţepeş.

**Iaşi**

**Iaşi** (*yash*) is one of the two historic capitals of **Moldova** (see page 243) and is a fairly large city.

Located in the extreme northeast of the country, **Iaşi** is just a few kilometers from Romania's border with the Republic of Moldova.

Unlike many of the cities in Transylvania, the Banat and Crişana, architecture in **Iaşi** is largely Slavic and Romanian in nature and this makes **Iaşi** one of the few cities which demonstrably "look different" because of this.

One of the greatest kings in Romanian history, **Ştefan cel Mare** (see page 253) ruled **Iaşi** and today there are monuments, churches, plazas, streets and boulevards named in his honor all over the city.

The national poet of Romania, **Mihai Eminescu** (see page 252) spent a lot of time in **Iaşi**, working and writing.

<u>Getting There</u>

Iaşi has an airport on the outskirts of town but has very few international flights. As far as I'm aware, the only domestic flights to/from **Iaşi** connect with **Bucharest**.

Considering just how far away **Iaşi** is (9-12 hours by car/train) from the capital, flying to **Iaşi** is probably the easiest and most economical way to get there.

**Iaşi** is a major rail hub on the domestic train networks and major lines run to this city from the capital, Transylvania and the Black Sea coast regions. Again, because **Iaşi** is literally sitting against Romania's northeasternmost corner, it is quite far away from most other cities in the country.

The city is generally flat but is surrounded by seven iconic hills.

Attractions

Again, because of the much different history in **Moldova** than the rest of (what is today modern) Romania, the city of **Iaşi** simply looks different than other places in the country. It also has a different "feel" to it, and seems almost to be in another land at times.

Due to the history of other regions, Moldova is exceptional in the fact that Romanians were allowed to practice their religion and construct churches much earlier here than anywhere else. One of **Iaşi**'s principle attractions is the numerous, elaborate and sometimes jaw-breakingly beautiful (Romanian Orthodox) churches.

Several of these are located in the "Golden Platou", a small area where many were built almost adjacent to one another, including the **"Three Hierarchs" Church** (Romanian: *Trei Ierarhi*) located about 1km north of the train station. Two or three other (only relatively) smaller churches are nearby.

Slightly beyond that (an easy walk on foot) is the **Palace of Culture** (Romanian: *Palatul Culturii*), actually a former royal building now housing several museums, including the Moldovan History Museum. The building is free to enter Tuesday through Sunday from 10:00am - 5:00pm but each individual museum charges an entrance fee. Directly in front of the **Palace of Culture** is an enormous statue of **Ştefan cel Mare**.

Heading just beyond that is the heart of modern downtown **Iaşi**, including several malls, a shopping district and the best of the funky, quaint cafes/bars that make a visit to the city so enjoyable.

Probably one of the most famous parks in Romania is **Copou Park** (Romanian: *Parcul Copou*) located just northwest of the train station. It is a large, verdant and beautiful area near several universities and easy to get to either on foot or by numerous bus/tram lines.

At the heart of the park is a famous linden[93] tree that were the legendary inspiration for the poems of **Mihai Eminescu** and it is now a popular destination for Romanian tourists.

The largest botanical garden (Romanian: **gradină botanică**) in the country is found in **Iaşi**, easily over 250 acres[94] in size and boasting a wide variety of flowers, plants and trees, including several tropical varieties.

Special Notes

Because **Iaşi** is so large, it is the only city (besides **Bucharest**) that is probably too large to adequately get around in entirely on foot and so you'll probably need to rely either on buses/trams[95] or else taxis.

All trains come into this city at the main train station on the city's southwestern edge, which is nearby the historic downtown but quite far from the universities and the student area. Unfortunately, much of the historic downtown area was destroyed and therefore has no significant tourist or historic attractions.

**Iaşi**, along with **Cluj-Napoca, Timişoara** and **Bucharest** is the home to several universities, drawing tens of thousands of students in every year from the surrounding areas. Because of this, the nightlife scene in **Iaşi** is very vibrant, with a wide variety of bars, clubs and discos to choose from.

Because **Moldova** is the heart of the country's wine-growing area, finding local and affordable wines in **Iaşi** is incredibly easy. Many corner stores (**magazin alimentar** – page 269) sell locally made wine "in bulk" wherein you bring in an old 2-liter bottle and they will fill it up for you at a set rate.

A wide variety of Ukrainian, Russian, Slavic and other regional foods can be found here that you can't get elsewhere, including even ordinary foods like **mămăligă** (page 46) served and cooked in the local style.

Very few people in this region speak or understand English, aside from the youthful university population. Furthermore, speakers of Romanian in **Iaşi** tend to use a very thick Slavic accent as well as regional idioms and slang

---

[93] British English: lime tree
[94] In metric this would be just over 100 hectares.
[95] Iaşi's public transportation network is called "RATP" but their website is abysmal at the moment and does not offer much useful information.

phrases that may be quite difficult to understand, even for Romanians from another region.

For example, many locals actually pronounce the name of their city more as *yesh* rather than the more common (nationwide) form of *yosh*.

What's Nearby

If you are heading to Russia, most parts of Ukraine or other points eastward, including the Republic of Moldova, then **Iaşi** will be your best starting point. There are multiple **autocar, minibuz** and train connections to Chişinau (the capital of RM) where you can connect to the rest of the former Soviet Union.

On the outskirts of **Iaşi** spread amongst the seven hills are several famous (Romanian Orthodox) functioning monasteries, including the "Fortress Monastery" (Romanian: *Manastirea Cetatuia*), the "Galata Monastery" and the "Beautiful Monastery" (Romanian: *Manastirea Frumoasa*). These are usually open to the public and charge no admission.

The city of **Suceava** (page 163) is only about 1.5-2 hours away by train/car to the west and has regular and frequent connections.

The city of **Piatra Neamţ** (page 162) is about 90 minutes away by car/train and has numerous and frequent connections.

The gorgeous natural area of **Cheile Bicazului** (see page 166) is roughly 2-3 hours away by car.

**Sibiu**

Easily the most "Western European" city in the entire country, and probably the hands-down favorite place to visit by most tourists, **Sibiu** (*see-be-you*) is a sparkling jewel of a little city, nestled in southern Transylvania.

Although the Germans (page 206) settled several cities throughout the region, **Sibiu** (German: *Hermannstadt*) is now the only place with a significant population of Germans still remaining. A German-language newspaper[96] is printed here and probably the most common language you will hear spoken (after Romanian) is German.

In fact, the current mayor of **Sibiu** is an ethnic German (Romanian citizen), leader of the small but regionally influential German political party. Thanks to many European Union funds as well as hard work and dedication, the city

---

[96] See page 198.

has been given a thorough makeover, enhancing and restoring its gorgeous historic center.

Lodging is plentiful at all budget ranges, from hostels to expensive luxury hotels. Because most of the attractions you will want to see are in **centru**, try to find a room as close to the city center as possible.

Getting There

Interestingly, **Sibiu** is located almost in the exact geographical center of Romania. This city does have a small airport but most of its flights run to Austria and Germany. Generally speaking, if you're already inside Romania, flying to **Sibiu** isn't likely to be your best option.

There are major highways connecting **Sibiu** to all points south (**Râmnicu Valcea, Pitesti** and then **Bucharest**), east (**Braşov**) and north (**Cluj-Napoca)** as well as west (**Timişoara** and **Arad**).

Furthermore, there are multiple train routes running through **Sibiu** as well as frequent **minibuz** (page 92) departures and arrivals.

Attractions

Essentially the entire downtown historic quarter is worth seeing, a delightful pedestrian-only zone where the visitor can casually stroll, stopping by sidewalk cafés for a cup of coffee or a leisurely meal.

This area is begins with the "upper city" (Romanian: **oraşul de sus**) between the river and the hill. The passage to the "lower city" (Rom: **oraşul de jos**) is via a spectacular staircase, winding in and sometimes through many standing medieval fortifications and walls.

The main square downtown is very easy to spot as it is huge, known in Romanian as **Piaţa Mare** (*pee-otza mar-eh*) literally meaning "the big square".

The northwest corner of the square leads to the entrance of the **Brukenthal Museum**, probably one of the finest in the entire country (page 173).

Elsewhere on the perimeter of **Piaţa Mare** are several medieval towers, including where the old town council used to meet.

Several buildings on the southern and eastern side of **Piaţa Mare** have unusual small windows on their upper stories. These are sometimes called "the city's eyes".

Many small, narrow streets lead off from **Piața Mare** and are wonderful to explore and see. One of these leads to another square, this one known as **Piața Mica** (or "little square"). This square leads (via **Strada Ocnei**) to the *Liar's Bridge*, the first iron bridge built in Romania.

On either side of the bridge are two historic buildings, one called the *House of the Arts* and the other the *Luxembourg House*.

Special Notes

By local ordinance, all taxis must be colored yellow and appropriately marked (see page 109). Elsewhere in Romania taxis can be any color.

In 2007 **Sibiu** was designed the "European Cultural Capital" and the entire city was restored for this year-long event, which drew hundreds of thousands of tourists.

As a result, **Sibiu** probably has today one of the liveliest cultural scenes in Romania, with many concerts, live performances, opera and jazz festivals occurring nearly year-round. Be sure to look at a current events' guide (page 34) to find out what will be going on during your visit!

I would say that hands down **Sibiu** is the city most visitors enjoy the best as it feels completely modern (western) European and has a relaxed, delightful charm.

What's Nearby

Just outside the city limits (to the south) is a complex of *ethnographic* museums, complete with an entire village of traditional (and authentic) Romanian dwellings.

The entire area is known as *Complex ASTRA* in Romanian.

Although other ethnographic and village museums exist in Romania, **Sibiu**'s is by far the largest and most complete. There are several working mills and other traditional Romanian handicraft industrial apparatus and it is a great way to see "the old way" of living in Romania. Also on the grounds is a museum dedicated likewise to the *Saxon* or German traditional lifestyle and handicrafts.

To get there from **Sibiu**, you can take the number 1 city bus as it runs right to the museum complex.

The nearby ski/winter resort area of **Păltiniş** (German: *Hohe Rinne*) is just 35km southwest of **Sibiu**, which is very difficult to get to with public transportation.

**Sibiu** is also the closest major city to the breathtaking **Făgăraş Mountains,** home to the world-renowned mountain road called the **Transfăgărăşan** (page 166).

## Sighişoara

Although almost every city in Romania and indeed Europe was founded during the medieval period, modernization and urbanization have largely destroyed everything except for a handful of churches and castle keeps.

Not so in **Sighişoara**, which appears almost like a magical dream, its entire city center untouched with medieval buildings, houses, bridges and walls still in their original condition.

Although the modern city of **Sighişoara** (*see-ghee-shwar-uh*) is still very small, the modern areas are all restricted to the lower part of the city. The small but steep hill in the center of town dominates the skyline and it is here that you will find the living, breathing medieval town that enchants visitors year after year. Indeed, the entire upper area of the town is a UNESCO World Heritage Site.

Because of its unique medieval preservation, every year a **Medieval Festival** is held in **Sighişoara**, breathing the past into life.

Lodging is fairly cheap and plentiful and because all of the sites worth seeing are in up in the historic **centru**, that's where you will want to stay.

The most famous Romanian of all time, Vlad "Dracula" Ţepeş (page 10) was born here and that house is still standing, open to visitors.

**Sighişoara** was one of the German (German: *Schäßburg*) fortified cities of ancient Transylvania (see page 206).

Getting There

**Sighişoara** has no airport but it lies on the main train lines (and automobile highways) connecting **Bucharest** to **Braşov** and northern Transylvania (**Cluj-Napoca**) so it is fairly easy to get to.

Additionally, there are several **minibuz** routes departing and arriving from nearby cities (mostly in Transylvania).

The nearest airport is in **Tîrgu-Mureş**, just about 40km away (page 164).

Attractions

Although there's not much left on the interior from his day, the childhood home of Vlad "Dracula" Ţepeş is available to visit (free of charge) just past the main entrance to the upper part of the city.

The main citidel is still largely intact, located just across from Vlad "Dracula" Ţepeş' childhood home.

The entire upper area of the town is covered in towers, some of them decaying but others open to the public. One of these is the Clock Tower (Romanian: *Turnul de Ceas*) which you can enter and for a small fee climb to the top to gain a 360 degree panoramic view of the entire city. Inside the tower is a history museum, access to which is included in the price of admission.

Just a few steps past Vlad Dracula's house is both the "Torture Room" and "Weapons Collection", one exhibit demonstrating (extraordinarily vividly) medieval interrogation techniques and the other boasting an impressive collection of weapons and armor from various historical eras.

Wandering around the entire upper area is simply delightful as even the "ordinary" homes are largely still in their original, medieval forms. One of the most famous of these is the "Stag Head" building, wherein an artificial deer's head was mounted high up on the corner of the building along with two paintings, giving the illusion that two deer bodies have one head.

Just two streets down from Vlad Dracula's childhood home is the famous covered stairs, an enormously long staircase that leads up to the very top of **Sighişoara**. Up there you will find the "Church on the Hill" and one of the city's oldest cemeteries.

The only main attraction *not* located in the upper, medieval center of **Sighişoara** is the birthplace of **Hermann Oberth**, one of the pioneers in space and aviation technology. His house is located down by the river and while it is marked (with a plaque), you cannot enter it.

Special Notes

Both Romanians and foreigners become bewitched by this city's charm, as it seems almost like a history book sprung into life.

Even though Vlad Dracula's childhood home is located here, the good news is that almost no vampire or Dracula tourism occurs here and there's almost no tacky or gimmicky promotions.

Instead, it is a quiet, beautiful city where you can easily stroll and soak in the atmosphere, pausing for a coffee or a local treat and never once feel like you're in the middle of a "tourist trap".

What's Nearby

**Braşov** is about 1-1.5 hours away by train/car (to the south).  **Cluj-Napoca** is about three hours away by train/car (to the north).

**Sibiu** is about 80 km away, but has no direct train connection (you must switch trains).

**Tîrgu-Mureş** is just 30km away and is the closest "big" city.

# Other cities

**Arad**

Located in southern **Crişana** (page 249), with just under 200,000 residents, **Arad** (*ah-rod*) is a gritty little town with a lot of character.

Frankly there's not too much to see here to tempt the busy tourist, although the "House of Cannonballs" in **centru** (with multiple extant balls in its walls) is quite interesting.  The City Hall is also located on a gorgeous square with some beautiful flowerbeds.

The city of **Timişoara** is about one hour away (to the south) with regular train connections.  Likewise, **Oradea** is about 90 minutes away to the north.

**Baia Mare**

A gorgeous little town in the heart of **Maramureş** (see page 249), the traditional region of Romania, although **Baia Mare** (*bye-a mar-eh*) is modern in every respect.

If you are planning on visiting the region, this is definitely where you want to base yourself.

The historic downtown is small but beautiful preserved and a lovely place to stroll and admire the sights.  Every October the town hosts a *Chestnut*

*Festival* when the many trees lining the boulevards produce their autumn crop.

Tucked away in one corner of the city is one of the most beautiful parks in Romania, complete with its own mini-train line called the "Ciuperci" (Mushroom train).

Note: The entire city skyline is dominated by a gigantic smokestack just outside of town, which looks almost identical to Sauron's lair in J.R.R. Tolkien's Lord of the Rings.

## Buzău

The city of **Buzău** (*buh-zew*) has about 130,000 residents and is northeast of **Piteşti** in **Wallachia** (see page 249).

The main downtown areas are centered around *Cuza Voda* Street, home to several bustling markets.

While this city has a lot of heart, there is not much to see here to tempt the traveler on a limited schedule.

## Cluj-Napoca

A gorgeous little city, now considered the capital of Transylvania, **Cluj-Napoca** (*klewj[97] neh-poke-uh*) was also one of the medieval German fortified cities (page 206) although little of that flavor still exists today.

Long ruled by Hungarians, the main downtown square **Piaţa Unirii** is dominated by a statue of **Mattias Corvinus** (page 255), one of the greatest kings in Hungarian history.

I have spent most of my life (in Romania) living in this city, so it's a little bit hard for me not to be biased in its favor, but I've yet to meet a tourist or visitor who was not beguiled by this modern, urbane city.

Although **Cluj**[98] is one of Romania's largest cities, it has little in the way of specifically tourist attractions, although it is home to many beautiful squares, museums (see page 173) and medieval walls and towers.

---

[97] This rhymes exactly with the sport "luge".

[98] There's a little confusion here because the judet (county) is called Cluj but the city's official name is Cluj-Napoca. The "Napoca" part was only added in the 1970's to refer to its ancient Roman name (Napocensis). Most locals drop the "Napoca" part when talking about the city.

Because it is home to tens of thousands of university students, there is an extremely active cultural and nightlife scene here and you can easily go out in the city and "party" every night of the week.

Increasingly, the summer movie festival (**TIFF – Transylvania Film Festival**) is becoming a draw for both Romanians and international visits alike (see www.tiff.ro for more details).

**Cluj** is also one of the wealthiest cities in Romania, boasting two world-class malls and one of the only **Starbucks** coffee outlets in the country.

## Constanța/Black Sea

The city of **Constanța** (*cone-stonce-uh*) is one of Romania's biggest urban areas and is the country's busiest port area as the city lies directly on the Black Sea (see below).

It is also the largest city in **Dobruja** (page 250) and is a great place to further explore the Black Sea, the Danube Delta (page 167) as well as find connections to Bulgaria, Turkey and Ukraine (page 113).

Because of its unique history, many of the monuments, churches, Roman ruins (page 167) and other historical markers are much different than the rest of the country. Indeed, **Constanța** is one of the few places where you can find mosques and it is considered the "Islamic center" of the country.

Be aware that this is a large, sometimes grimy, industrial city but is one of the major tourist destinations for the country and the people generally are friendly, helpful and knowledgeable.

The entire Black Sea resort/coast area begins at the southern limits of **Constanța** and there are regular city buses as well as trains connecting these areas.

As far as tourist attractions inside the city itself, don't miss the country's largest acquarium (Rom: **Acvariu**), the "Dolphinarium"[99](Rom: **Delfinariu**) and the many fine museums, statues and buildings all clustered around **Piața Ovidiu** (Ovid's Square).

Black Sea

The entire strip of land on the coast south of **Constanța** running down to the Bulgarian border is home to Romania's oldest and most popular resort areas. In the Communist era, most Romanians (and other Eastern Bloc

---

[99] Similar to but far smaller in scope to "Sea World" adventure parks in the United States.

countries' residents) took their holidays here, and this is when most of the facilities were built.

This strip of resorts is often collectively known in Romanian as **Mangalia** (*mun-gall-e-uh*) named after one of southernmost points.

Sadly, today this means that the infrastructure is largely worn and outdated and often tacky, run-down or else unappealing.  Honestly, the resorts just across the border in Bulgaria are cheaper, nicer and often times in much better shape.

One exception is **Mamaia** (*muh-my-uh*), considered to be the luxury boardwalk style resort town in Romania.  It has an enormous (and modern) water park, including slides and a "lazy river" and an overhead cable car system to get from one side to the other.

Lodging in **Mamaia** and other prices may be quite expensive, so you're much better off staying in **Constanța** or one of the cheaper resort towns and simply taking the bus to **Mamaia**.

The other exception is the enclave on the coast known as **Vama Veche** (see below).

Vama Veche

The name **Vama Veche** (*vah-muh veck-eh*) in Romanian means "the old customs post", as in historical times it lay on the actual border with Bulgaria, although today that's actually a few kilometers further to the south.

Even during the Communist era, the authorities took a "hands off" approach to **Vama Veche** and so it became a gathering place for dissidents, intellectuals, "hippies" and other free thinkers.

Today it is home to one of Romania's only full nude beaches.  Camping directly on the beach is still permitted (although technically illegal in some places but the rules are always flaunted here) and it has a very youthful, iconoclastic "party" vibe to it even today similar to Mardi Gras in New Orleans or "Spring Break" in the United States.

The summer season in Romania officially kicks off on **May 1** (page 117) and tens of thousands of young people flock to **Vama Veche** for the large festival slash party.

Because of its historical freethinking spirit, one of Romania's most celebrated musical acts is named **Vama Veche** after this area.

## Craiova

A large, sometimes grimy city located in western **Oltenia** (page 249), **Craiova** (*cry-oh-vuh*) is the industrial heart of Romania, producing both Dacia brand cars as well as train engines for Romanian railways.

Although limited in terms of tourist attractions, it is a lively, bustling and very thriving city.  It also has a delightful botanical garden as well as the gorgeous downtown **Nicolae Romanescu Park**, complete with a lake.

The region outside of **Craiova** is somewhat mountainous and is the heart of Romania's mining industry (especially near **Tîrgu-Jiu**).

## Galați

Located right on the Danube River on the border of Ukraine, **Galați** (*guh-lots*) is one of Romania's biggest cities and is a major shipping port.  It is located in southern (Romanian) Moldova.

There is a lovely riverwalk that stretches for a few kilometers along the water and some delightful bars and restaurants that allow you to take in the panoramic view.

While there isn't much of interest to see in the heart of downtown, the streets are shaded with leafy trees and just about every modern urban convenience is at hand.

Due to its large size, there are regular connections between **Galați** and the rest of (Romanian) Moldova northwards as well as **Tulcea** and other points southward.

A few kilometers east of the city is a border crossing into the Republic of Moldova (the country).  This crossing must be done in an automobile but regrettably there are no buses running between the two countries so if you're trying to cross here without your own car you'll have to flag down a ride.

Note: This city is briefly mentioned in Bram Stoker's <u>Dracula</u> (page 12) although there are no marked references to this in the city.

## Oradea

Located right on the Hungarian border in northwestern Romania in the **Crișana** (page 249) region, **Oradea** (*oh-rod ee-uh*) is a small but thriving, wealthy city with an unusually high number of English speakers.

Anyone coming to/from northwestern Romania and Transylvania will likely cross via **Oradea** as it is a major rail rub for trains and vehicular traffic heading to Budapest and points westward.

**Oradea** has a lovely, pedestrian-only downtown zone in its historic **centru** and a delightful park that runs by the river, in plain view of many impressive historic buildings.

## Piatra Neamț

Many people consider **Piatra Neamț** (*pee-otra neigh-omtz*) to be one of the most picturesque and lovely small towns in the (Romanian) Moldova region.

As one of the oldest inhabited places in the entire country, many ruins and remnants from the previous **Dacian** culture still exist, some on display just outside the (modern) city limits.

The surrounding areas in the region are some of the most beautiful in the entire country, including the spectacular **Cheile Bicazului** (page 166).

## Pitești

One of the most beautiful cities in the **Wallachia** region, **Pitești** (*pee-tesht*) is situated just a short distance northwest of **Bucharest**.

Because there is now a modern, high-speed highway connecting the two cities, it is far faster to travel by private car than public transportation, about the only place this is true in Romania.

This city has an absolutely lovely downtown park, complete with a winding, snaking fountain and wide open plaza for pedestrians.

## Ploiești

The city of **Ploiești** (*ploy-esht*) played a significant role during World War 2 as it is the home of Romania's petroleum producing region.

The oil industry continues to thrive and **Ploiești**, just a short distance north of **Bucharest**, is one of Romania's larger cities, a bustling, modern metropolis.

It should be noted that the Peace Corps' main training facility in Romania is in **Ploiești** although they will cease operations at the end of 2013 because the country is now deemed modernized enough to no longer require their services.

## Suceava

**Suceava** (*sootch ah-vuh*) is the ancient capital of the **Bukovina** region (page 243) of Moldova, the northern half of which is now in modern day Ukraine.

During the days of **Ştefan cel Mare** (page 253), **Suceava** was the capital of all of Moldova and is home to probably the greatest quantity of medieval Orthodox churches in the entire country.

Because of its location in **Bukovina**, the city of **Suceava** is a great place to base yourself for day trips to explore the world-famous **Painted Churches of Bukovina** (page 165).

## Târgovişte

Located precisely halfway between **Piteşti** and **Ploieşti**, **Târgovişte** (*turg-o-veesh-teh*) is a city of about 100,000 people and was an important fortress town in medieval **Wallachia**, including during the rule of Vlad "Dracula" Ţepeş, who build the *Chindia Tower*, which still stands and can be visited today.

During the 1989 Revolution, Nicolae and Elena Ceausescu were captured and executed in **Târgovişte** (sometimes spelled **Tîrgovişte**).

## Timişoara

One of Romania's largest cities, **Timişoara** (*tee-mee-shwar-uh*) is the capital of the Banat and one of the most popular destinations for visitors.

Due to its long-standing role in the Austrian-Hungarian Empire, there are very strong connections even today to Germany and Austria and **Timişoara** remains a place where German-speaking visitors can find a lot of accommodation in their language.

It should be noted here that the main train station, called **Timişoara de Nord** (meaning "north") is not actually in the northern part of the city and is in fact due *west* of **centru**.

The train station is dirty, grimy and chaotic and can be very intimidating to visitors, although it is generally safe. Lodgings very close to the train station are often over-priced and of extremely poor quality.

Walking out of the train station, turning towards your left (towards an OMV gas/petrol station) and continuing for just one mile will take you straight into the absolutely gorgeous, sparkling downtown, complete with **Piaţa Operei**, an enormous plaza where the 1989 Revolution began.

This area, between **Piaţa Operei** and **Piaţa Unirii** (just north via the pedestrian-only street) is full of lovely buildings, fountains and architecture and should not be missed.

There are also a delightful series of parks and restaurants adjacent to the **Bega River**, which begins just south of the main (green) cathedral of **Piaţa Operei**.

**Timişoara** also has an international airport (albeit far outside of town, and reachable only by taxi/private car) with multiple connections to Western Europe.

Please be aware that there are some exorbitantly expensive taxis operating in **Timişoara**, especially around the train station (see page 109 for much more). The cheaper taxis at the train station can all be found by crossing the main street (a very busy thoroughfare).

## Tîrgu-Jiu

This city, sometimes spelled **Târgu-Jiu** (*turgoo-jew*) is located in **Oltenia** in southwestern Romania.

Probably the number one attraction in this hard-working industrial city is numerous statues by the famous sculptor **Constantin Brancuşi** (page 253).

## Tîrgu-Mureş

Again, due to Romanian spelling changes (page 275), this city's name is sometimes spelled **Târgu-Mureş** (*tur-goo moo-resh*) but is always pronounced the same.

Located on the edge of Szekely Land (page 197), this city is divided almost equally between Hungarian and Romanians.

It has a lovely, gorgeous downtown bursting with flower arrangements and mosaics, especially on the Palace of Culture.

## Tulcea

Located right in the heart of the Danube Delta (page 167), **Tulcea** (*tulch-ee-uh*) is a city of about 100,000 people nestled in the upper northeastern part of Romanian **Dobrogea** (page 250).

Because of its unique history as a shipping port for centuries, **Tulcea** and the surrounding regions are home to many minorities, including the **Lipoveni** (page 209).

# Top 8 Recommended Rural Places to Visit

Even though there are many amazing and wonderful cities in Romania, by far the most spectacularly beautiful and gorgeous spots are in the countryside.

The list below is only a small sampling of what you can find here as Romania is one of the most unspoiled, natural, "wild" lands in all of Europe, with a wide variety of diverse flora and fauna, with every kind of geographical feature from misty mountain crags to beaches to waterfalls to musical rivers and streams.

Unless otherwise noted it is very difficult to reach these areas with public transportation.

### Bâlea Lac/Lake

It's almost impossible to write out phonetically how to pronounce the name of this lake, something akin to *buh-lee-uh lock*, a glacier lake at over 2,000 meters altitude in the **Făgăraș Mountains** in central Romania just north of **Sibiu**.

Due to the altitude, the water in the lake is always very cold and is considered some of the freshest, purest water in the entire country. To me personally it tastes exactly like fresh-fallen snow and is the most delicious beverage I have ever consumed in my entire life, bar none.

Because of its location, access to this lake can be quite difficult except in the middle of summer as the roads leading to it are closed (by heavy snowfall) the rest of the year. It is accessible both by car (from the **Transfăgărășan**- page 166) as well as a "ski" type cable car.

### Painted churches of Bucovina

Recognized by the United Nations as a UNESCO World Heritage Site, the various painted, wooden churches of southern Bukovina are world-renowned for their beauty and craftsmanship.

Spread throughout the region near **Suceava** (page 163) are several wooden churches, miraculously having survived the intervening centuries, their exterior walls painted in loving detail with many scenes from the Bible, intended as a kind of "visual sermon" to the parishioners.

With private transportation, it is possible to see these all in one day. For more information on the exact location of each church and where it is located, look online[100].

## Sinaia/Predeal/Buşteni – hiking trails

The Bucegi Mountains region just south of **Braşov** is home to a series of small owns all in a row that follow the main rail line.

Due to their elevations, this region is home to ski slopes as well as some of the best hiking in Romania, with well-marked trails of varying lengths for hikers at varying degrees of expertise.

Note: be aware that the cable car to ascend at **Buşteni** is often very busy and there can be significant delays. Access from Sinaia is usually the best option whenever possible.

Likewise the road between **Buşteni** and **Sinaia** is often very crowded and thus a short drive can sometimes take a considerable amount of time.

There are *minibuze* that operate between these three towns that cost just a few lei.

## Cheile Bicazului

Translated into English as the Bicaz Gorge, this is a spectacular canyon almost 8km long in southern Moldova, close to the city of **Piatra Neamţ**.

At the center of the gorge is the Red Lake (Rom: **Lacu Roşu**), which has camping facilities as well as modern hotels.

## Transfăgărăşan

The **Transfăgărăşan** (*trans fug uh ruh shawn*) is a paved highway, the second highest road in Romania, and it goes over and crosses the **Făgărăşan Mountains,** starting just north of **Sibiu** and ending near **Piteşti**.

This road gained international attention in 2009 when the British show *Top Gear* featured it as possibly the "best road" in the world.

Due to the altitude, this road is usually closed during the winter months.

---

[100] http://www.romaniatourism.com/painted-monasteries.html

**Iron Gates – Danube River**

As the Danube River exits Serbia and crosses into Romania, it passes through the Iron Gates (Rom: **Porțile de Fier**) via a spectacular canyon, now home to two hydroelectric dams.

**Danube Delta**

After wending its way throughout much of Europe, the Danube River fans out in a large, delta-shaped region in the **Dobrogea** region (page 250) of Romania, forming a large wetlands/marshy area similar to the bayou in Louisiana, before terminating in the Black Sea.

These wetlands are the home to millions of migrating birds and tourists come annually to observe these.

Likewise, this is the fishing and aquatic center of Romania, with many people living in villages raised up on stilts to avoid the seasonal flooding. Indeed, some regions of the Delta may be accessibly only by watercraft.

Many organized tours abound, focusing on the local culture, birdwatching as well as fishing and hunting.

**Orăştie/Sarmizegetusa**

Near the modern city of **Orăştie** is the former capital of the Dacian Kingdom, **Sarmizegetusa**, which was conquered by the Romans under Emperor Trajan (Rom: *Traian*) in the year 106 after an epic, five-year struggle against King Decebal(us).

The complex at **Sarmizegetusa** is now an archeological park, where visitors can see various ruins, both Dacian as well as Roman (see below).

This region has been inhabited for hundreds of thousands of years, and some of the oldest human remains in all of Europe have been discovered here, including what may be the oldest form of writing ever found on the continent.

**Roman Ruins/Fortifications**

The ancient Romans had two settlements in what would be classified as modern Romania today – one being the Province of Dacia Felix, centered around (what is now) **Orăştie** and containing most of Crişana, the Banat and Transylvania (see page 240 for more).

The other settlement, called **Moesia**, was on the Black Sea coast (especially around the modern city of **Constanța**) and formed part of Rome's maritime empire. Note: the poet Ovid was sent into exile near the end of his life to this city after offending the emperor.

Primarily in Dacia Felix, the Romans started or improved upon existing mines as the region is very rich in mineral resources, including salt and gold. Romans also expanded upon the multiple rich, naturally-occurring thermal springs and turned them into baths and spa resorts, a practice which continues to the present day.

Note: Some Roman ruins and items are preserved in museums, particularly the National Museum of History in **Bucharest**.

Dacia Felix Roman Ruins

Located 8km outside the modern city of **Zălau**, just 45km north of **Cluj-Napoca**, is the former Roman fort of Porolissum. While not extremely impressive (especially as compared to medieval castles), this is probably the best-preserved Roman fortification in Romania and on the grounds are the remains of several Roman residences.

Built 8km away from the Dacian capital of **Sarmizegetusa**, the Romans built their own capital and called it Ulpia Traiana. Today several temples, an amphitheatre and the remains of other buildings can be viewed.

There is a small extant fortress from the Roman city of Apulum just outside the modern city of **Alba Iulia** (see page 120). Also nearby is the former Roman gold mine of Alburnus Maior, which visitors today can descend and explore.

Moesia Roman Ruins

Spread alongside the banks of the Danube River are several long, earthen walls called "Trajan's Walls" although they were actually built at a later period.

Next to one of these walls is the Roman-Byzantine fortification called the **Cetatea Pătului.**

Near **Constanța**, one can find the ruins at Adamclisi, built during the reign of Emperor Trajan and dedicated in his honor.

Located outside the city of (modern) **Tulcea** is the former Roman city of Isaccea, which contains the citadel of Noviudunum.

The fort of Halmyris (actually the Greek name, the Roman name was Salmorus) is located near the city of **Tulcea** today and several buildings still remain although this area is still undergoing excavation.

# Best Castles/Palaces to See

### Hunedoara Castle

Also known as **Corvinesti** or **Hunyadi Castle**, this amazingly well-preserved castle was the seat of power for the Hungarian nobility for centuries.

It was here in this castle that Vlad Țepeș (page 10) was imprisoned for seven long years by Mattias Corvinus (page 255) until he was released and later became an ally of the Hungarian king.

The interior of the castle was refurbished in the 1950's and is in impeccable condition and considered a museum today. Visitors enter via a long drawbridge over a moat and the size of the fortifications is simply immense.

Reaching this castle with public transportation is difficult, as it is located atop a steep series of crags just outside the city of **Hunedoara** in western Romania. Another nearby city is **Deva**.

As with **Poenari** below, this castle is considered by many to be haunted.

If you are interested in seeing a genuine castle and getting the full "medieval fortifications" experience, this is definitely the place to visit.

### Bran

If you are at all interested in Bram Stoker's Dracula (page 10) and vampires and the rest, the castle in the town of **Bran** (*brawn*) is where you want to go as it often referred to as "Dracula's Castle".

At the bottom of the hill is a small market selling every kind of vampire and Dracula-related souvenir and knick-knack known to mankind, including "blood wine".

At the top of the hill itself is the castle, beautifully preserved and seemingly untouched over the centuries. Visitors can freely wander all over the grounds, looking in various rooms and seeing a very close approximation of historical accuracy from when this castle was a vital defensive fortification.

Nonetheless, there is little to no evidence that the real Vlad Țepeș ever spent any time there. In fact, the ruler who actually resided here was none other than **Queen Marie**[101] of Romania, the country's last ruling female monarch, and much of the castle's furnishings come from the period of her residence. Not only did **Queen Marie** die while living at Bran Castle but her heart still remains buried on the grounds.

The castle is only available for visits during daytime hours but every year on Halloween tourists are allowed in at nighttime for a themed party that many foreigners enjoy.

There is regular bus service to and from **Bran** from the nearby city of **Brașov**.

### Peleș

Located on the outskirts of **Sinaia** (page 166), **Peleș** (*peh-lesh*) is the formal royal palace of the Romanian monarchy. It is one of the most surreal palaces I've ever seen, as the king in the days when this place was built was a German who did not speak any Romanian. Inside is a private movie theater (the first one in Romania) as well as many other ornate luxuries beyond description.

After King Michael (page 254) was forced to abdicate in 1947, the palace became a property of the state but it was returned to the royal family in 2005.

Nonetheless, the palace is open for tourists to visit but only on guided tours for a somewhat hefty admission fee.

The palace at **Peleș** is just a short 10-minute walk from the train station in **Sinaia**. It is regularly voted as one of the top 10 most beautiful castles/palaces in all of Europe and is visually stunning, especially from the outside.

### Elisabeta Palace

Located in **Bucharest** just north of the city center, this is the formal royal palace of the Romanian monarchy and the seat of power during their reign. After King Michael (page 254) was forced to abdicate in 1947, the palace became a property of the state but it was returned to the royal family in 2005.

---

[101] Marie was born in England of British royal blood and married into the Romanian monarchy in 1893.

Nonetheless, the palace is open for tourists to visit but only on guided tours.

**Poenari Castle**

Considered to be the "real" Dracula's castle, **Poenari** (*poy-nar*) today is largely in ruins, although there is plenty to see and explore. It is considered the most authentic of Vlad Țepeș' castles because he upgraded previous fortifications on the site and actually used this castle during his rule.

Located high up on a crag near the **Transfăgărășan** (page 166), the castle sits directly on a cliff and you will have to walk up quite a long, steep flight of stairs (1,048 total) to reach it.

Many people considered **Poenari** to be one of the most haunted places in the world.

It is extremely difficult to reach this castle without private transportation. The nearest city is **Curtea de Argeș**. It is also close to both **Brașov** to the north as well as **Pitești** to the south.

# Best Festivals to See

Romania is a land of many festivals, some of them modern musical concerts and some traditional agricultural holidays.

There are far too many of them to be listed in their entirety here, but below are some of the best.

**Cerbul de Aur - Brașov**

Pronounced *chair-bull day our* and known in English as the "Golden Stag" Festival, this is probably the most famous annual musical celebration held in Romania, with artists coming from all over the world to participate.

While for decades it was held in summer, recently the organizers have changed the scheduling a bit, so now it is held in early autumn.

The headliner concerts are held in **Piața Sfatului** in the city of **Brașov** (page 142) and are shown on national television.

The official website for the concert is: www.cerbuldeaur.ro

## Junii - Braşov

Probably the most famous festival held in Romania involving people on horseback, this is a weeklong ceremony culminating on the first Sunday after (Orthodox) Easter in **Braşov**.

The name of this spring rite in Romanian, **Junii** (*jew-knee*) comes from an old Latin word for "youths", so traditionally this is translated into English as "Feast of the Youth".

Men in carefully selected fraternities ride out to all corners of **Braşov** on horseback, elaborately decked out in traditional costumes and raiment throughout the entire week up until the final moment, performing an elaborate set of rituals that can be traced to the Dacian, pre-Roman days.

## Târgul de Fete - Muntele Gaină

The name **Muntele Gaină** (*moont-eh-lay guy-ee-nuh*) literally means "Hen Mountain" and is the name of a large peak near the city of **Oradea** (page 161).

Every year on or around June 20, various men from surrounding areas gather for the **Târgul de Fete**, translated literally as something akin to "Marriage Market" where men go to "shop" for wives.

These kinds of "marriage markets" used to be held all over Romania in the past as a way to ensure that rural, scattered villagers could find an appropriate mate.

While some matches are still made today, these are now festivals held for the pure joy of it, meeting and mixing with neighbors, wearing traditional costumes and cooking and enjoying delicious, homemade food.

## TIFF film festival – Cluj-Napoca

Every summer, when the rest of the town seems emptied out of university students, one of the most renowned film festivals in the country occurs every year in **Cluj** (page 158) called **TIFF** – the **Transilvania International Film Festival**.

Hundreds of films are shown from around the world over a period of weeks, all of them either in English or subtitled in English, allowing visitors from many nations to enjoy them.

For more information, the official website is: www.tiff.ro

## Medieval Festival – Sighişoara

As **Sighişoara** (page 155) already has the most intact medieval city center in Romania, it is only natural that once a year they hold a medieval festival.

Locals dress up in period costumes, including ladies in gowns and men on horseback, armed with swords and shields. Demonstrations of medieval life, from music to weaponry, are held and before your very eyes it seems as though the medieval spirit of the city has sprung into life.

Unfortunately, exactly when this festival will be held can be sometimes difficult to determine as currently there are no official websites with dedicated information. Generally though it is held some time in either June or July.

# Best Museums to Visit

Romania, a land with so much history, clearly has a lot of its past to preserve and exhibit in museums. There are usually several museums in every larger city with a wide collection of exhibitions to satisfy the tastes of almost any visitor.

### Pharmacy Museum - Cluj

It may sound a little strange to be recommending a museum about the history of pharmacology as one not to be missed, yet the one in **Cluj-Napoca** (page 158) is definitely unique.

Located on the northeast side of the main downtown square, it is a small, unobtrusive building that can easily be missed if you're not looking for it. It has an impressive display of medical instruments, equipment, medicinal jars and even "magical recipes" once used to cure people.

The finishing touch is the unusual curator of the museum, who gives his own special spin to the tour, using his unique grasp of English to weave tales of this city's wonderful alchemical past.

### Brukenthal National Museum - Sibiu

It is no mystery that **Sibiu** is probably one of the most culturally enriched cities in the entire country and the enormous **Brukenthal National Museum** is one of the oldest and largest, actually composed of six separate museums.

One museum contains an impressive art gallery, with paintings, engravings and other masterpieces collected over the past 250 years from a wide variety of artists.

There is also a history museum, a library (containing both archaic works as well as modern ones), a history museum, a museum of natural history and finally a pharmacology museum, which contains the very laboratory in which Samuel Hahnemann first invented homeopathy.

These museums are located right off of the huge **Piața Mare** and could easily take days to explore in their entirety.

### Village Museum – Sibiu

There are several "village museums" in Romania, including a very impressive one in **Bucharest**, wherein entire villages have been preserved for the visitor to wander around and peer at.

That being said, the ANTRAC complex just south of **Sibiu** (see page 152) is probably the best one to see. Not only does it have an entire Romanian village preserved but also a German/Saxon one. There are also operational mills and people weaving, spinning and doing other tasks in the old way, making it truly a "living history" museum.

# Music, TV and the Media

Very little of the Romanian media, whether radio stations, television channels or printed media is owned by Romanians.

Larger European media conglomerates control most of it and there is very little to no original programming on Romanian television or radio even if some content is in the Romanian language.

Nonetheless, there are about 3 "national channels" which primarily sandwich news broadcasts in between syndicated foreign television shows (subtitled in Romanian) and action movies.

There are dozens of newspapers with many differing viewpoints, each about 20-30 pages in length.

Music on the radio will be mostly in English but all of the talking will be done in Romanian.

Please note that in Hungarian areas, there will always be Hungarian-language media of all kinds. Furthermore, English, German and French-language television channels are common, especially in larger cities (and in hotels).

## Radio stations

Effectively there is nothing on the AM band.

FM stations follow the European standard, meaning they end on an *even* number, i.e. 94.2 FM.

The vast majority of radio stations are going to be nearly identical with a "morning zoo" crew of jokesters and then the type of music will be bland pop (see page 176).

Other stations will be nearly all talk, mostly about sports and/or politics, quite popular with taxi drivers.

There are a couple of government radio stations which may play traditional music (see page 179) and/or classical music.

While most of the music will be in English, none of the programming will be. Be aware that in many cases curse words or swearing in English songs will *not* be censored or bleeped out.

## Television

The situation concerning television in Romania has undergone some dramatic changes in the last few years. In the Communist era, television broadcasts were few and far between and primarily political in nature.

After the Revolution however, owning and watching television has become a national obsession. Just about every Romanian who can afford to owns and watches a generous amount of television programming.

Since both cable and satellite service are ubiquitous, most Romanians have access to several dozen channels, the majority of them American.

Almost all foreign-language programming is broadcast in its original language with Romanian language subtitles on the bottom of the screen, making this a handy way to learn the language.

The foreign visitor speaking English, Spanish, German and possibly French or Italian will find at least some content in their language on Romanian television.

There are three national Romanian television channels who have a little original programming (in Romanian) but generally broadcast American-made content.

The three domestic channels' most popular programming to a Romanian however are their news broadcasts, particularly the one at 7:00 pm (1900 hours). A large percentage of Romanians are <u>addicted</u> to the 7:00 pm news broadcast, which is usually gory and sensationalist with a heavy emphasis on death and dismemberment. These news broadcasts are quite lengthy (about 45 minutes) with no commercial interruption until just before the sports news, which comes last, and are quite lengthy themselves.

If you don't speak Romanian, these can be quite tedious to sit through, especially if your hosts or colleagues are staring, slack-jawed throughout the entire thing.

Note: Many sports reporters are women, often young, attractive women, and some visitors find this "mysterious" or "odd".

**Prevalence Of Music In Everyday Life**

If you spend just a couple of weeks in any kind of urban environment in Romania you're going to find that certain songs will get hammered into your consciousness whether you like it or not.

What am I talking about?

Scanning the Romanian FM radio band, you will find the vast majority of (musical) stations to be extremely similar, based on just a few formulas:

**Budinca[102] Hits** – Designed to be extremely smooth and relaxing, a mélange of commercial hits of the last 40 years.

**Morning Zoo** – Has a "wacky crew" doing "hilarious" jokes in the morning and then the rest of the day the music is 80% English, 10% Romanian, 7% Spanish, 2% Italian and 1% German and always zero percent Hungarian, Russian, Bulgarian or Polish.

The music itself is a standard blend of what is called "Top 40" in many places, the same commercially-driven hits that half the globe is listening to simultaneously (I know).

---

[102] See page 292.

**Techno Variant** – Same as above except sometimes they'll play "techno" music exclusively, especially that kind that barely has any singing and is mostly just interesting electronic rhythms and sounds.

If you combined the entire playlists of all the radio stations in these two genres I doubt it would be even one thousand separate songs. There is clearly someone, somewhere, or a group of "someones" who is choosing this playlist because it is surprisingly limited and updated simultaneously when new songs are added.

What is indisputable however is that the songs playing on Romanian radio follow the power law, which in layman's terms means that **a few songs get played one heck of a lot**.

This fact combined with the reality that in (urban environments in) Romania it is nearly impossible to escape the range of these radio broadcasts means you will be forced to memorize these songs. Radios in Romania are playing almost everywhere and at nearly every hour of the day and night.

Just a few of the endless places you are quite likely to hear a radio blasting:

- Inside a taxi
- Playing at the corner **magazin mixt** (page 269)
- Sometimes quite loudly in a grocery store or hypermarket
- At a café
- At a bar
- At McDonald's
- During any kind of public event or festival
- From overhead speakers at large bus stops
- On some nicer trains
- From cars driven by guys who enjoy playing loud music
- At a restaurant
- At a friend's house

And many, many more…

Therefore about the only way to avoid this (in a city) is to always stay at home, close your windows and never, ever turn on your radio. You can basically never conduct any kind of business, commercial or social, without this music going straight into your cranium.

Over the years, I've met a lot of visitors and sometimes as early as the third day they'll turn to me and ask, "What *is* the name of that song?"

If you're at all sensitive to having songs get "stuck" in your head, Romania is not the country for you.

## Pop music

This will be played just about everywhere (see page 176) and is mostly English with a little Romanian, Spanish and Italian mixed in.

Most of this music will be upbeat with a catchy chorus and a great deal of lyrical simplicity.

## Manele

If you walk up to any normal Romanian and say "hey that **manele** song is really catchy. It's got a beat and I can dance to it" they will immediately scowl, spit in your face and most likely never speak to you again as long as you live. They will disinherit you, scratch out all the cartouches with your name on them in the family tomb and tell everyone you are "dead to them".

Yet at the same time, **manele** music is *everywhere* in Romania, it has its own TV channels and CD sales are super brisk. And yet absolutely no one will ever admit to liking it or listening to it. What gives?

To begin with, you need to understand what a *rroma* is, aka a "gypsy" in ordinary English (see page 200).

Before the modern era, one thing many gypsies specialized in was called **muzica lăutărească**. Essentially, bands of gypsy musicians would amble around the countryside of Romania and sing and play this kind of music for weddings and other festivals.

Note: Many Romanians will freely admit they like **muzica lăutărească**. Nothing shameful about it.

So what's **manele** then? Well essentially some gypsy musicians decided to blend old-school **muzica lăutărească** with some Balkan type music, add some electronic synthesizers and "jazz it up" a bit.

Just imagine a metaphorical blender where you take violin-heavy wedding music, cheap 1980's synth rhythms, Turkish/Middle Eastern wailing and BZZZZZZT make a musical smoothie out of it. That's **manele**!

Or the musical part of it, which is half the fun. The other half of the fun is the lyrics, which are essentially *exactly the same* as "urban rap" in the United States. You know, fast cars, getting wasted, lots of chicks, I'm a bad ass, you name it.

So to most Romanians, manele is a "cheap" and "corrupted" form of traditional music (the **muzica lăutărească**) mixed with very vulgar and trashy lyrics. All true. No doubt about it.

Fun fact: *Many other Balkan countries, especially Serbia (called "turbofolk") and Bulgaria, also have their own kinds of manele.*

Now when you hear a **manele** song, you will have one of two reactions:

*Puke! It's horrible! Sounds crappy and stupid and I hate it.*

This will win you many smiles and hands of friendship from your Romanian associates and they will breathe deep and smile and consider you a wonderful and enlightened person and give you the password to their super secret but awesome salon where you can sit in leather chairs by a fire and sip fine brandy out of a decanter brought to you by a butler in "coat and tails" and debate the finer points of philosophy and just be loved by everyone.

OR....

*Wow! Catchy tune! I like it. Where can I get my hands on more examples of this finely crafted musical genre?*

Run for the hills! The only Romanians who will ever speak to you again are filthy bums with two teeth in their mouths who constantly cadge cigarettes and drive burnt-out scooters at 5 kph up hills and wear ugly track suits and put tons of gel in their hair. And they're just being nice to you so they can wheedle money or smokes from you. Even they don't like you!

YOU HAVE BEEN WARNED!

**Folk Music**

There are no "hard lines" between what differentiates various types of Romanian folk music because each genre freely borrows from and is inspired by another.

**Muzica Lăutărească** – Essentially the "traditional" songs performed by gypsies for festivities and social occasions.

**Etno** – Literally meaning "ethnic", this refers more to what would be called "folkloric music" in English. These are the ancient, traditional peasant songs of Romania, often performed in the traditional way.

**Muzica Folclorică** – Generally identical to **etno** music above.

**Muzica Populară** – There were two waves of this genre, one beginning during the Communist era and one in the post-Revolution era.

Both waves of **muzica populară** involved taking **etno** songs and re-working them to be catchier, more upbeat and/or easy to sing. Many modern versions are done in a "techno" or pop style.

In the Romanian language **muzica populară** means both "pop(ular) music" as well as "music of the people", making it a nice ideological fit with Communist doctrine.

**Horă** – Often thought of as a "Jewish dance" outside of Romania, in this country it is a popular group dance for everyone, often featured at weddings, baptisms and any large social festival.

## Live music

Between cover bands, concerts, cafes and bars, specialized venues, public parks and concert halls, there is a great deal of live music in Romania.

Some clubs specialize in **muzica lăutărească** (page 178).

For a list of concerts and live music in most larger towns, check out one of the online entertainment guides (page 34).

There are usually orchestral, operatic and classical music concerts given on a regular basis in cities as well. Your best bet is to contact the venue in question for a list of upcoming performances.

## Newspapers and Print Media

Generally sold via kiosks and small newsstands, there are literally dozens of competing newspapers, financial papers, sports digests and other publications in Romania.

The oldest English-language Romanian newspaper is called **Nine O'Clock**[103] and can generally only be found for sale in **Bucharest** although it has a streamlined website online.

There are several Hungarian-language daily papers in Romania, published in cities with a large ethnic Hungarian population.

The only German-language Romanian newspaper I'm aware of is the **Hermannstädter Zeitung**[104], only available online and in kiosks in **Sibiu**.

---

[103] http://www.nineoclock.ro

Some Romanian newspapers like **Evenimentul Zilei** and **Adevărul** have some news online in English as well although not in the print editions.

Newsstands in larger transportation hubs (like train stations and airports) will often sell a variety of foreign newspapers and magazines, especially in French, German and English.

Magazines are sold almost everywhere newspapers can be found and are extremely popular in Romania, especially amongst women. Most of the most well known international magazines (Cosmopolitan, Vogue, FHM, etc) have a Romanian-language version.

**Classified Ads**

By far the most popular way to advertise in Romania is via specialized "advertisements only" newspapers called **publicitate** (*poobly-chee-totty*) or sometimes **anunțuri** (*anoonce-oor*), published once a week (or month).

Whether you're looking for a secondhand car to buy, an apartment to rent or other business services, these specialized newspapers are your best bet.

Very few of these publications are online or have updated listings so generally you're going to have to stick with the "dead tree" version.

At the moment there is no one, commonly-used internet site for classified advertisements nationwide like **Craigslist** or **Gumtree** although some Romanian newspapers have an accompanying website with advertisements.

There is an "Ebay" style website called **Okazii** (www.okazii.ro) that is starting to be used by some Romanians but the majority of buying/selling is still done via local classified ads.

# Romance
## Romanians online

Due to a number of factors, a great number of Romanians have computers in their home and spend quite a lot of time using them. In fact, there are many companies which open branch offices in Romania precisely to hire software developers and engineers because of this.

Romanians (living all over the world) can be found online and are a great resource for the language, culture, food, customs and helpful tourist information.

---

[104] http://www.hermannstaedter.ro

I'm going to be extremely frank and admit I've dated a few women I've met online. That being said, I must warn you that generally speaking, this is not a good idea.

Romanian culture is still highly social in the face-to-face sense so meeting (or dating) people met online is still a relatively new phenomenon.

Again, as with all online activities anywhere (from any country), beware of fraud, con artists, thieves and tricksters.

## Dating in Romania

Yes children, cover your eyes!

In your travels through Romania, you're likely to meet some very attractive white people. I mention this because while many nations have absolutely gorgeous people of color (hello Pakistan!), a nation of good looking white people is becoming something of a rarity these days.

So you, the horny traveler or business person is likely to see someone you find very attractive that you want to match your fleshy parts with their fleshy parts.

As many writers have noted, the dress code is very liberal in Romania (see page 23) and you're likely to see a lot of skin on display, further causing your hormones to surge. You want to hook up with the object of your desire but sadly, your efforts come to naught, leaving you very frustrated.

It's not just hyper-caffeinated doofuses like Leif Pettersen[105] who have come to this sad conclusion. I first became aware of how widespread this phenomenon was when one of the so-called leaders of the "sex gurus", Neil Strauss, wrote a book called The Game, detailing his exploits with fellow "guru" Mystery[106].

In this book, the author goes into great detail about all the attractive women they met in Eastern Europe and "picked up" and flirted with. Yet inexplicably, they travel all throughout Romania and don't get laid once.

So if the "masters" are getting sexually frustrated, it's likely you are too unless you read the following. In fact, I really should be charging you $20 apiece to read this but frankly that's not my kind of work.[107]

---

[105] One of the current writers of the Romanian edition of guidebook **Lonely Planet**.
[106] One of several people who refer to themselves as "pick-up artists".
[107] Although such guides are a good business for Thailand apparently.

Before I go any further, a couple of things to get straight. While this is a useful and straightforward guide to dating, it isn't a manual to *prey* on anyone, nor is it intended to be lecherous in any way. What goes on between consenting adults, regardless of nationality, is the only thing of concern in this section.

Gay Man

Quite frankly, your best options are in **Bucharest** although there are an increasing number of options in larger cities (**Cluj-Napoca** currently has two gay discos). At the moment there are at least three clubs open in **Bucharest** catering to gay clientele (male and female), which you can find online (see page 34). Even "straight" clubs in Romania close and open quite frequently so all nightlife information is temporary at best.

Outside of **Bucharest** any kind of sexual contact is going to be extremely problematic and is often given hostile opposition if discovered. Conversely most people barely believe homosexuality exists so all secondary "indicators" such as prissy behavior, mild cross-dressing, hand holding etc will literally never be identified as homosexual.

Lesbian Woman

Again, **Bucharest** is going to be your best bet by far. Other than that, there's a much more lenient attitude towards lesbian behavior (touching, kissing, etc), especially if you're young and/or appear more "traditionally female".

On the other hand looking "butch" is going to be problematic anywhere outside the capital and get you a lot of stares unless you're over 50 years old, in which case almost every Romanian woman on the street looks fairly "butch" herself.

Child Molester

What used to be quite a bad problem has now been vastly improved with Romania's accession to the European Union. Paying a street urchin one pound sterling to blow you behind a dumpster is going to get you serious jail time these days.

Heterosexual Woman

If you're reasonably good looking, getting a date should be a cinch. You'll be hit on constantly in any part of the country.

If you're *not* reasonably good looking, or especially if you're anywhere close to overweight, things are going to be a lot tougher. Your best bet is to stick with your "own kind", i.e. your fellow **Filthy Backpacker** (see page 212).

During the long and lonely journey, those guys from Belgium bunking in with you at the hostel get mighty lonely as well. Buy a good bottle of the local wine and you can save yourself the price of going out on the town for one night.

Heterosexual Guy

Ah now we're getting down into the meat and potatoes of the thing because everybody's getting on quite well but us. I say "us" in the figurative sense because while right now I am quite satisfied with my partner's lavish attentions, at one time I too stood among the ranks of the frustrated foreigner.

Right up front I'm going to say the word **escort** and be frank about it. Any large city in Romania has free entertainment guides (ex: *24-Fun, Şapte Seri* - see page 34) in all bars and most restaurants. At the back of that guide are going to be some adult ads.

Either through the ads or some online searching of great searchiness, you should find whatever it is that appeals to your taste if that's your sort of thing. Romanians and Europeans in general have a much less Puritanical stance on these sort of things so it is what it is – deal with it if that upsets you.

Although this has never been my cup of tea, so to speak, throughout my long residence here I can tell you second-hand that the "customers" I've spoken to were all fairly satisfied with the service they received, to put it delicately. As far as law enforcement is concerned, it's technically illegal in some cases but the onus is always on the escort, never the customer.

Frankly though, this costs money and also may not be the route some foreign guys want to take. What else is there to do?

First and most importantly, **go to Bucharest**. It is Romania's largest city and the most cosmopolitan, open-minded and "forward" thinking place. It also has a lot of very attractive residents, among them a subset of Romanian women that you can't find anywhere else.

**Bucharest** is the one place Romanians *relocate to* in any quantity. Everywhere else in the country, the vast majority of the residents are either life-long locals or from somewhere relatively close by.

**Bucharest** on the other hand is absolutely full of people who moved there from all kinds of smaller locales. This is fundamentally critical because it makes **Bucharest** the only place where people are used to (and often quite welcoming to) foreigners or newcomers.

Being the most cosmopolitan means, amongst other things, that you're going to meet both a lot of ambitious people as well as people who speak English. It takes some serious guts to move from a small, peaceful village to the car honking maelstrom of **Bucharest**. Therefore that hot girl you're flirting with has already demonstrated a very high level of boldness.

For these reasons (and many others) **Bucharest** is going to be absolutely your best bet all around.

But what else? And what about if you're elsewhere in this land besides the capital?

From a Romanian song:

*N-ai tupeu? Stai acasa!*

Roughly translated, this means "If you have no balls, stay home". Here's the magic formula you need to remember:

### She's Shy So You Be Bold

Really that will work wonders in this regard. A lot of "westerners" are used to a much higher level of boldness from women and as a consequence, have become less bold themselves.

Note: This is why most, but not all, Western Guys Married to a Romanian are married to a *very bold woman indeed* :P

Conversely, a lot of western guys have become *unaccustomed* to a high level of shyness when it comes to women and fail to respect it when interacting with Romanians.

Here's a common mistake to analyze in this regard:

*Mistake*: You give her your phone number.

Why is this a mistake? Because she's shy and it would be considered extremely forward to call you first. Get *her* phone number and then call her. Then if she likes you, she'll save your number and might call *you* one day.

By the way, I am fully licensed to laugh like a loon because believe me, I've made every mistake in the book.

Therefore, be bold and go for it. If the chick at the cash register is hot and you like her, don't come back to visit her and flirt 50 times. Ask her out right on the spot, or at least get her phone number (or online info, etc).

Having some balls really is necessary because in most cases you're actually putting a tremendous *stress* on the girl in question. In the first place, you're speaking English, forcing her to respond back to you in what is, to her, a stressful language to speak. Secondly, the fact that you are demonstrably foreign means entering into what is uncharted territory for her.

Almost all Romanians, male or female, have crushing inferiority complexes and therefore find it generally quite stressful to have to "live up to" what a foreigner expects. Therefore dating one requires a certain level of ambition and boldness that if she had, she'd likely be gone to **Bucharest** or somewhere overseas by now.

Furthermore, Romanian guys are some pretty bold bastards themselves. Old Timmy the Timid Wallflower isn't going to get much attention, if you dig what I'm saying.

What's next? Oh yeah.

Get Some Male Friends

In this regard, it's perfectly fine to "cruise" with other foreigners but whomever, get some male buddies to go out with you. For one thing, you're likely to be bolder when out with your male friends.

Secondly, your male friends are likely to know people (yes, including attractive women), leading up to the next most critical thing:

The More People You Know, The Better

Period. Outside of **Bucharest**, everyone knows everybody and it's quite an odd thing meeting someone who doesn't fit into that social network (you!). You can play that "Kevin Bacon in 6 links" game[108] quite easily in any Romanian town (besides **Bucharest**) and probably fewer than six with most people you meet.

Therefore, get to know people!

Assuming you have few other options, or perhaps in addition to the other ways you have of meeting people (work, host family, etc), a good route to take is to pick a bar/club and stick with it.

---

[108] Called the "Six Degrees of Kevin Bacon", easily found online.

That is to say, find your nightlife establishment of choice and go there regularly, perhaps several times a week, until you begin to know the staff and recognize repeat customers. This is a great way to make male friends amongst the other regular patrons.

It also means you need to be somewhat of a drinker unless you can hang out in a place sober while the majority of the people around you are drinking and listening to loud music.

Learn Some Romanian

This is absolutely the most helpful thing to do, even if it's just a little. Even if she mostly speaks English to you, if she feels confident you *could* understand her in Romanian, that's going to go a long way towards reducing the stress of dating a foreigner.

Furthermore, a great deal of attractive women speak little or no English at all and so therefore you're missing out on many delightful opportunities from the get-go. Seriously, Romanian women are amazing so get your nose in a dictionary, fool!

Also of critical importance: Dress And Smell Nice

It pains me to write this but nonetheless I shall:

Wear clean, unwrinkled clothes that fit and are not baggy, saggy, full of holes (yes, this means your jeans!) or food stained.

If you can wear something that is fashionable and makes you look more attractive, all the better.

Be clean as in shit, showered and shaved.

Wear a good-smelling *parfum*[109]. If you don't know what one is, go to the nicest *parfumerie* store in town and ask the female clerk to choose one for you.

And last but definitely not least:

Be Respectful

There's a way to be bold and respectful. Being bold but *not* respectful will simply make you a lecher and then you'll have to go back to your two-star *pensiune* and write angry blog posts before relieving yourself in the lumpy bed.

---

[109] See also page 25.

Again, it pains me deeply to write this but here we go:

*Don't do things that make people stare at you in public!*

Whatever those things are, from your "musical armpit" to drunken yodeling to other embarrassing, attention-getting behavior, don't do them (see also page 131).

Furthermore, the tact that you want to take is the "dashingly bold gentleman" rather than the "arrogant foreign jerk". Being considered rude is going to get you absolutely nowhere but being sassy yet respectful will get you everywhere.

And as a very important addendum, if you want any kind of relationship of substance at all, **be honest**. Whatever that entails, whether your quirks, desires or monetary status, be honest.

That last one there is the key to the golden door, fellas. Being truthful is in itself a kind of boldness and women here in Romania find it *very* attractive.

Well there you go, and I wish you good luck in making the beast with two (or more!) backs in this fine country of mine. In addition, I wish you hundreds of fat children.

A Few Practical Notes

Condoms are sold in every pharmacy, hypermarket[110], large grocery store and gas/petrol station. Use them!

In case of accidents, the "morning after pill" is available at all Romanian pharmacies without a prescription or doctor's note (or anything else, like identification) for about **20 lei** (approximately 7 USD or 5 Euros).

Completely legal and in every city are "sex shops" (always identified like that, in English) which sell just about anything you might need in terms of lubrication, toys and accessories. That being said, if you want something ornate, bring it from home.

Alas, sadly if you're a "person of color", getting a date is going to be difficult regardless of your gender or orientation. I've even seen some pretty good looking black guys go a-begging because a different skin color on top of everything else is quite a hurdle to overcome.

---

[110] See page 295.

### Marrying a Romanian

Marrying a Romanian is a fairly simple procedure, either in Romania or in another country.

If you are planning on getting married *in* Romania and are not a citizen, contact your own embassy for further details. Generally speaking you will be required to provide documentation that you're not a criminal, are not married to anyone else and have no contagious diseases.

Once you have the documentation, it is just a question of having the forms approved in the Romanian's hometown city government office.

For Romanian marriage customs, see page 233.

Note: Marrying a Romanian is but one step in a long line to acquiring citizenship[111] and does not come automatically once you're married. Generally speaking if you reside in Romania for 5 years after being married to a Romanian you are eligible to acquire citizenship.

Getting permission to reside permanently in Romania is however, thankfully much easier if you're married (see page 230 for more).

# People in Romania

According to recent statistics, approximately 90% of the people living in Romania self-identify as Romanians, 6.5% as Hungarians, 2.5% as Rroma (gypsies) and the rest a mixture of smaller groups.

Below are descriptions of the people you will meet here. There is also a section on foreigners (as some 8-9 million come every year) as well as dogs, as you will likely meet both during your visit.

For a history of the country of Romania, see page 240.

### Romanians

Clearly anything I could say can and probably does have an exception to it. I'm also under tremendous pressure because I have an inherent pro-Romania bias *and* I'm putting my name on this while living here, hardly a recipe to encourage strong criticism.

---

[111] Becoming a citizen of Romania is far more difficult than in many countries, including the United States and requires at least 5 years of continuous marriage, among other things.

The good news is that while I do have an inherent pro-Romania bias (after all, I do *choose* to live here) it is not exactly the same as having a pro-Romanian bias, as in sometimes I like Romania a lot more than I like the people living in it.

I think the only way to explain this is that there is a *tremendous* cognitive dissonance going on here. What you (the visitor) see is *completely different* than what the (average) Romanian sees. The very essence of this is that Romanians are *unbelievably* pessimistic *and* resistant to new ideas on any subject. It's a lethal cocktail.

The only metaphor I can think of is a guy I once knew years ago, ethnically "white" but he felt he was some kind of "re-born" Native American Indian so he made everyone call him "Two Moons". He ended up becoming a bonafide alcoholic, losing his job and his wife and everything else until he became borderline suicidal.

Convinced that his life was entering an inescapable downward spiral, he began to give everything away in his house, including large and valuable appliances like a washing machine as well as some good quality furniture.

I'm telling you this story because Romanians are quite similar to Two Moons. They're often convinced life is locked in an inescapable downward spiral and therefore they give away and heavily discount the truly valuable things they have.

The good news is, as far as I know, that Two Moons never took that final step. What happened to him after that, I don't know. Likewise, Romanians for the most part still cling tenaciously to life, even if they're not convinced yet that there's light at the end of the tunnel.

Quite simply put, as a nation, Romanians have an extremely battered psyche. As a people they had their rear ends kicked for nearly 2000 years straight, spending the long centuries mostly as serfs, peasants, cow herders and sometimes literal slaves to Poles, Russians, Turks, Greeks and Hungarians.

Only 150 years ago did (some!) Romanians even break away from the Slavic alphabet and begin to gain a sense of "nationalism" and a sense of political unity was even first accomplished (of any duration) based on "being Romanian".

Nor did that ascendancy into power come easily. Romanians still celebrate **December 1** (see page 120) but the truth is that a third of what was

Romania in 1918 is split up into four (and a half[112]) separate countries now. And a number of Romanians (thankfully not too many) still worry about Transylvania going back to Hungary even today.

Not to mention *both* world wars opened up a can of misery on Romania, especially WW2. If you can get any elderly person to open up to you and tell you stories from those days, it'll knock your socks off.

I was quite blessed to know an elderly man (now deceased) and the stories he told me about the *Battle of Stalingrad* still gives me goose flesh. Most documentaries and history books focus on how bad the Russians and the Germans had it but the Romanians had it even *worse*.

Since parts of Transylvania *were* briefly wrested away from Romania during WW2, the unbroken continuity of Romanians exercising governance over what is today's Romania is barely 70 years old.

And the first 50 of those years were under Communism, starting off with massive reparation payments to the Soviets and then the utter lunacy that was the Ceauşescu regime.

Therefore let's list the group of peoples who have at one time conquered and ruled the people who became today's Romanians:

- Romans
- Scythians
- (Other) Goths
- Avars
- Bulgars (later Bulgarians)
- Cumans
- Gepids
- Hungarians
- Tatars
- Turks
- Russians
- Polish-Lithuanians
- Greeks
- Germans
- Austrians
- Soviets
- Fascist Romanians

---

[112] The "half" a country is the only partly recognized Republic of Trans-Dniestr, called "Transnistria" in Romanian and Приднестровская Молдавская Республика in Russian, an area in what is technically today the Republic of Moldova, not discussed elsewhere in this book.

- Communist Romanians

And then finally, only now, in the last 25 years has Romania awakened with Romanians in control of all political and social power. Wow!

Like my friend Two Moons, Romania has had a difficult childhood. There are many grandmothers (and fewer grandfathers) who were raised and spent their *entire* lives under the heel of someone else's boot.

And those grandmothers had daughters, who likewise spent all but the last 20 years bearing the yoke of someone else's control. And it was they who raised today's young adults – who grew up with one foot in the modern, commercialized MTV world and one still in the land of the "old days and old ways".

Therefore it's only the very youngest Romanian children and some expatriates who have spent a significant amount of time abroad who have had full exposure to new ways of thinking.

Communism favored the color red, which definitely is appropriate in its context of meaning "stop", as social progress in those days was definitely not encouraged.

Perhaps the traffic signal appropriate for today's Romania would be yellow, as in caution, slow down and approach carefully. There is a general sense of extreme inflexibility in Romania and it is only cautiously and slowly that it begins to bend.

The other important aspect to understand about Romanians is that they are a *country* or rural/agricultural people through and through.

Although of course Romanians came to live in cities, accelerated somewhat under Communism, for centuries they were generally the peasants out in the field while the noble (of a different nationality) on a horse rode off to the town and the castle.

Even under Ceauşescu the pace of "urbanization" was actually fairly slow. Only in **Bucharest** did a tremendous amount of real estate get re-arranged for the glamour of the ideology and the state. Tens of thousands of villages still existed and life went on, in some cases, nearly unchanged as it had for centuries.

But just about *everybody* today has a cousin, a granny, an uncle or an aunt living out in the countryside. Very young children from urban areas often spend the first few years of their life with a relative in the country and frequent visits throughout the rest of their life are common as well.

And that's not to forget the millions of Romanians who still live in rural areas, just slightly under half of the current population. They're still there, still making soup the old way and still having a very strong influence even on the people in the urban areas.

While this culture of rural traditions, including dress, songs, handicrafts, music and foods is revered partially or in whole by most Romanians, it does leave a tremendous gap in cultural identity. Most Romanians know quite well their *traditional* side but what is their *modern* side?

Aside from perhaps gymnasts/gymnastics and maybe hacking/computer use, there's not much. There is of course a great fascination with technologies and cars and all of that but very little of it is *domestic*. It's not made in Romania and it's not designed by Romanians. It is simply *consumed* by them.

So what are you if all you do is drive the same cars, drink the same drinks, wear the same clothes, watch the same movies, listen to the same music and eat the same (fast/junk) foods as everyone else around the planet?

It's a tremendous vacuum to fill and therefore it becomes terrifying. Likewise, all urban things as well as all the hustle and bustle of modernity frighten the pants off most Romanians. Some will deny it but most will openly admit it. When you've got roots that deep, it's very difficult to transplant them very quickly.

Romanians are not, to put it lightly, very astute business people, as a rule. It's just not their priority. Working industriously to make money and/or keep money is simply not number one on a Romanian's personal priority list.

This can sometimes lead to "baffling" situations for visitors when for example a restaurant owner would rather *not* make money than serve them some food/drink or provide some other service. This often even comes across as *rude* for some capitalist visitors (see page 134).

But even when Romanians *think* they're all about the money, they're not. Bills go unpaid here. Salaries go unpaid. Government projects or payments (like retirement money) go unpaid sometimes. Invoices and contracts go unpaid. A lot of very "unprofessional" and money-losing acts go on here, simply put, and this is just the tip of the iceberg.

This ties perfectly into the other result of this "money isn't first" mentality, which is what is generally called "corruption". Is there plenty of it in this country? Darn right there is. Sometimes it's "little corruption" like in the form of bribes. Other times it's blatant and cheeky as hell.

So what *is* your average Romanian's priority if it isn't money? Actually it's two things: material objects and power over others.

Rule #1: Wear/display your wealth at all times.

When you first see the dismal architecture in Romania (the endless gray concrete *blocuri*) it's always a shock to see such clean, well-dressed and frankly often glamorous people exit out of those buildings.

The kind of clothes you wear and their quality is an extremely important visual cue for Romanians to determine your *social status*. If you dress as a high status person, you will get good service and respect. Dressing like a "bum", even if it is "comfortable" is not my recommendation for any visitor.

Of course if you can afford to, make everything else that's yours look good as well, from your car to your house/apartment to your garden to whatever else. It is better to have 100 nice things in the house and no money in the bank than money in the bank and nothing nice in the house.

Rule #2: Power Over Others

The number one obsession in Romania, played by contestants of all ages.

One odd contrast you will often see in this country is a low-wage employee taking their job extremely seriously, even if they aren't exactly a "hard working" employee. Everyone who has the authority to tell someone else what to do can and will do it.

Which parlays right into the <u>Scolding of Righteousness</u>[113], used specifically in *cultural* contexts, whereupon one person enforces social uniformity on another.

Besides the scolding, there's also a lot of snitching and tattling going on in this country. Sometimes my friends and I like to sit around comparing all the malicious gossip and tattling going on, especially with our neighbors living in the same *bloc*.

Whew, it seems like I've gotten into a lot of the perhaps "negative" things about Romanians, so let's talk about a few of the nicer ones, shall we?

To begin with, they're poor liars. They tend to go for the "I'll tell you a bald-faced lie and you pretend to believe it" route (*eşti un mare mincinos dar mereu ma minţi frumos*) rather than the truly sneaky, duplicitous route, so that's actually kind of refreshing.

---

[113] Page 150

Also, in general they're not too physically large or violent, which for me personally is a *very refreshing* change. They're often quite trusting and naive, which while sometimes tempting to abuse is actually quite nice. I cannot even begin to number the times I've met Romanians and two seconds later trusted them in return.

In general, when they say things, they mean them. This is partly due to the language, which is in itself direct and beautifully concise, but also because there's less inclination for "pretty, polite" talk here. It takes two Americans about 90 seconds (or more) to say goodbye on the telephone and Romanians about 1 second.

Romanians are also remarkably low-key people. Most of the time everything they're doing from ambling in the park to working on the job is kind of at a "steady as she goes" pace and is rarely frenetic. They kind of just float along through the day and that's just how it goes.

Romanians are terrible workers (from the corporate overlord perspective) but they are champion partiers. Whether parties and outings for little kids (including June 1 – **Ziua Copilor**[114]) to adult parties of all stripes, Romanians like to throw down. They greatly enjoy drinking, dancing, good music and above all else, good food.

There is no such thing as a festival, holiday, wedding, funeral, graduation, vacation or a good party without lots and lots of good food. Yes, the quality of food here (and drink) is exceptional.

And despite their scolding, most of the time you can actually do exactly what you want and nobody will bother you, hassle you, harass you or try to control you.

Sometimes, when it comes to wearing what kind of clothes you want to wear (and sometimes very little at all), it might be great to be this "free" (page 23). Or the fact that you can find a bar open at 6am to keep the party going (page 31).

Other times however, it leads to a much greater sense of responsibility. A perfect example of this is the unmarked or poorly marked hole or ditch or gap in the pavement or sidewalk where someone is doing some kind of repair or construction work.

I once fell smack into a ditch because it was completely unmarked. Of course it stung both my pride as well as my knee, but what does all this

---

[114] See page 132 for more.

teach you? When it's up to you to be responsible, you start to look out for yourself.

It's not just the fact that jagged pavement might tear you up, it's that even in more "abstract" realms, Romanians are quite self-reliant people, being particularly driven to stay clustered together largely by family and geographical origin.

So Romanians are rather tough and resilient people. I'm quite fortunate to know many young adults and while they're definitely filled with youthful energy and drive, in many ways they also seem more adult to me precisely because of this toughness and resiliency.

A year (or two?) ago, a friend of mine and I were down deep underground in an extremely slippery salt mine with only minimal handrails to keep an *adult* from plunging into the nearly limitless depths. A group of Romanian school children passed by us, perhaps each about 9-10 years old, completely fearless, each kid's head barely the same or *less* than the height of the handrails.

I turned to my friend (an American) and said, "Do you think a group of 10-year-old Americans would ever be allowed into this mine?" Our consensus was a unanimous "heck no".

Romanians are also extremely generous *when they know you*. Sometimes it's an overwhelming generosity that far exceeds the bounds of one's previous experiences.

And last but definitely, definitely not least, and despite the rudeness, the corruption, the snitching, the constant grumbling, complaining and whining, Romanians have absolutely gigantic hearts.

If they open those to you, wow. Just wow. Sometimes it's hard to see it behind the brambles of an indifferent, frosty exterior but trust me, it's there.

I don't want to be misconstrued when I say Romanians have a *lusty* heart, but they do. The things that truly touch their soul are done with great gusto and passion and likewise with the people that they care about.

Once you are on the receiving end of that passion and heart and soul, whether through fellowship, family, friendship or romance, it's impossible to let go.

## Hungarians

Ahh, the Hungarians. They currently comprise about 6-10% of Romania's population but I lived here a long time before I even began to gain the slightest understanding about them and I don't think I ever will fully understand them all the way.

To understand the Hungarians in Romania, it's essential to travel back through time to the beginning of the Hungarians as a separate race or ethnicity of people.

Around the end of the 10th century, there emerged seven tribes (Hun: *hetmagyar*) of Magyars amidst the pan-Asian slash Turkish peoples living in what would be the steppes of Ukraine and southern Russia today.

In both the Romanian and the Hungarian language, the original name, *magyar* is still used but the English version of "Hungarian" comes from the name Hun, as in Attila the Hun, although the Huns are ethnically unrelated and came at a much earlier time into Europe (about 500 years earlier), albeit from the same direction and in a similar manner (on horseback, bearing weapons).

Through a wide variety of circumstances, these semi-Asian people, the seven tribes of Magyars, pushed their way west into an area comprising what is now modern day Hungary as well as some other nearby areas (including a large portion of what is now Romania) around the year 950 AD.

It is due to this Asian origin that the Hungarian language is completely unrelated to all other European languages, with the exception of a remote link to Finnish and Estonian. I can tell you that just from the little bit I've learned of Hungarian, the grammar is absolutely and completely different and even the vowel sounds are too different for me to properly get a handle on.

The only two Hungarian words that made it to English are "biro" (more of a British usage, meaning ink pen, from the name of the guy who invented it) and the word "coach", especially the old meaning of an enclosed carriage drawn by a horse, from the town of *Kocs* in Hungary (pronounced roughly "coach") where they were first made.

This territory settled by the Hungarians in Europe became known to the Hungarians as the *Honfoglalás*, literally meaning "the conquest". I mention this because this is still the term many modern-day Hungarian politicians use to refer to Transylvania.

By the year 1000 AD (or possibly 1001), Saint Stephen (Hun: *Szent Istvan*) was crowned king of all the Hungarians and had all of the various tribal factions united under his rule.

Stephen is the most important Hungarian in their history[115] and it's easy to see why – not only did he convert a people long-accustomed to nomadic pastoralism to a life of farming but he was also the first ruler to convert to Christianity – in this case, Catholicism, which became very important later on as most of the neighbors (and subjugated peoples) were Orthodox Christians. The Hungarian symbols of state (including the flag) also still carry his unique double-armed cross today.

Although not given much credit now, the Kingdom of Hungary lasted from the year 1000 to the end of World War 1 as a very large and influential player in Europe. The kingdom included what is now the nation of Hungary as well as what the magyars called the military frontier (Hun: *Határőrvidék*), which includes parts of Ukraine, Croatia, Serbia and Slovakia (today) as well as Transylvania (Hun: *Erdély*).

Most of the medieval period was spent uniting and allying with various other Catholic nations and fighting off the Turks until the late 17th century, when the much better known Austro-Hungarian Empire was formed, which was formally defeated and broken up at the end of World War 1.

So that is the simple and unedited version of Hungarian history but I've left out both the mystical "pre-history" of the Hungarians as well as some of the more controversial bits, especially concerning Transylvania.

Finding information in English on the mystical origins of Hungarians is almost impossible but I've spent enough time talking to Hungarians (especially those born and raised in the Republic of Hungary) to know that they're still being taught about it and I can't properly do it justice here. It does involve a story of a spirit deer leading the way and a kind of special rune alphabet that the Hungarians invented to communicate with each other. All I can really tell you on that is ask a Hungarian and then hold onto your hat as it's quite a complicated story.

The controversial bits, especially concerning Transylvania, involve whether or not anyone of note was living in the various regions before the Magyars got here, and whether or not that included Romanians, and whether or not who brought civilization to whom. I'll just leave it at that.

What isn't mysterious however is the **Treaty of Trianon**, signed in 1920, which broke up the Hungarian Kingdom and left huge swathes of ethnic

---

[115] For more on who he was, see page 281.

Hungarians living in countries where they were no longer the majority – including the (modern state of) Romania.

The Hungarians left inside the new borders of Romania fall into two groups – one is the "regular" Hungarians (magyars), who mostly live in **Crişana** (page 249), along a belt of ethnic Hungarians that goes from modern day Serbia through southwest Ukraine, and in **Transylvania** (page 242).

In Romania there's also *another* group of Hungarians, called the **Szekely** (pronounced *sek-elly*), who live in a contiguous zone in central Romania known as "Szekely Land". I've asked about 50 Hungarians to explain to me who the Szekely are and gotten about 50 different answers.

What I can tell you is that:

1) The **Szekely** speak Hungarian and are considered ethnically Hungarian,
2) They're a separate ethnicity of "warrior" Hungarians; and
3) They're often the least-integrated into Romanian society in the present day. They often tend to live in villages or towns that are ethnically homogeneous and keep to the "old ways".

It's confusing enough that in 1438 the Union of Three Nations (in **Transylvania**) meant the three "nations" of Germans, (regular) Hungarians and Szekely.

There is a heck of a lot of Hungarian history and culture still tied to Transylvania, including in **Cluj-Napoca**, where one of the most famous and influential kings of their history was born, Matthias Corvinus (page 255).

His birthplace and large statue in the central square are still big tourist draws in **Cluj** today. Matthias is most famously known (to the outside world) as being one of the princes who variously allied with, controlled or fought against Vlad the Impaler, aka "Dracula" (page 10).

It is extremely difficult understanding Hungarians and their situation in Romania, even when you live here.

On one hand, you've got cities like **Cluj**, where I know lots of Hungarians who speak fairly good Romanian, sometimes marry Romanians, go to work with Romanians and are otherwise as integrated as can be.

Likewise I know many Transylvanian Romanians (and from **Crişana**) who get along just fine with Hungarians, work with them, go to school with them, sometimes date or marry them, occasionally even speak their language and everything is just peachy.

And then at times you have extreme anti-Hungarian sentiment, such as Corneliu Vadim Tudor and his goons over at PRM (see page 250), including the former mayor of **Cluj**.

And from the other direction, I've met plenty of Hungarians who keep their children in separate schools (including up to university level), never learn Romanian and exist in almost a parallel, separate world. I've also noticed that it seems that the Hungarians born and raised in Hungary (the modern day nation) tend to be a little more "ultra patriotic" than do the Transylvanian-born and raised Hungarians.

So it's very confusing and it is easy to get lost in the morass of all the various loyalties and cultural identities. Years ago, I was in Budapest (the capital of Hungary, but you know that!) and was flying to **Cluj**. The guy at the airport gently chided me and wrote the word "Kolozsvár" on my baggage tickets, because that is the Hungarian name for the city.

Likewise, there is a Hungarian name and "way of doing things" for just about everything in the parts of Romania they used to control. And to the uneducated eye, it's easy to be completely unaware of the boundaries between them.

Perhaps due to their minority status, the Hungarians (but not **Szekely**) in Romania tend to often be quite multi-lingual and I've noticed lately that they tend to use a lot of English outside their bars, pubs, restaurants and the like – perhaps to avoid confrontation with choosing either Hungarian signage (angering some Romanians) or else Romanian (so as to not submit to that either).

If you see a public place with all-English signs, it's likely owned and/or largely frequented by Hungarians (or some other non-Romanians).

I can tell you as a completely uninterested party to the proceedings (so to speak), Hungarians tend to be very welcoming and friendly to strangers and perhaps more generous (at first) than Romanians.

They are, however, a far less emotional people and far, far quieter than Romanians and about a million times quieter than the Gypsies.

For information on Hungarian food, see page 68.

**Gypsies**

Probably the one thing I get asked the most, by far and away, is about gypsies. Who are these people? Why do they do the things they do?

If you're going to visit Romania, you need to know whom the gypsies are.

The legal, politically correct name is "romany" people (*rromi* in Romanian) which sounds almost exactly like "Romanian" (*români* in Romanian) and confuses everybody so everyone just calls them "gypsies". Apparently the peasants in Europe a long time ago thought they were from Egypt so in almost all languages (including English and Romanian) the name "gypsy" comes from a contraction of the word "Egyptian".

Gypsies are apparently all over the place in Europe (and the USA somewhat) but many thousands of years ago they decided Romania was the bestest and most funnest place to live so about 90% of them live here in Romania. Why? Nobody knows. Quit asking questions like that!

All throughout "Eastern" Europe and the Balkans there are nationalities, ethnicities and sub-groups of ethnicities, many of whom you've never probably never even heard of[116]. If you walk around with your ignorant, tourist eyes you wouldn't even be able to tell the difference between them.

EXCEPT for the gypsies. The gypsies always stand out because the gypsies are both a separate "ethnicity" and a separate culture. Gypsies have their own way of doing absolutely everything and I do mean everything. They live in their own special places and do things their own special way and dress in their own special way and that's just how it is.

Note: *During World War 2 both Hitler AND Stalin tried to completely kill every last gypsy. Didn't work. All the other dictators in Europe tried it too. They're unstoppable. Just accept it.*

Even though I know almost nothing about gypsies, I'm going to give you a crash course in identifying gypsies. All terms are completely my own invention, by the way, so don't quote me in the footnotes of your scholarly paper.

Westerners, particularly USAmericans, have a very bizarre notion of what gypsies are. For instance, if you're vaguely into "hippy" or "New Age" things and are female, calling yourself (or being called) a gypsy is some kind of *compliment*. It means you're free! You're a noble spirit, floating on the wind, unchained by crass modern limitations!

REAL gypsies are totally different so pay attention.

Gypsies are organized into tribes and are usually identifiable at a distance by their dress:

---

[116] http://en.wikipedia.org/wiki/Gagauz_people

**Cowboy gypsies** – Especially popular in Transylvania. They wear a lot of black leather vests and large, black leather gypsy hats. They don't actually work with cows though so don't get confused!

Note: For some reason, most male cowboy gypsies refuse to drive a car or a wagon or anything else. So the oldest and most powerful (male) cowboy gypsy rides up front in the passenger side.

**Rainbow gypsies** – If you're a woman you must wear a super mega colorful skirt (never pants). You must wear an equally super mega colorful shirt. Third, you must wear a super mega colorful head scarf OR braid your incredibly long hair with mega colorful braids. ALL ITEMS MUST BE OF DIFFERENT COLORS. This is the law for rainbow gypsies!

**Manelişti gypsies** – These ones can confuse you if you're not prepared. They are fans of manele music (page 178) and therefore, by gypsy law, listen to it 24 hours a day. If they're out and about in the streets, usually they have their telephone playing manele music through its one tinny speaker.

Male version – Dresses in track suits (if wealthier) or knock-off jeans. Usually has gel in the hair. A large thick gold chain around the neck is preferred.

Female version – Knock-off jeans and cheap Chinese shoes as well as a T-shirt or other shirt with incomprehensible English language words on it. Abundant (usually cheap) jewelry is preferred. Rarely wears skirts or dresses. If they're indoors (aka at a club) listening to manele, their clothes must be as skin tight as possible.

**Italian Mafia gypsies** – They're not actually Italian or in some kind of genuine "mafia" but they dress like they are. Cheap suits and overly tight shirts are worn that barely restrain their beer bellies.

Note: All "Italian mafia" gypsy boys over the age of 8 wear the full regalia, the suit, the business shoes, etc.

**Filthy Vagrant gypsies** – Literally as filthy as possible, wearing any kind of ragged clothes, be it more traditional woolen clothes or else a 1986 Superbowl Shuffle Chicago Bears T-shirt that even God himself doesn't know how they got a hold of. Stains of all kinds are fine, both on clothes as well as on their face and/or body.

Showers and washing are to be abstained from at ALL TIMES.

Ok now that you can identify the gypsies, time to know when and where you will encounter them.

First Iron Rule of Gypsies – they never work indoors. NEVER. As in never, ever, never. Therefore they will all be making their money in some kind of way where they don't have to sit indoors inside a maze of cubicles and listen to soft jazz and type under fluorescent lights.

So how do gypsies survive? If you're considering becoming a gypsy, what career options are option to you?

**Flower Seller** – Gypsies pretty much have cornered the market on selling flowers. Sometimes they do this at an established spot (like in the market) or sometimes just on a random street corner.

Sometimes the flowers are roses or other flowers you'd be happy to buy for your wife/girlfriend and other times the "flowers" are some kind of plant that looks like they was just ripped out of the dirt from alongside the train tracks two minutes ago.

Note: female Rainbow or Filthy Vagrant gypsies mainly perform this job.

**Manual Labor** – Anything from literally digging ditches to re-tiling a roof to cleaning gutters to paving streets to construction work. Sometimes it's fairly skilled work but usually it's not.

Note: this job is for male Filthy Vagrant gypsies only.

**Spoon Seller** – All traditional Romanian recipes can only be made with the use of a wooden spoon. True fact. And therefore there are people whose sole job is to sit at home and whittle spoons and then stuff them into a plastic bag and hawk them on the street. If you are a tourist in Romania, you really should buy one.

Note: selling wooden spoons is for male Filthy Vagrant or Manelişti gypsies only. I don't know who carves them though.

**Musician/Singer** – This is the best-paying line of work for a gypsy. You can form your own band and play either **manele** or **muzica lăutărească** (page 178) and make tons of money singing at weddings, festivals or making videos for TV.

Note: you must be an Italian Mafia gypsy in good standing to be a manele musician/singer.

Note: while female Italian Mafia gypsies can become manele singers, only male gypsies can become manele musicians. Why? Quit asking questions, that's why!

**Fruit/Vegetable Seller** – You get to stand behind an enormous pile of vegetables and/or fruits at the market. The food you're selling may or may not come from your own actual farm and be food you've grown.

Once a year when the watermelon harvest is in, sometimes you get to move to another town for a few weeks and sleep and live next to your enormous pile of watermelons as you desperately try to peddle them in the baking summer sun.

Note: for Filthy Vagrant gypsies only, usually female.

**Gold Dealer** – Gypsies have been around forever so they don't trust any modern currencies – only gold. Therefore they're always wheeling and dealing in gold, whether chains, necklaces, medallions or other sundry bits of jewelry. In any large town in Romania there's usually a 24-hour non-stop gold dealer just for this very purpose.

Note: one of the few gypsy jobs where both male and females of every variety are involved with in some form or fashion.

**Scrap Metal Recycler** – Go around town from place to place, collecting old scrap metal of all kinds and then hauling it to the recycler for cash. Sometimes the metal isn't quite "scrap" as you are allowed to pry metal off of just about everywhere, including manhole covers.

If you're super poor, you have to do this by hauling a flimsy cart (or possibly a bicycle) around town, overburdened with too much scrap. If you're a little richer, you can use your horse and wagon to do it.

Note: for male Filthy Vagrant gypsies only.

**Leather Coat Peddler** – Much like the flower seller above, you walk up and down the street, peddling leather coats (for men).

Note: this job is for female Rainbow gypsies only.

**Rambo Knife and/or Fishing Gear Peddler** – Same as above. Why only women sell these products is a mystery to one and all.

**Perfume Peddler** – Same as above.

Note: sometimes the perfume is heavily watered down. Sometimes it's a cheap Chinese knockoff. Good business though as Romanians LOVE perfume. Love, love, love it! (see page 21)

**Pickpocket** – A very, very skilled profession and you're likely to never know it happened to you until after they're long gone.

Note: this job is restricted to male Manelisti gypsies.

Note: Gypsies are champion *thieves* but not robbers. What's the difference? It means they'll steal anything not tied down but never use force to rob you.

**Beggar** – Roam around the streets, begging and pleading for money. It requires extreme persistence and learning to "never say never". If you can learn to never give up in the face of adversity, curses and occasional spitting, this might be the job for you!

Note: Mostly children have cornered this market but there are opportunities for adults as well, especially if you can feign or show some kind of hideous deformity. This job position is only open for Filthy Vagrant gypsies.

**Fortune Teller** – Probably one of the few things "in the movies" they got right about actual, real gypsies. Only there's not some nice, friendly lady with a neon sign of a palm hanging outside her window in her home. No way.

Real gypsy fortune tellers (Romanian: **ghicitoară** literally meaning "the guesser") are creepy, eerily accurate women who stare into your soul and tell you things you don't want to know. *Really* don't want to know.

Note: this job is for female gypsies only.

**Stolen Electronics Peddler** – One of the few sales jobs open to male gypsies, particularly Cowboy gypsies. If someone tries to sell you a video camera for only 20 euros, you know where it came from!

## 11 THINGS YOU MUST KNOW ABOUT ROMANIANS AND GYPSIES

1. All Romanians hate gypsies, spit on them, never have anything nice to say about them at all and constantly pray they all die. Even the most tolerant Romanians are just that, *barely tolerant* of gypsies.
2. Even if you see a very beautiful Rainbow gypsy with lovely braided hair and a colorful skirt you must never, ever, ever compliment them to your Romanian friends. They (the Romanian friends) will resent you forever and ever.
3. Romanians who don't know you will NEVER EVER talk to you or pass the time of day with you or otherwise act like you're alive. Gypsies on the other hand are chatty, cheerful people and will be glad to talk to you. If you're lost and need directions, ask a gypsy!

4. Romanians constantly complain about how wealthy gypsy singers and musicians are but they simultaneously acknowledge their musical genius and hire them for weddings and festivals and pay them large sums of cash to do so.
5. Gypsies (almost) never mind having their picture taken and will grin and mug for the camera with no problem. Romanians are surly and suspicious of such activity.
6. Rich Romanians live in beautiful houses. Rich gypsies live in bizarrely beautiful houses with ornate roofs and window holes but no glass in the windows. It's like "semi-indoors" living.
7. Romanians constantly curse and bewail the fact that gypsies are thieves but then they (Romanians) will gladly buy stolen electronic goods from the self-same gypsies.
8. Romanians and gypsies share the same religion but nobody will ever tell you that or admit it could possibly be true.
9. Romanians are sometimes monolingual (speaking just one language). Gypsies on the other hand are masters of multiple languages (including their own gypsy language) and could probably kick Noam Chomsky's ass in a linguistic showdown.
10. If you ever see or hear about "Romanians" outside of Romania, i.e. in Italy or Spain or somewhere, chances are about 99% certain that they're actually a gypsy (from Romania) rather than a Romanian (as in an ethnic non-gypsy Romanian).
11. Romanians can be loud at times but gypsies are ALWAYS louder. If it's possible to shout out an entire conversation, they'll do it. If the volume on the stereo goes to 11, it will be cranked to 11. Louder = better for gypsies.

**Germans**

One day you might find yourself tooling around southern **Transylvania** in your fine motor car, enjoying the fresh air and suddenly come around a bend in the road and enter the town of **Sibiu** and you're going to think, "Mein gott in himmel, have I just arrived in Germany or what?". Yes, pretty much you have.

One of the surprising populations inside Romania is the Germans, otherwise known as the "Transylvania Saxons" in English or the *Siebenbürger Sachsen* in German.

Around the year 1200 the Hungarians were getting their southeastern flank bedeviled and continually harassed by wily band of semi-nomadic Turks. What to do, what to do?

Well, the Hungarians made a few Germans back in the "home country" an offer of a lifetime: move to the wild and woolly frontier (of the then Hungarian Kingdom), fend off those dastardly Turks and we'll reward you with riches and gold.

Historically this was part of a larger movement called the **ostsiedlung**, wherein German settlers founded many cities all through Eastern Europe.

The Germans, being the particularly industrious people that they are, built up seven fine fortified towns (called the *Siebenburgen* - literally the "Seven Towns") in (what is now) Romania and settled in and grew fat and made many fine sausages and twirled their mustaches gaily and drank large steins of beer and listened to oompah-loompah music, etc, etc, as Germans are wont to do.

Fast forwarding to around 1490 or so, the good German folk of the town of **Braşov** entered into a dispute with **Vlad "Dracula" Ţepeş** (page 10) and got on the wrong side of his Impalin' Sticks, creating the legend that everyone "knows" today.

And all was well until a little fellow named Adolf Hitler decided to rampage across Europe in the 1940's and then pretty much everyone in Eastern Europe quit loving the Germans quite as much as they used to. And so 99% of all the Germans who used to live in Romania got the heck out of Dodge and went back to the "old country".

But they left behind a lot of architecture and beautiful buildings, the *Black Church* in **Braşov** being exceptionally beautiful and completely worth a visit when you come to Romania (page 142).

Back to **Sibiu** though. The few Germans still left in Romania have mostly all congregated in Sibiu and even have their own political party. In fact, the mayor today is Johannes Klaus, the (Romanian) German mayor of **Sibiu**. Furthermore, **Sibiu** is the only town in Romania (I think) that has its very own German language newspaper (page 180).

Mayor Klaus and his merry band of Germans have been incredibly busy elves and have used their Germanic industriousness and artistry to wangle funds to improve **Sibiu** and the city is just absolutely amazing. It's a gorgeous town that looks like something out of a fairy tale and well worth a visit. And yes they have bratwurst and every other kind of sausage you'd ever want to eat as long as you ever shall live.

Even though most of the Germans are gone from the rest of the country, Germans from the Fatherland still maintain strong ties to Romania and so you will find many Germans traveling in Romania and doing business in this country. There are usually good deals on flights into Romania from Germany (and Austria) precisely because of this. Germany is *by far* Romania's largest trading partner today.

After English, German is probably the second-most commonly studied foreign language and so if you speak German, you can probably get around and do fairly well for yourself.

Interestingly enough, signs and maps still in use in Romania refer to towns and places by their German names, where applicable.

## Aromanians

Just when you thought you've finally got a handle on who the Romanians are, their language, their culture and their long and tortured history, up pops the Aromanians.

Say what? Yeah, you know, the Aromanians. It turns out Romanians come in a wide variety of flavors: there's the Aromanians, the Bromanians (my personal favorite), the Cromanians, the Dromanians, etc. Collect them all!

Nah, I'm just joking. In reality there are "regular" Romanians and then there are groups of people who somewhere in the last thousand years got separated from the main group and developed their own distinct sub-group of Romanian language and culture.

The biggest of these sub-groups is the Aromanians, whom I had never heard about until one day I was walking in downtown **Bucharest** and saw a sign written in what looked like crazy, bizarro-world Romanian language, close to the real thing but just slightly different enough that my already weakened mental hinges began to slide open and worlds began colliding.

The sign was written in Aromanian and was an advertisement for a big upcoming meeting of Aromanians to speak in their language and get together and hang out and have fun (I'm assuming) and let others get to know them a little bit better.

Most Aromanians are simply people who, for whatever reason, long ago moved to the highlands of the Albania, Greece, Macedonia region of Europe and decided it was a fine, fine place to raise their sheep. Over time they developed a distinct series of changes to their language from "regular" Romanian (officially known as Daco-Romanian). I can pretty much *read* Aromanian but hearing it spoken (to me) sounds like a really drunken guy slurring his speech.

In Greece and elsewhere in the lower Balkans, the Aromanians are called the "Vlachs", which is where the term "Wallachia" (in English) comes from as well, just meaning "them foreign bastards"[117] rather than any kind of true derivative of what they call themselves.

Most remaining Aromanians still live in the lower Balkans area, surrounded by a sea of people speaking vastly different languages (i.e. not derived from Latin).

There are a few Aromanians in Romania today but not very many, mostly because they've been absorbed (culturally-speaking) but the ones that are left can be found primarily in **Dobruja** (page 250) as well as their occasional meet-ups in **Bucharest** of course.

If you really want to know more about the Aromanians, they have a nice website online in English[118]. For a nice comparison of "regular" Romanian and Aromanian languages, see Wikipedia[119].

Note: the most famous Romanian soccer (football) player of all time, Gheorge Hagi, was an ethnic Aromanian.

There is also a gigantic debate and controversy over whether "**Moldovan**" (from the nation of Moldova) is or is not a separate and distinct language than "regular" Romanian. All I can say on that is "Moldovan" has a heck of a lot more Slavic words than Romanian does, as well as using much more Slavic pronunciation (especially the letter "E") but for all intents and purposes, it's the same language.

That being said, during the Soviet period and continuing to today, Moldovan is/was written in Cyrillic letters rather than the western alphabet.

**Lipoveni**

Even though both Russia and Romania begin with the letter "R" and were both at one time Communist nations, there's actually nothing very Russian about Romania at all.

Yes, it's true that at one time Russian was a language studied in high school. But the same is true that in America people used to study Latin. Have you ever met anyone who actually *speaks* Latin though? No. And you won't find anyone who speaks Russian in Romania either.

---

[117] The Greeks referred to anyone who could not speak Greek as "barbarians" and the word "vlach" is related to this.
[118] http://www.farsarotul.org/newslett.htm
[119] http://en.wikipedia.org/wiki/Aromanian_language

Except for these guys – the **Lipoveni**, better known in English as the Lipovans or in Russian as the **Липоване**. So who are they?

Well, a long time ago (1652 to be precise) the head of the Russian Orthodox Church (aka the "Russian pope") decided to modernize and update the religion. A whole bunch of Russians got royally angered about it and swore by the hairs of their long grey beards that there weren't going to stand for such heresy. And a group of them decided to move down to eastern Romania and have been here ever since – the Lipoveni.

The Lipoveni mainly live in **Tulcea**, mostly in small villages that are in the middle of a giant flooded zone known as the Danube Delta (page 167). Just imagine Cajuns deep in the Louisiana swamps and that's roughly what we're talking about here. Many Lipoveni live in villages which are literally only accessible via boat, especially in the village of **Jurilovca**.

If you speak Russian (or Romanian), the Lipoveni even have their own newspaper[120], complete with lots of nice pictures and updates on culture events.

There are only about 30,000 Lipoveni in Romania but they are a well-established community here.

## Moți

Although some people believe the inhabitants of **Tara Moților** (see page 250) are genetically different because of a propensity for blue eyes and blonde hair, generally the **Moți** (*moats*) are considered Romanians.

As the region is a mountainous highland zone, in many ways the foods and traditions from this area are quite different than in other parts of Romania. It is said that the altitude and low oxygen makes both the livestock and the residents of this region much heartier and robust.

## Foreigners

Ah yes, we cannot forget the foreigner in Romania, of which there are far more than one would guess at first glance. Considering that between 7 and 8 million people visit Romania every year, this means there is one tourist for every three Romanians.

Because Romania isn't a "top tier" tourist destination, many visitors often seemingly believe they're among the first to come here. I can tell you that it

---

[120] http://zorile.ro/russian/

is quite normal to hear 5 or 6 different languages being spoken on any given day (in a larger city).

So whom shall you expect to meet on your travels besides the native peoples? Let's start with groups.

**Missionaries** – Ah yes, praise the Lord. Save up your pennies and come stand on the street corner in Romania, passing out pamphlets and having fun singing.

Enjoy total acceptance by the local culture, zero threat or hassle or intimidation, especially if you're some kind of Christian as *most of the people in Romania already are Christian*. It's a little bit like asking someone to switch from vanilla ice cream to caramel ice cream.

On the other hand, beware the ever-tenacious Mormons. They go the extra mile and learn the language.

**Peace Corps** – Almost always stuck way out in the country, digging those wells. Sometimes they write good blogs but the organization often sends them out in the field with basically zero useful practical knowledge.

Since these (usually) kids are coming straight out of academia in a western nation, even their "commonsense skills" are fairly useless here.

I was partly inspired to write this book precisely *for* all the Peace Corps Volunteers I kept meeting here, who were let loose with very little education or background on this country and culture. Sadly (especially for them) it looks like 2013 will be their last year of operations in this country.

**University Students** – This is what I call "Team Cinnamon" because their skin hues range from a light dusting of mocha to downright swarthy. A real hodgepodge of people from Arab and African nations, sometimes with multiple citizenship issues.

In general, these students tend to stay in fairly homogenous groups amongst themselves for a wide variety of reasons. Nonetheless, the best foreign speakers of Romanian I ever met were all members of Team Cinnamon.

While these people are often somewhat estranged because they are different, outright hostility towards him is a very rare occurrence.

Romania has a long history of cultural and educational exchanges with Arab and African countries.

**Sports Teams** – Often from far-away countries to play sports you may have only vaguely heard of.

**Asian Workers** – Only in a few, isolated areas for now but it's potentially on the increase. Usually brought in all together from one place to work at one specific factory.

**Foreign Restaurant Family** – Quite often Italian but sometimes other things like Japanese, this is an entire family from a foreign land who have opened their own restaurant in Romania, serving food from their homeland.

**Horny American Soldiers** – Mostly stationed out at the big airbase near **Constanța** although a few are scattered throughout **Bucharest** and a few other places in the south of the country. Clearly, page 182 was partly written with them in mind.

Now let's talk about some of the common individuals you will find (including you!)

### Filthy Backpacker

A tourist from a wealthy country, usually young, quite filthy and ragged but carrying expensive equipment, especially cameras, other electronics and the backpack itself.

These people can be *tenacious* conversationalists so only engage one when you are fully prepared. They are incestuously tied to other members of their kind, whom they continue to meet up with and split apart from at various places around the globe.

They are impelled to keep moving however and will soon be gone.

### Stern European Businessman

Wears a suit, usually ensconced in a car. The only place you're likely to run into one in the wild is at a higher-end hotel, especially the kind with available escorts and casinos in the basement.

Watch out for these types in the airport as they are pushy, demanding and arrogant.

### Western Man In Love/Married to a Romanian Woman

All over the place, salted away if you know where to look for them.

The boyfriend/husband is usually always employed and bringing in a sizable sum, especially for Romania. He's usually also the more supplicating of the two and she is more dominant, bossy and "wears the pants".

The man on the other hand will rarely learn the Romanian language and live a fairly isolated social life with the exception of fellow speakers of his language. He will be completely dependent on his Romanian partner to handle daily tasks.

## Western Woman In Love/Married to a Romanian Man

Almost always a sad case usually involving a much older woman. Not always though, thank goodness.

## Wealthy Resident Foreigner

Usually in his 30's or 40's, he has some kind of business or income that might be normal in his home country but in Romania goes a lot further. He's usually holed up with his fellow language speakers who are also usually at his same income level.

Almost always becomes an alcoholic or at least a heavy social drinker.

## Drunken Lecher

Can also be a member of any of the above types. There is an enormous amount of physically attractive people in Romania and this can draw a certain kind of perverted, lecherous type to hang around.

Due to the way Romanian culture is, it can be quite difficult to gain acceptance if you are foreign. This means that a lot of the time, your desired sexual/dating partners are out of reach. Drinking, seeing, wanting and not getting has deleterious effects on some men, especially those from cultures where they're used to getting their way.

## Temporary Paying Volunteer

This is when people in western countries save up their own money and then spend it to come to Romania to help people for a set period of time. Almost always the Temporary Paying Volunteer is a woman.

A lot of this involves taking care of babies or children, especially orphans and gypsies.

## Westerner Visiting Family Homeland

Also known as someone who is at least partly Romanian by birth, although they've never lived here and are visiting Grandma's hometown, etc. Mixed bag here although the younger children seem to enjoy it tremendously while young adults often get resentful and whiny.

## Hungarians from Hungary

Arrogant, ultra-patriotic and uber-ferocious about their culture. They will gladly speak English but consider learning even a single word of Romanian to be beyond useless. Literally bursting with nationalistic pride and will gladly go on at length about it.

## European Union Do-Gooder

Quite often a student and young. As part of either a school activity or else boosting one's CV, they come here for a set period of time to do some social good. There are multiple EU and other agencies devoted entirely to this.

They usually find Romania quite a lark because the prices are insanely low but life is otherwise normal and recognizable to them, especially clubs, bars, shopping and discos.

## Wandering German

For a long time, a lot of Germans lived in Romania. A few still do. There are always Germans coming from various German areas here in Romania to visit their ancient "homeland" and to connect with remaining German culture (see page 206).

Probably amongst the calmest and genial of the foreigners, with a gentle sense of curiosity and a heart without rancor.

## Vampire Porn Lovers

A small but utterly creepy cohort of people who are overly fascinated with vampires, Dracula and blood drinking. A lot of them gather in Romania for Halloween but can be found throughout the year in certain zones (see page 13).

## Conference/Competition Attendee

Due to their business back home, they have to come to Romania temporarily to either attend a conference/competition or else complete a project.

Can be very grumpy and disoriented due to culture shock so beware. Often complains about the food.

## Ambitious Moldovan

In other words, a person from the Republic of Moldova who somehow got permission and the ability to be in Romania. If they made it that far, they're the savvy type. Don't tangle with these people!

## Dogs

While dogs may or may not be considered "people", you will definitely meet some of them while you are here.

There are dogs absolutely everywhere in this country, including in the streets (even in big cities) and they will be a part of your daily life.

The situation in Romania today is drastically different than it was just a few short years ago, so my first piece of advice to you is that unless you are pathologically afraid of dogs, you should be okay.

The current president of Romania, Traian Basescu, cut his teeth politically back when he was the mayor of **Bucharest** by wiping out most of the feral (wild) dog population in the capital. As an animal lover myself, I cringe at the memory of what went on but in terms of political astuteness, Basescu made the right decision. Quite simply put, the wild dog situation in Romania was quite out of control for many years.

Things came to a head in 2006 when a Japanese businessman in **Bucharest** was attacked and killed by a wild dog, unleashing a firestorm of controversy because a significant portion of the population sided with the dog in question, partly because Romanians are a very passionate about canines and partly because of racism.

I myself have been bitten (nothing serious, thank goodness) by two different dogs at two separate times in public when I was doing absolutely nothing but walking down an ordinary sidewalk minding my own business.

Again, let me stress, these incidents happened years ago and the situation is much better than it was.

Today, everywhere you go, there will be loose dogs wandering around the streets (and countryside) and these fall into roughly four categories:

## House Dog on Patrol

Lives somewhere close by and has a proper home and "owner", this dog will be patrolling his/her territory and will let you know if you get too close. There isn't too much to worry about though as public sidewalks and streets are far too heavily traveled for the dog to actively defend.

That being said, watch out for the dog behind a fence who will charge you from out of nowhere, snapping and growling, scaring the snot out of you but luckily unable to hurt you because he is thankfully behind the fence.

Note: any owned dog will always have a collar, always. Romanians are obsessed with demonstrating that their owned dog is not a **boschetar** or "vagabond" or homeless animal.

## Fed Regularly But Not Owned

A great number of Romanians enjoy putting food out for dogs but not actually taking them in and properly caring for them. So the dogs in question circle around the area where they are fed, sometimes being quite defensive and territorial.

I live near a government-owned weather station and the workers there feed a German shepherd dog, who roams freely about the compound and nearby streets, quite territorial and a little intimidating, although he's never attacked anyone (that I know of). Nonetheless he's quite a fearsome looking dog.

One place to be especially vigilant is around dumpsters or where trash cans (rubbish bins) are stored as often people feed dogs there (in combination with scavenged food from the trash itself) and so the dogs in question may start to "defend" this area.

## Pure Homeless Dog

Sad, miserable, suffering, ill, mangy, covered in fleas, often times injured, hobbling and otherwise heart-wrenchingly pitiful, these dogs roam around looking for any scrap of food or kindness from humans.

Because they've been so miserably abused, these dogs are usually the least dangerous (in terms of spontaneous attacks) but they will break your heart just seeing them.

## Romanian Sheep Dog

There are actually several breeds of domestic sheep dogs in this country and I can tell you from personal experience that they are extremely aggressive when defending their territory or homes or people or wards (sheep, etc).

These dogs are most dangerous when found in the countryside, as I found out myself once (luckily I was not bitten). Once these dogs get it into their head that you're encroaching on their territory, the best choice you have is to back up and head another way.

I am on very good terms with my veterinarians and often hang out at their office for hours, talking to them and other customers so I can definitely report that there are enthusiastic, caring and kind people in this country who treat dogs (and cats and other animals) very well.

That being said, I've seen a plethora of animal cruelty in Romania, most often against dogs. I once saw a dog run over by a car, the said car not even stopping, which left the dog whimpering awfully and shaking on the sidewalk, clearly unable to move. An unrelated passer-by unceremoniously lifted it up and threw it back in the street because it was blocking the sidewalk. Just hideous.

Sadly, most street dogs (today) are not a threat precisely because other people have been cruel and vicious to it long before you came across its path. A good friend of mine told me a spine-chilling tale of a group of teenagers who tormented and nearly killed a homeless puppy behind her *bloc*. The good news is that my friend called the police and the laws against animal cruelty were actually enforced this time.

There's also a lot of the kind of "ownership" of dogs that involves staking or chaining the dog permanently in the back yard, regardless of weather or miserable living conditions, just because you can do that. There's a guy living in my neighborhood with such a dog and I can only assume the reason he keeps the poor creature out there in his miserable patch of bare dirt is to "guard" the house.

Also, spaying or neutering animals is still considered offensive[121] to a lot of people here (or too expensive to be worth doing). The good news is that this year I saw there were a couple of free clinics for castrating dogs, although that's still a pretty new thing.

Likewise, due to expense and general Romanian hyper-zealous "thriftiness", even a lot of otherwise well-treated pets are never brought in for shots, general medical care or given proper diets and attention. Some of the pet food sold in stores here is execrable, brightly dyed crap manufactured in Poland or Ukraine at rock-bottom prices.

---

[121] Or just plain emmasculating.

Sadly, there is often little one can do about the general plight and suffering of animals here as shelters are rare to non-existent although thankfully this situation is improving. A friend of mine got involved with a local shelter in his town after visiting and finding out that the animals there were so miserable and ill-treated that they would've been better off living on the streets.

Between the bitterly cold winters, the deliberate policies of exterminating feral packs, the increase in owned pets (which drive off strays) and general human cruelty, the "good news" is that walking around this country is a much safer enterprise than it was just a few, short years ago.

That being said, yes about once a week I cross the street to avoid a dog and yes sometimes it can be a little intimidating or scary to walk past certain areas where dogs are sleeping but in general, things are pretty safe. It still breaks my heart though to see any animal suffering.

If, by chance, you do get bitten please see a doctor right away and get treated for rabies, as this is a very real risk.

ATTENTION ROMANIANS: I am quite aware that animal cruelty happens everywhere from Nepal to the United States and isn't specific or unique to this country. I am only writing about Romania specifically because this is where I live and I am preparing a guide for the visitor or newcomer to this country.

And on a final note, I do see plenty of cats wandering around, from well-fed pets to canny street animals. The only real difference is that cats never attack people so it's not much of an issue (in terms of safety) to the visitor.

**Romaniophile**

Last but not least, this type is elusive and difficult to find in the wild. The reason they came to adopt Romanian culture and live here voluntarily is generally considered to be a result of incurable madness.


# Urban Tourism
## Introduction

A few years ago in Romania, I taught a small class of 12 and 13-year-olds a course in English over the summer. At one point, I asked them to imagine that they had a friend from another town who was going to come and visit. What activities and places to visit would you recommend to them?

The answers were slow and hesitant in coming, as Romanians find it a novel and sometimes counter-intuitive idea that their city or country is actually a worthy tourist destination.

Part of Romania's indescribable charm is precisely that it is not beholden to an overly commercial, gimmicky image (apart from some Dracula and vampire paraphernalia) and a fetish for commercialism at all costs, churning out their history and lifestyle into pre-packaged chunks for visitors to consume.

That being said, the historic center of most Romanian cities and towns has many fine treasures from gorgeous examples of architecture, medieval city walls, fortresses and castles, sublimely beautiful churches, lush and peaceful city parks, fountains, pedestrian zones perfect for strolling and houses of high culture, including for theater and opera.

In every city in Romania, including **Bucharest**, the main urban attractions are clustered around the downtown (city centre), known in Romanian as the **centru** (*chen-true*), most easily negotiated by foot. Therefore it is usually worthwhile to obtain lodging in **centru** as you can easily get to all the sites you want to see in a short amount of time.

## Lodgings

The cheapest lodgings in most cities are hostels, which you can easily find online[122], providing shared or single rooms at a rock bottom price. I highly recommend you read reviews by other travelers, as sometimes the quality of service can be spotty.

These are often the preferred choice of **Filthy Backpackers** (page 212) as hostels are where you can easily mix and mingle with fellow travelers and they are a great way to make instant connections.

Hotels in Romania use the star rating system, with one star being the worst and five stars being the best. Four and five star hotels can be quite pricey indeed but often have many modern amenities, including indoor pools, spas and high-class restaurants.

The only place I would feel reliably comfortable in paying with a credit or bank card in Romania would be at a four or five star hotel.

---

[122] http://www.hihostels-romania.ro/index.php?lang=eng

Reservations can usually be made either online[123] or via telephone <u>without</u> a credit card to "hold" the rooms or any other kind of cash payment down, with some noted exceptions, especially in smaller cities during annual festivals which bring in a lot of tourists. During busy seasons a cash deposit into the hotel's bank account is required in advanced.

Generally speaking, the nicer the lodgings and the more popular a tourist destination you are visiting, the greater the likelihood that employees will speak or understand a modicum of English (or other foreign languages).

Another option is the **pensiune** (plural: **pensiuni**) meaning "inn" or "pension"[124], often run by a family and consisting of 4-20 guest rooms and usually at least one meal per day[125].

For information on eating at hotels and **pensiuni**, see page 62.

Usually these are slightly cheaper than a hotel and much more homey and nicer, with a deeply personal touch as each one is decorated and run according to the owner's tastes.

Some **pensiuni** are rated with stars while others are not so this information is less useful in this case. It's a good idea to research online beforehand and see other travelers' reviews.

Rural **pensiuni** and villas are (sometimes) rated on a system of 1 to 5 flowers, known as **margarete**. For more on this, see page 224.

Internet service via wi-fi is usually available (for free) in most hotels and **pensiuni** in Romania and is commonly listed on their amenities list. Occasionally this may be an Ethernet connection only, meaning you will need a physical cable to plug in your computer.

Another option, particularly good for lengthier stays, is renting someone's apartment (flat), known in Romanian as **regim hotelier**. These can be found via advertisements either online or printed in special Romanian newspapers (see page 181).

This is actually my favorite personal choice even for a weekend visit because it gives you a greater sense of privacy as well as the freedom of

---

[123] There are far too many hotel booking websites for me to recommend one particular one. A few basic online searches will get you where you want to go.
[124] Or "Bed and Breakfast" in some parts, although in Romania the breakfast part doesn't always happen.
[125] The most comprehensive site I've seen with information on finding *pensiuni* is http://www.infopensiuni.ro but be aware it is in Romanian language only. It does however show you on Google Maps the location of all their listings.

being able to wake up in the morning and make a cup of coffee in your pajamas.

If you're planning to stay three or more days, renting someone's apartment (flat) is usually the most economical option after a shared room at a hostel.

**Eating Out**

Generally speaking, there are six types of restaurants you will find in Romania.

**Fast Food**     Can be a simple walk-up window on a sidewalk to a full-service sit down restaurant with a wait staff. For much more on this, see page 56.

**Traditional**   Sometimes they go the extra mile and decorate the interior in the old style, dress up the wait staff in traditional clothes and serve only traditional Romanian foods on hand-carved dishes as well as having traditional drinks, including **țuica** (page 73).

Although the meals in a traditionally themed restaurant may be pricier, they are usually frequented predominantly by Romanians so the food is quite tasty and authentically prepared. Definitely worth at least one visit!

In other cases, this is a legacy restaurant from the Communist era, still serving a basic fare consisting of soups (page 76) and other Romanian food staples.

**Pizza**         Probably the most common full-service restaurant in Romania. For much more on this, see page 50.

**Upscale**       Perfect for a "date" night or else just a quality meal in a relaxed setting. The prices in these establishments can often be exorbitantly high so check the menu before ordering.

**Hungarian**     Anywhere you will find Hungarians living (see page 68), you will usually find a number of cafes and restaurants that serve Hungarian dishes.

**Foreign Food**  Quite often run by an immigrant family, the most popular varieties being Italian (pizza and pasta) and Chinese, although you can often find German, Austrian and even Japanese food available in larger cities. By far the most rare foreign cuisines to be found in Romania are Russian, Mexican and British.

A few other places to get food are:

**Grocery**   Stores selling food, whether pre-packaged snacks or fresh fruits and vegetables are everywhere in Romania.

**Market**    All Romanian cities have markets where agricultural products are sold, the cheapest way to get the freshest foods. For much more on this, see page 63.

Reservations are rarely mandatory for restaurants but are occasionally used so check ahead if you've got a particular spot in mind.

Smoking is generally permitted inside most restaurants. For more on this see page 86.

For a list of expressions and words to use in a restaurant, see page 266.

For a list of meats, see page 262.

For a list of vegetables, see page 264.

For a list of fruits, see page 265.

For a list of drinks, see page 263.

**Attractions Off The Beaten Path**

Although visiting palaces, museums and old churches is fun and interesting, sometimes I like to wander off the main tourist paths to see what kind of other things can be found.

Almost every city in Romania has a park of some kind and many of them are quite fantastic. The little gem of a park in **Baia Mare** is tucked away in the corner of the city and you'd miss it if you didn't know where to look for it.

Usually parks in Romania are quite broad and shady from many, many old trees. Generally there's a fountain or maybe even much more, but certainly a place where you can stop to get a sip of water. There are benches dotted up and down the quiet footpaths.

It may seem strange to come a long way just to sit and be still and relax but sometimes that's the very best part. And what's this? Is that a bee sailing lazily along, heading towards that bunch of fragrant flowers? Why yes it is, as Romania is incredibly fertile and bees are numerous and plentiful in this land.

If you have a local person along with you, ask them to identify the wild, edible plants growing everywhere in the park.   One of a Romanian's greatest delights is to meander along the verdant lanes, wiling away the time in sparkling conversation, meanwhile bending over and picking and nibbling on wild plants.

Hint: Amongst other plants, the very best strawberry you will ever eat in your entire *life*, with a taste that will make you collapse on the ground, tears streaming down your face, thanking your maker you lived long enough for that moment, can be found growing wild in Romanian parks during its season.

Every city, no matter how large (yes even **Bucharest**) is always right on the edge of the countryside.  Pick a street, any street, and if you follow it long enough (and many times, not long at all) you'll suddenly emerge to pure countryside, sometimes breathtakingly gorgeous.

It's not just the *cuisine* or the prepared dishes that make Romanian food so good, it's also the main ingredients.  If you've got any way to prepare or cook food while you're here, it's definitely worth a visit to the **piața** (page 63) to try the very freshest and highest quality meats, dairy products, fruits and vegetables.

Quite frankly, I treat all of my tourism travels in Romania as a kind of spa treatment.  Instead of making a specified building, monument or church the main attraction, I make what I consider to be all the pleasant things in life to be the main attraction, with the palace or whatever as the benefit.

What does that mean?   It means I always make time to enjoy a leisurely meal.  There's time to read a book and sip a coffee at a gorgeous café.  And yes, there's also time to get a haircut, a massage and then take a leisurely stroll in the park enjoying a delicious ice cream.

Walking, in and of itself, is a real pleasure in Romania often times because it's what everyone else is doing as well, so you're rarely alone.   A great number of Romanian attractions, including monuments, parks, fountains and even stores, cafes and restaurants are designed for pedestrians.

It's also a great way to "people watch", to simply bathe in the simple pleasure of watching ordinary humanity pass you by, going on about their ordinary business, special and unique and wonderful in its vitality.

### Architecture

There are, generally speaking, two types of urban architecture prevalent throughout Romania.

Because large parts of **Transylvania** were part of the Austro-Hungarian Empire until 1920, the architecture in this region tends to be heavily Germanic.

Around the beginning of the 20$^{th}$ century, anything and everything French was considered especially trendy and admirable and large parts of some cities (especially **Bucharest**) were remodeled in these styles.

The architecture in **Moldova** on the other hand is much different, showing a Slavic influence, with many more turrets, minarets and spires.

Besides peasant dwellings and medieval churches, there are few truly domestic Romanian architectural styles and many cities are a mish-mash of different, often clashing, designs and influences.

Quite often long rows of grey, crumbling buildings give Romania a darker and more depressing appearance than it truly deserves. Since the effect of these buildings has such a strong appearance, it is often the very first thing that visitors notice.

I guess what I want to say here is that it is quite important to understand that it is perhaps the exteriors of these Communist-era structures that are amongst the *last* things to change in Romania.

# Rural Tourism
## Introduction

Many visitors to Romania report that it looks like a "fairy tale", as the rolling, verdant hills are gently nibbled on by roaming flocks of sheep, herded in the old way by a man and his dog, leading them down to greener pastures, farmed by hand, and small, thatched cottages, warm and cozy as smoke burbles up the chimney.

As half the population still lives an idyllic, agricultural lifestyle, a trip to Romania is incomplete without a visit to the countryside.

### Rural Lodgings

Besides camping (page 35), you have two options in order to find lodgings in rural environments.

A few specialty inns or *pensiuni* cater to foreigners and often have specific rural experiences designed for visitors. Some of these are quite well known and can easily be found online.

Other *pensiuni* are harder to find as they usually only cater to Romanians but nonetheless can be charming and cozy, a great way to spend the night as you explore the countryside.

Some *pensiuni* are rated by stars (1 to 5) and some by "flowers" or **margarete** (1 to 5) and some are not rated at all.

Furthermore, in some small areas it is possible simply to hearken upon a stranger and barter or work out lodging on an ad hoc basis.

Please be aware that most rural people, besides those working in foreigner-designed facilities, tend not to speak English or other foreign languages.

### Getting Around

Many rural Romanians walk great distances.

Public commercial transportation can be very infrequent or non-existent, and your only option in some areas may be either a private motor vehicle or hitchhiking.

Seeing horse-drawn wagons entrances a lot of visitors. It is a rather simple affair (especially if you are with someone who speaks Romanian) to negotiate a brief ride on one of these, if you so desire.

### Bicycling

A great number of biking enthusiasts have been coming to Romania as there as so many idyllic, rural roads one can explore in this country. Many large cities now also have reserved bike lanes as well.

Renting a bicycle can be problematic in rural areas but most large Romanian cities sell and/or rent bicycles and bicycle parts.

It should be noted, however, that due to the angle of descent and the roughness of the road, the downhill portion of the **Transfăgărășan** (page 166) may be unsuitable for some bicycles.

### Hiking

Especially in Transylvania and the area from Sinaia to Busteni, there are many marked hiking trails, each using specific symbols to designate trail length and difficulty.

For specific details it is advised to acquire a local map of the area that you want to explore.

The name for "Search and Rescue" in (esp mountainous) hiking areas is usually referred to as **Salvamont**.

**Costs**

Generally speaking, most parks and wilderness areas are free to enter and explore. Camping in designated areas may require the payment of a small fee.

Lodging in *pensiuni* and other rural hotels should be cheaper than urban rates, except near ski resorts and other popular tourist destinations. Many times breakfast is included or offered for a good price, and is generally home-cooked and of high quality.

# LIVING IN ROMANIA

If you are planning on living in Romania due to a job relocation or to attend school here, you should look to your employer/school for guidelines on most things.

Be aware that while you should encounter no difficulties with your paperwork being accepted, this is a very bureaucratic country and multiple stamps/visits to multiple offices may be required.

European Union citizens should have a lot easier time as they automatically have a right to stay and setting up other permissions (such as working here) is relatively easy.

Long-term residents in Romania are given a **permis de şedere** (see page 230) literally "permission to reside", a kind of all-in-one identification card. It is recommended that once you have this card, you leave your passport at home permanently as you can conduct any and all business in Romania with only the **permis de şedere** card.

Foreigners (non-EU) marrying Romanians will likewise be granted the right to reside for five years before acquiring citizenship rights (see page 189).

**Viaţa La Bloc**

In urban areas, you may likely find yourself living in an apartment (UK: flat) inside a larger building called the **bloc** (*block*).

You may have an address that includes street, street number, *bloc* number, *scara* (stairway), *etaj* (floor[126]), and apartment number.

Usually there will be a series of postal boxes on the ground floor entrance, each one locked and accessible only by key.

The main entrance to the *bloc* is often electronically locked, which can be opened with a fob/barcode or else someone inside can "buzz" someone in, similar to the show *Seinfeld*. This buzzer/lock device is known as the **interfon**.

The lights inside the main staircase are invariably on a timer. Climbing or descending these at night may require careful calculation so as to not get stranded mid-landing. Make a note of where the stair light switches are, as often they are adjacent to and identical in appearance to doorbell switches.

Each apartment may have its own separate (air) heating system and/or water heating system or it may be centrally controlled by the *bloc*. If it is centrally controlled, you will have no control or decision over how much heat is pumped into your apartment nor how much hot water you will get or when you will get it.

Stores today sell rather inexpensive heaters for "instant on" hot water, especially useful in old or inefficient *blocuri* with central hot water control.

Once a day, the staircase and public areas of the *bloc* will get swept and mopped.

At the end of the month, each apartment owner (or renter) must pay the **intreținere** (maintenance) fee, to cover the electricity for the stair lights, cleaning, maintenance and upkeep of public areas as well as perhaps the central heating and hot water. The cost per resident will be posted on a board near the building entrance.

Gas stoves usually do not come with a pilot light or an ignition switch/button and so are lit with matches or cigarette lighters.

The light switches for all bathrooms are on the *outside* of the room.

Especially in colder months, teenagers and other young people may congregate in the stairwells for lack of other suitable entertainment venues.

---

[126] The ground floor is called the **parter**. The next floor above that is the first floor, and so on.

# Education

Generally speaking, Romanians are extremely educated and literacy is almost 100%. Romanians are avid readers of books, news and sports papers as well as magazines. Crossword puzzles and "word jumbles" are also quite popular.

A great number of people in Romania are conversant in two, three or more languages.

The school year runs from approximately mid-September to early June. At the moment, schooling is technically mandatory for all children and thus homeschooling is not an option except via a loophole (i.e. proof that a child is registered for an approved correspondence course, a difficult procedure).

## Children

There is a common (not slang) expression used in Romania that seems a little weird at first – **7 ani de acasa** (*shop-tay awn day ah casa*) because it literally means "seven years at home".

What does it mean?

Even today, a child legally does not need to go to (full-time) school until s/he is seven years old. That is because the child is supposed to be at home learning *how to act right*.

Essentially anything you can later righteously scold[127] them for not doing "correctly" is what you were supposed to have learned in those 7 years – manners, politeness, decorum and "proper" behavior.

Therefore saying someone *doesn't* have **7 ani de acasa** is equivalent to saying they're rude, ill-mannered and poorly brought up as a child. Like this:

**Me:** (sticking my tongue out)
**Offended Old Lady**: Nu ai 7 ani de acasa! (You don't have 7 years at home)

The phrase "7 ani de acasa" therefore means something like "proper behavior" and anyone who is rude or uncouth doesn't "have" the seven years at home aka the proper training and therefore a proper scolding is required.

Nonetheless, in urban areas it is becoming increasingly common for children to attend a variety of "pre-schools", called sometimes a **gradinița** or a

---

[127] See page 150.

**cresa**, a kind of part-time activity that's more focused on playing and creative exercises than "academic" learning.

Note: It is a common tradition for children to bring a bouquet of flowers for their teachers on the first day of school.

Around age 7[128] the studies truly begin at the school, called a **şcoala.** Students in **şcoli** (schools) are referred to as an **elev** or "pupil", from the French.

Around age 14, the **elevi** begin to attend a high school, called a **liceu**, which is often focused on a specialized discipline like music, the arts or perhaps a foreign language.

Although school attendance is mandatory in Romania for all children[129], it is often not adhered to in some rural communities and by many gypsies.

To graduate from **liceu** and to be eligible for higher studies, every student must pass the **bacalaureat**, an extremely difficult and comprehensive test.

**Adults**

If you are a citizen, you are eligible to attend any number of universities at no cost, assuming a number of requirements are met[130].

Tens of thousands of foreigners come to study in Romanian universities, with some classes taught in English, German or French. The costs for tuition are not free but the prices are quite competitive for some foreign students compared to the costs they would have to pay in their home country.

If you are residing in Romania purely on a student visa[131], you will be unable to seek employment but the paperwork, cost and hassle with this visa is quite low.

Students at the university level are known as **studenţi** in Romanian, differentiated from the term **elevi** above.

Tests and examinations, especially at the end of term, are extremely numerous in Romanian universities.

---

[128] Again, some parents opt to enroll their children in "grade zero" at an official school as early as 5 years old.
[129] Indeed, home schooling beyond age 7 is actually illegal.
[130] First you have to sometimes pass a test or satisfy eligibility requirements but after that it's a question of maintaining your grade point average.
[131] And not say, a citizen of another EU country, etc.

# Identification

Once you get the visa to stay here, called the **permis de şedere** (see below), you can suddenly do a lot of things in Romania.

Without it, however, you will be required to use your passport for many things, a practice I don't recommend (see page 22) and will be unable to do much beyond exchange money, rent a car or check into hotel rooms.

If you have an identity card from another European Union country, many more options will be open to you. Certainly this will handle all of your travel-related needs as well as any issues having to do with banks.

For things like signing contracts and doing business in Romania, however, you may need a Romanian ID document.

### Permis de Şedere

Literally meaning "permission to reside", there are several ways to get this.

If you are a European Union citizen, you already have the right to reside in Romania (barring certain criminal convictions) so this won't be an issue for you.

If you are coming from elsewhere to Romania either as a student or as part of your employment, check with your school or employer as they will be handling that paperwork for you.

It is always best to check the Romanian Embassy in your home country first for the latest information on visas.

There are several other ways to get a **permis de şedere,** including being a business owner. For this option it is best to consult with a lawyer familiar with Romanian judicial proceedings.

Note: sometimes even when all of your paperwork is in order, you may encounter a problem. I strongly advise resilience and patience and to try to go back on a different day and submit the paperwork with a different employee. Romania is a quirky country and so it's best not to get too discouraged if you encounter some initial setbacks.

This "permission to reside" card is effectively a **buletin,** which is what Romanians call their (citizen) ID cards and can be used in all situations (domestically) in lieu of a passport or other ID document.

### Getting a driver's license

If you're a citizen of the European Union with a valid driver's license from your home country, you don't require anything else.

Otherwise there are two ways to get a driver's license for long-term use in Romania, both of which require a **permis de şedere**.

The first is to take your (currently valid and foreign) driver's license to the local traffic police[132] precinct in your area and have it "converted" into a permission to drive here.

I wish I could tell you there was a set formula for what the police will require of you but frankly there isn't. The people you have to satisfy work at the central police precinct and they'll each have their own requirements.

In Romanian a driver's license is called a **carnet** (or **permis) de conducere**.

The second way to get a driver's license is to go through the same procedure Romanians do to get a license. This requires taking a class, having several supervised hours of on-street driving and then taking a very lengthy written test.

Please be aware that this second route is quite expensive (and the written test is extraordinarily difficult). I'd estimate that it would cost you at least **1000 lei** and quite possibly even more.

As with any government procedures, it is recommended that you bring a Romanian with you to help you with translation. Many, many Romanian government officials get quite *nervous* and *stressed* when having to talk to foreigners, even in the Romanian language.

# Subscriptions/Plans

Signing a contract with a Romanian company for such things as telephone, internet, electricity, gas, sewage, water or other services can be very difficult, even for Romanians.

Usually what's required is both an identity document[133]and some kind of proof or residence in Romania.

---

[132] The traffic police (Politia Rutiera) are a separate and distinct branch and not to be confused with the "regular" police who handle criminal matters.

[133] Like the **permis de şedere**, page 254.

If you don't own property in Romania (along with the papers proving that you do), then you will need a stamped and signed rental contract, something you may not have.

If a Romanian property owner files a rental contract with the government, s/he is then required to pay taxes on the rent money they are collecting. This is a strong disincentive for property owners to want to give you the signed and stamped rental contract, something that you may need.

The solution is to ask them to draw up a contract that is correct in every way except that the reported rental price (per month) is at the legally minimum price. Then they are not on the hook for higher taxes and you have the documents you need.

Please note that even things like "loyal customer" cards at hypermarkets require proof of residence + an identity card or document.

While some things, like mobile telephones and internet service, can be obtained fairly easily (on a prepay or pay-as-you-go basis) without needing to sign a subscription contract, many other services are only obtainable with a contract.

It may be far easier to have your landlord (if you are renting) put these services in their name and you reimburse them. A human being signing a contract in their name is referred to as a *persona fizica* (physical person).

The only other way to get a subscription or monthly plan is if you own a business in Romania and thus the business is the entity signing the contract. The business is referred to as a *persona juridica* (legal person).

And yes, you will need a ton of paperwork to prove this every time you want to sign a contract.

## Doing business in Romania

Although I know people, both Romanian and foreign, who have opened businesses here in Romania, I strongly recommend against doing so, unless you're a multi-national corporation and then you certainly need to consult with your team of high-paid lawyers.

The paperwork to open a business is relatively straightforward and not even very expensive. This is probably the easiest route to gaining a visa to reside here (semi) permanently assuming you aren't here for other valid (long-term) reasons.

I have heard it theorized that it is impossible to conduct business 100% legally in this country and I'd wager that this is largely true. Quite frankly, there are a great number of contradictory, conflicting and seldom-enforced regulations and laws and even the most earnest of ethical merchants would be hard-pressed to ever be in full compliance.

Permission to do things, whether given from the government (on its various, multiple levels) or from the nearby community, is primarily based on relationships. If you know the right people and have the right relationship with them, things will go smoothly. Otherwise, they won't.

Foreigners working *for* Romanians is virtually unheard of. I've certainly never heard of it except in the case of some Asian workers sent here to work in a factory.

Employing Romanians seems to go fairly well for investors and business people here, as long as one knows what to expect when beginning such an undertaking. Clearly this is just a general guide and one should always consult a lawyer before doing anything.

Tax avoidance is a national sport in Romania with just about every business participating in it on one level or another, including self-employed people.

# Major events in a Romanian's life

By far, the three most important days in a Romanian's life are their baptism, their wedding and then their funeral.

Lesser events include their personal birthday, graduation from school and when they turn 18 years old.

## Marriage
**Customs**

Marriage customs in Romania vary from couple to couple and region to region.

The Romanian word for marriage is **nuntă** (*noon-tuh*).

Generally speaking though, once the couple is engaged, they will seek out a "godfather" (**naş** – *nosh*) and a "godmother" (**naşa** – *nah-shah*) to "assist" them and be their "spiritual guide". Oftentimes it is a close friend or relative of the family who adopt the roles of "godparents" and it is never the actual parents of either the bride or groom.

The "godparents" may also help in arranging and designing the wedding as well as paying for it.

Generally speaking, most weddings are held on Saturdays although in some regions (particularly **Maramureș** – page 249) they are held on Sunday.

On the morning of the wedding, the groom, his family, his friends and wedding party will get dressed and then form a convoy of decorated vehicles, which proceed to the bride's house, all the while honking their (car) horns and flashing their lights.

Once they arrive at the bride's house (traditionally her parents' house), a group of musicians will begin playing a variety of traditional songs using a saxophone and an accordion.

The groom (and his party) will enter the bride's house and once he meets his bride-to-be, it is customary to "ask for her hand" one more time (on bended knee) in front of the parents.

Once she says yes, the musicians play more traditional songs and the entire wedding party files outside to their convoy of vehicles. Flashing their lights and honking their horns, the convoy then heads to the **primăria** (city hall).

The actual legal, civil ceremony at City Hall is extremely short and consists of signing a document.

If the couple wants a religious wedding, the entire party then heads to the church or house of worship where that is performed, including the wearing of crowns (Romanian Orthodox) and other religious traditions.

Throughout the entire day, there are usually (hired) people who are filming and lavishly photographing every moment.

At the end of the day, the married couple host a party, complete with music, food (see below) and dancing, which can easily last until the wee hours of the night.

As in "western" countries, the bride usually wears a very elaborate, white dress and the groom some kind of suit, tuxedo or other formalwear. There's also a "first dance" for the couple (usually a waltz) and a fancy cake to cut.

For those who can afford it, the couple then leaves on a honeymoon, described literally the same way in Romanian as **luna de miere**.

Note: The most traditional salutation to greet someone who is engaged (or just married) is to say **casă de piatră** (*casa day pee-ott-ruh*) literally meaning "house of stone" but meaning "I wish you a long and happy marriage" or something along those lines.

**Costs**

The entire cost of the wedding itself will be borne by the hosts, the actual wedding couple (and their families) and/or the **naşi**.

Please be aware that <u>guests are charged money</u> to attend the wedding. You will be informed ahead of time what the sum is, which can be quite large, as it is considered a gift to help the newly married couple begin their life together.

Presents such as appliances and other gifts are not customary – the cash fee is designed to go towards that. Nonetheless, a nice bouquet of flowers is always welcome.Foods

Generally speaking, guests at a wedding will be served multiple courses of standard Romanian foods. Indeed, there is often "too much" food served during these festivities but it is considered obligatory to dazzle your guests with an overabundance of things to eat and drink.

# Funerals

Probably the single biggest event in a Romanian's life (besides their wedding day) is their funeral.

It is customary for the services to be *extremely* lengthy, often many hours in length, as the depth and breath of the eulogy is considered a reflection on the deceased's worth, therefore the more the better. Usually their entire life history will be reviewed with a thorough emphasis on all major accomplishments.

The priest does all of the speaking and there is generally no music or euologies done by the deceased's friends and family.

As with all Orthodox ceremonies, there is no seating so the entire funeral service is held with all attendees standing up.

Every family member and important person in the deceased's life will usually be mentioned during the service of the priest.

Generally speaking, there was a rural custom for the deceased to be laid out "in state" for a few days in someone's house before burial. Nowadays, especially in urban areas, the procedure is for the deceased to be embalmed at the mortuary and kept there until the funeral service and burial.

After the service, the very closest relatives and loved ones of the deceased will follow the priest in a procession to the burial site.

**Foods**

There are several special foods served only at funerals (or anniversaries of people's deaths), many of them based on bread.

The most common of these is the **colac** (*coe-lock*), literally meaning a "ring" as it is a large, ring-shaped piece of bread, extremely tasty.

Usually one very large **colac** is mounted to a cross during the ceremonies. As the bereaved guests leave, usually they are presented with a small, individual **colac** of their own.

After the service, refreshments are usually provided as well.

# Baptism

Romanians take their religion very seriously and a few weeks after a child is born there is an important baptism ceremony, called the **botezul** (*boat-ez-ool*) in Romanian.

Generally speaking, the family will throw a quite elaborate party where friends and relatives witness the baptismal ceremony.

The child in question is dressed in fine clothing and there is a nice ceremony involving candles for the guests.

Although not obligatory, it is common for the child's family to rent out a special place and have music, catered food and dancing for a party after the baptismal event.

Many times there is also a pair of godparents (see page 233) who play a vital role in this ceremony as well. If they are included, it is usually the godfather who holds the child at the moment of baptism.

Note: As with most Romanian celebrations, it is up to the *host* to provide the food, drinks and entertainment and there is no cost to the guests.

# Lesser events in a Romanian's life
## Graduation

Traditionally the only graduation celebration that was held was for graduating university but it is becoming increasingly more common to celebrate graduating high school (**liceu** – *lee-chow*) as well.

This graduation ceremony is known as **(bal de) absolvire** (literally "graduation ball").

The members of the graduating class will pay to fund an elaborate dinner, usually at a rented facility, along with drinks and dancing and everyone is dressed in formalwear.

## Age Of Majority

When you turn 18 years old in Romania you are legally an adult in every way – you can drink alcohol, start a business, vote, marry, drive a car, join the military and sign your own legal contracts.

Some Romanians, but not all, throw a private party on this day for their friends, quite often with alcohol, to celebrate this occasion, called the **majorat**.

It is not unusual for parents and other family members to attend and even participate in the festivities with their (now adult) child.

As with most Romanian celebrations, the *host* who invites you to the party will be responsible the costs of the event. That being said, a small present or token of appreciation is always warmly welcomed.

## Birthday And Name Day

There is a common tradition in this country to name a child based on the day he/she was born, according to the Orthodox Christian calendar (if Romanian) or the Catholic calendar (if Hungarian), each day of which honors one (or more) saint(s).

On the day that honors the saint that shares the same name as someone you know, they will celebrate their "name day", which is a low-key affair consisting of not much more than calling (or writing) the person and wishing them **la mulți ani** (see page 257). Nonetheless, the person will expect a greeting from everyone they know on their name day.

A person's "proper" birthday is usually a very low key and simple affair in Romania except for with very small children. Usually the person who is celebrating their birthday will invite over a handful of family and friends and have a small party, where a light, airy (usually fruity) cake is served. Only token gifts are brought by the visitors (if at all).

It is however, traditional for a woman to receive flowers on her birthday from her boyfriend/husband and male relatives.

If you are invited either to someone's home or out on the town by them to celebrate their birthday, it is the custom in Romania that the birthday boy/girl is the host and therefore pays and is the host(ess).

The role of the individual is not as cherished here as in some other cultures and so birthdays (and name days) are not a big deal except to your very, very closest friends and loved ones.


# Medical care

Once again, the emergency number nationwide in Romania is **112**.

**Insurance**

If you're planning on staying in Romania for any length of time, it is entirely possible for non-citizens to buy into a private medical insurance plan for relatively little money.

You will not be able to receive state assistance until you become a citizen, which is an extraordinarily lengthy process (page 226). That being said, a number of public clinics offer free services, including consultations with doctors, even to visiting foreigners.

Depending on your home country and insurance rules there, you may or may not be able to coordinate coverage from home and have it applicable in Romania. Check with your insurer at home for more details.

**Facilities**

In larger cities there will be larger and better-equipped facilities.

For minor ailments and illnesses, consult one of the many drugstores/pharmacies/chemists (Romanian: **farmacie**), always denoted with a green cross. By law, all cities above a certain minimum population will have a 24-hour or non-stop pharmacy.

Pharmacists are trained to diagnose and dispense medicines for minor ailments and illnesses and the "consult" is free. Most pills and capsules can be bought on a "as needed" or "a-la-carte" or "one at a time" basis –

negating the need to buy a whole box of pills when all you need is one or two.

Note: the "morning after" pill is available at a pharmacy without a doctor's note or order required.

For more urgent cases, many larger cities have **clinici** (clinics) where specialized doctors are available to consult and diagnose certain conditions.

The Romanian word for hospital is **spital**. Sometimes on signage, the international "H" symbol written in white on a blue background is used.

Although many of the *buildings* are quite old and often in various states of repair or neglect, usually the treatment provided inside is quite good.

Various doctors also have private practices, denoted with a large sign outside saying **cabinet medical**. Generally speaking, consultations in a private practice are by appointment only.

This is not to be confused with a **cabinet stomatolog**, which refers to a *dentist*'s office.

Especially in larger cities, some doctors do make house calls. The easiest way to get a list of these is to consult your home country's embassy (in Romania) and/or the most luxurious hotel in the city where you're staying.

Romania also has a network of entirely private clinics and medical facilities, which usually accept any patient willing to pay the (listed) fees and costs. Some of these are incredibly modern, luxurious and up to date.

Because of crowding (in public facilities), there is a higher chance of infection and this can sometimes be a serious risk. Long-term internalization in public facilities is definitely not recommended.

Rural areas may have a visiting doctor or other healthcare provider who travels around a given region, doing check-ups and preventative medicine.

Note: Please be aware that if you are "checked into" the hospital and remain there overnight, you will be required to wear pajamas (page 131). You will also be responsible for providing all of your own food and beverages.

## Costs

The costs for medical care are extremely low. Consultations at public facilities are usually free for everyone, including foreigners.

The cost for most medicines and other supplies from pharmacies is also fairly low.

Some elective procedures, such as dental work, are of such high quality and affordable price that some foreigners come here primarily for that reason alone – known as *medical tourism.*

Whether pills, splints, medicines or other treatment, almost all medical care in Romania is "a-la-carte" or sold and priced on an individual basis.

Note: It is customary for the family of any interned patient in a hospital to provide most of the "daily needs", including meals, or pay someone else to provide them.

# History of Romania

There have been people living in what is now Romania for tens of thousands of years. Indeed, some of the oldest human remains ever unearthed in Europe were found in Romania.

Starting in the year 82 of the modern era, a Thracian people had settled in what is more or less modern Romania. They were called the Dacians.

As this land bordered what were then vassal states of the Roman Empire, a series of crises occurred and after several attempts, Roman legions under Emperor Trajan (Rom: **Traian**) entered the Dacian capital at Sarmizegetusa (page 167) and destroyed it in the year 106.

The Romans then occupied what is now northwestern and southwestern Romania and called it the province of **Dacia Felix** or "Happy Dacia". Interestingly enough, Dacia was the last province to be added to the Roman Empire and the first one to be abandoned – around the year 275.

The history of what happened after the Roman Empire pulled out its legions and government officials is highly debated in Romania today, due to conflicting claims based on ethnicity.

**Romanian Version** – Although the government of Rome left in the year 275, a lot of Romans stayed behind, inter-mixing with the local population and retaining their Latin language.

Over time, this changed into what we now know as the Romanian language. As Romanians are the direct descendents of those Roman colonizers, Romania clearly is and shall always be a Roman(ian) nation.

**Hungarian Version** – After the Romans pulled out, the local population largely dispersed and became a nation of cow herders.

Around the year 1000, the great Magyar horde swept through what is now Transylvania and Hungary (see page 197) and began to build cities and settle the area.

From the year 1200 to 1920 in an almost continuous, unbroken pattern, the Hungarians were the feudal lords, monarchs and nobility in most of what is Transylvania, the Banat and Crişana today.

Since the Hungarians dominated the Romanians for so long, most of what you see today (especially in Transylvania) is largely due to Hungarian influence and direction.

The Treaty of Trianon in 1920, in which Hungary lost a third of its land, was a great tragedy and remains a thorny issue even today but what is not in dispute is that the Hungarians are the rightful heirs to these lands.

**Romanian Version** – After years of feudal serfdom in vassalage to Hungarian, Polish and Turkish overlords, a rising wave of nationalism culminated in 1918 with the declaration of union between the three majority-Romanian regions – Moldova, Wallachia and Transylvania.

This is celebrated as **National Day** every year on December 1 (see page 120).

Although these three regions had been briefly united once before (see page 254), 1918 marks the first time that anything that could be called a truly Romanian nation ever existed.  Prior to that, the three regions had almost entirely separate histories and have therefore each developed their own slang, dialects, clothing, food, traditions and dances.

In chronological order, the modern nation of Romania went from being a monarchy to being a vassal fascist state (to Nazi Germany) to being Communist to being democratic.

At the conclusion of World War 2, the region known as **Bessarabia** was absorbed into the Soviet Union and became the (Soviet) Republic of Moldova.  After the disintegration of the Soviet Union in 1990-1991, the Republic of Moldova became a sovereign nation and chose to remain separate from Romania.

The Republic of Moldova has several severe ongoing civil issues even today (which won't be covered in this book) and it remains a deeply divided and very poor nation.

Note: From about the early 15<sup>th</sup> century into the first half of the 16<sup>th</sup> century, there was a brief surge of various Romanian princes gaining all or full autonomy, including Vlad "Țepeș" Dracula, Ștefan cel Mare and Mihai Viteazu.

## Ardeal/Transylvania

From the year 1000 until 1920, Hungarian nobility ruled most of what is today's Transylvania with Romanians as their serfs. At times, the Hungarian nobility was itself under the suzerainty of the (Turkish) Ottoman Empire.

During a very brief period during World War 2, Transylvania was re-incorporated back into Hungary as part of a political deal with Nazi Germany.

During the long centuries of Hungarian rule, a large number of Germans (page 206), referred to collectively as "Saxons", were brought into settle this region as it was on the frontier of the Hungarian empire.

They built and maintained seven[134] fortified cities, known in German as the *Siebenbürgen*, comprising what are today the Romanian cities of Medias, Sebes, **Sibiu**, **Cluj**, **Sighișoara**, **Brașov**, **Bistrița** and **Orăștie**.

Even today in the German language this region is still referred to as *Siebenbürgen*. In Romanian it is known either as **Transilvania** or **Ardeal**, borrowed directly from the Hungarian name for the region – *Erdély*.

Some of the most famous Hungarian monarchs and rulers were born and ruled in Transylvania, including **Mattias Corvinus** (page 255) and **John Hunyadi** (page 256).

The vast majority of ethnic Hungarians living in Romania today are located in Transylvania and Szekely Land.

Today, Transylvania is the most prosperous and modern of the three major regions in Romania.

---

[134] It really was just 7 at first but depending on how you count them, there were at least 9 and possibly more that ultimately were built.

For geographical information about Transylvania, see page 248.

For geographical information about Transylvania, see page 248.

Principal Cities

- Cluj-Napoca
- Braşov
- Sibiu
- Sighişoara

## Moldova

The first thing to understand about Moldova is to clear up a little confusion about the name.

Historically there is a region known as Moldova. Today, part of those lands are the separate, sovereign nation of **Republic of Moldova** and part of it is the *region* of modern Romania which is *also* known as "Moldova".

Technically speaking, in English-language guidebooks the Romanian province is called Moldavia and the separate country called Moldova to differentiate the two. That being said, Romanians have never heard of this term (Moldavia) and won't understand you if you use it. Therefore, for clarity's sake, I will indicate exactly what I mean when I refer to Moldova.

Having escaped Roman conquest in 106 (see the history of Transylvania on the preceding page), Dacians continued to occupy this area although only held weak and intermittent political control, the area lying on many important trade routes and therefore subject to frequent attack.

Starting around the year 1300, a series of Romanian princes seized and maintained control, although at various times were forced into vassalage to either the Ottoman or Polish Empires.

In 1812, the eastern region of Moldova (known as Bessarabia – page 241) was absorbed into the Russian Empire and largely remained separate from western (and modern day Romanian) Moldova, although it did join with the other regions to form the first modern nation of Romania in 1918.

In 1859, Moldova joined with the region of Wallachia to form the first Kingdom of Romania and (Romanian Moldova) has remained united with Wallachia ever since.

As Russia and Ukraine have had centuries of influence, there is a much stronger use of Slavic pronunciation and vocabulary in this region.

Probably the most famous[135] Romanian of all time, **Ştefan cel Mare** (page 253) ruled this province in the second half of the 15th century, renowned for fending off multiple attacks from both the Tatars and the Ottoman Turks.

Although **Iaşi** and **Galaţi** are very large cities, much of the rest of Moldova is rural farmland, particularly famous for its high-quality wines.

Principal Cities

- Iaşi
- Suceava
- Galaţi

**Wallachia**

The term "Wallachia" in English comes from a Greek word that just means "foreigner" and isn't used by Romanians at all. Instead, this region is known in Romanian as **Ţara Românească**, literally "Romanian Land".

Historically speaking, this is the region where (ethnic) Romanians maintained the most power, starting with a series of ruling princes around the year 1310, breaking away (more or less permanently) from the Hungarian Empire.

Nonetheless, by the year 1415, all the Romanian princes of Wallachia were subject to the suzerainty of the Ottoman Empire, along with intermittent control by Russia until 1859, when Wallachia joined with (western) Moldova to form the first Kingdom of Romania.

Although Vlad "The Impaler" Dracula is best known in connection with Transylvania, he was actually the ruling prince of Wallachia during his various (and short-lived) reigns.

The region of Wallachia is further divided into two parts, with **Oltenia** forming the western (and more mountainous) region and **Muntenia** forming the eastern region, including the national capital, **Bucharest**.

Principal Cities in Muntenia

- Bucharest
- Buzau
- Piteşti
- Ploieşti

---

[135] To Romanians.

Principal Cities in Oltenia

- Craiova
- Râmnicu-Valcea
- Drobeta-Turnu Severin
- Târgu Jiu

**Other regions**

Although smaller in size, there are several other key regions in Romania, each with their own history.

Crişana

In Romania's extreme northwest, this area differed from that of nearby Transylvania in that Transylvania was a province ruled by the Hungarian empire while Crişana (*cree-shawn-uh*) was part of Hungary proper.

After 1920, eastern Crişana became part of Romania while the western half remained part of Hungary. Even today there is a strong Hungarian presence in this region, with much cross-border traffic with (what is now) the Hungarian side, including the city of Debrecen (in Hungary).

This area was the northern limit of the Roman province of **Dacia Felix** and is home to several thermal baths, many of which are still used today.

Principal Cities

- Arad
- Oradea
- Salonta

Banat

On Romania's extreme western flank lies the Banat, a flat expanse of territory that is geographically a continuation of the Hungarian Plain, although it borders what is now the nation of Serbia today.

This region was part of the Roman province of **Dacia Felix** and after the Roman pullout it was subject to several invasions by neighboring tribes, including a number of Slavs (modern day Serbians).

After the Hungarians moved into neighboring Transylvania, the Banat became a separate province of the Hungarian Empire, and many of the most famous Hungarian rulers from that historical period came from this region (see page 245).

After the year 1552, the Banat fell under direct Ottoman control until 1716 when it was absorbed into the greater Hungarian-Austrian Empire.

Therefore this region is remarkable in that it has a much stronger Austrian influence than anywhere else in Romania, especially in terms of architecture. Outside of **Sibiu**, the Banat is probably where more German is still spoken today anywhere in Romania.

After World War 1 and the Treaty of Trianon in 1920, the Banat was awarded to Romania and has remained part of it ever since.

In 1989 in the city of **Timişoara** the events began that led up to the revolution and the end of Communist era.

Principal Cities

- Timişoara

Maramureş

Squeezed into the extreme northwest of modern-day Romania, Maramureş (*mar-uh moo-resh*) is sometimes referred to as the "land that time forgot".

Although historically it was part of Hungary proper (and not a separately ruled province like Transylvania), this area is a large valley encircled by mountains and therefore has remained agricultural, isolated and largely unaffected by Hungarian and other influences.

Even Communist-era "reforms" largely passed by Maramureş and this region is quite well renowned for its unspoiled, natural beauty.

Many, many traditional customs, including time-honored crafts and traditional dress are still adhered to in this region.

Although its capital and largest city, **Baia Mare**, is a modern (if small) town, many of the surrounding villages remain largely unchanged, a great source of pride for many Romanians.

Principal Cities

- Baia Mare
- Sighetu Marmaţiei

Bucovina

For most of the historical period of Romania, this area was part of the principality of Moldova.

However in 1775 it was annexed into the Austro-Hungarian Empire, where it remained until the end of World War 1, when it was united with the other regions of Romania.

After World War 2, the northern half of Bucovina was absorbed into the (Soviet) **Republic of Ukraine** and remains part of the (independent) nation of Ukraine today.

The southern (and now Romanian) half of Bucovina is where the world-famous painted churches (page 165) are located.

Principal Cities

- Suceava
- Vatra Dornei

Dobruja

Known in Romanian as **Dobrogea**, this is the name given collectively for the coastal region bordering the Black Sea (see page 159).

This area is also where the vast, marshy wetlands of the Danube Delta (Romanian: **Delta Dunarii**) are located.

Because this region is home to several ports, its history is vastly different than other regions in Romania. Dobruja was conquered and ruled by several different empires, including a brief (but important) stint under Greek Byzantine rule.

Completely separate from **Dacia Felix** (see page 240), the Romans controlled parts of Dobruja beginning in the year 15 AD, calling it **Moesia**, and ruling[136] it until around the year 580.

After a long and turbulent history, Dobruja was conquered by the prince of Wallachia in 1319 and then almost immediately fell under Ottoman rule. Even today, there is a much stronger Turkish and Muslim presence in this region.

After a series of wars in the Balkans in the late 19th century, the southern half of Dobruja became absorbed into what was then Russia and is now modern-day Bulgaria.

At the end of World War 1, (northern) Dobruja united with the other regions to form the modern nation of Romania, where it has remained ever since.

---

[136] After the split of the Roman Empire into West and East, it was ruled by the Eastern or Byzantine Empire.

Principal Cities

- Constanţa
- Tulcea
- Mangalia

# Geography of Romania

Imagine if you were a little kid and you loved a certain brand of goldfish crackers sooooo sooo very much that you got out your trusty pencil and paper and decided to draw an example of your very fine snack, swimming from right to left.

Well that's what the country of Romania looks like on a map – a goldfish swimming towards the viewer's left.

Romania essentially has four separate regions, which are incredibly distinct from one another, both due to geography and terrain as well as to the historical fact that up until 1920, there was no such thing as the modern Romania that we know and love.

Each of these four regions had a different history under different rulers and with different outcomes (page 240).

### Ardeal/Transylvania

Most of Transylvania is either mountainous or quite hilly and includes the Carpathian (Romanian: **Carpaţi**) Mountains as well as the **Apuşeni** mountain chain.

Its southern zone, starting near **Braşov**, is where most of the well-known ski resorts in Romania are located.

If Romania were a "fish" then Transylvania would be the entire head of that fish, comprising roughly the northwestern third of the country.

### Moldova

Moldova is largely a series of rolling hills, perfect for the growing of their world-renowned grapes.

If Romania is a "fish" then Moldova is the entire "back" portion of the fish, comprising roughly the northeastern third of the country.

## Wallachia

Almost entirely flat, Wallachia would be the "belly" of the fish.

Because it is further south, and generally at lower elevations, Wallachia has warmer temperatures than the rest of the country. It is also prone to earthquakes, occasionally very strong ones.

The western parts of Oltenia, especially near **Târgu-Jiu**, are very mountainous and home to a very large mining industry, especially coal.

A great deal of agricultural foodstuffs are grown in Wallachia.

## Dobruja

If Romania were a fish, Dobruja (Romanian: **Dobrogea**) would be the tail of the fish, comprising the coastal area of the country bordering the Black Sea.

Much of northern Dobruja is a marshy, swampy wetland area known as the Danube Delta.

Romania has a few other smaller geographical regions:

## Banat

Very flat and extremely hot in the summertime, this area is geographically a continuation of the Great Hungarian Plain.

If Romania were a fish, the Banat would be the "chest" of the fish.

## Crişana

Ringed on its southern and eastern flank by the **Apuşeni** Mountains, this area is generally flat and part of the Great Hungarian Plain.

If Romania were a fish, Crişana would be the "forehead" of the fish.

## Maramureş

This area is a valley entirely encircled by mountains, wedged into the extreme north of the country.

If Romania were a fish, Maramureş would be located at the very top of the fish's head.

## Ţara Moţilor

A mountainous region located in Transylvania and abutting the region known as Crişana, this area is quite similar to the Scottish Highlands.

Populated by what many consider to be a distinct sub-group of Romanians (page 210), this region is home to a lot of animal husbandry, particularly cows and sheep.

This area lies exactly between Crişana and Transylvania.

# Romanian Government

Since 1989, Romania has been a parliamentary democracy and its Constitution and political framework are almost identical to that of France.

The head of state is the president (currently Traian Basescu[137]), directly elected to a five-year term, with a maximum of two terms possible.

The president in turn chooses a prime minister (from amongst the parliament members) and the prime minister in turn assembles the cabinet.

There is a monarchy in Romania (see page 254) but the king holds no official power or status in the government.

### Political Framework

There are dozens of political parties in Romania, including:

**PSD** – Probably considered to be the "old guard" party, it is one of the two parties that continue to hold a significant chunk of the parliament and are the "conservatives".

**PNL** and **PD** – Now two separate parties, these two continue to hold the other large slice of the parliament. Generally considered to be the more "leftist" or "progressive" wing.

Currently the **PNL** is united with the **PSD** to form the ruling coalition but was previously aligned with the **PD** and other parties.

**PRM** and **ND** – Rabidly nationalistic and often virulently anti-Semitic and anti-Hungarian.

---

[137] First elected in 2004 and then re-elected in 2009.

**UDMR** – The most popular Hungarian political party, known by its Hungarian initials as **RMDSZ**[138].

Corruption, inefficiency and the passing of unfunded, unrealistic and complicated legislation are legion for politicians in Romania. Very few Romanians have any trust or confidence in the political system and voter fraud continues to be a nagging problem.

Almost all prominent politicians in Romania were also well situated during the Communist era and much of their mentality and way of doing business has remained unchanged.

The "good news" is that the relative inefficacy of the government leads to a less state-dominated society. Minor bribes, connections and persistence give one "wiggle room" to bend or avoid onerous rules, laws and enforced traditions.

While some people view this fluidity and inherent contradiction as frustrating and chaotic, it does allow the average person to find a way to get things done, even if that "way" isn't exactly orthodox or necessarily legal.

There is a vast gulf between the laws and regulations "on the books" and those that are actually enforced. Therefore sometimes it is better to actually "break the law" (see page 22).

# Famous Romanians
## Vlad "The Impaler" Țepeș

For the full chapter on this man, see page 10.

That being said, it's important to understand that in modern Romanian culture, Vlad Țepeș is a national hero and represents a widely admired mentality of an unflinching, tyrannical stance against corruption and thievery.

For Romanians, there are absolutely zero associations between the man and vampires or being "Dracula"[139]. In fact, Bram Stoker's book was not even translated into Romanian until after the 1989 Revolution. Here in Romania he is only known for his actions when he was the ruling prince of Wallachia.

---

[138] Romániai Magyar Demokrata Szövetség
[139] The famous fictional vampire count.

## Nadia Comăneci

Most famously known for being awarded the first perfect 10 for gymnastics in the 1976 Olympics, she is easily the most famous Romanian alive today.

Despite the fact she still speaks Romanian and still has close ties to her community, she has lived in the United States since 1989.

In English her last name is often pronounced *coma-nEEtch* but in Romanian it would be closer to *coma-netch*.

## Henri Coanda

One of a group of Romanian emigres in the early 20$^{th}$ century who moved to France to escape persecution at home, **Henri Coanda** was one of the most important early pioneers in aviation and airflow dynamics.

The main international airport in **Bucharest** is now officially called "Henri Coanda" Airport but is still universally referred to as **Otopeni** (for information on this airport, see page 102).

There is some debate about it but general consensus is that **Henri Coanda** built the first working jet engine in the world.

## Aurel Vlaicu

Similar to **Henri Coanda** above, **Aurel Vlaicu** was an early pioneer in aviation history, although **Vlaicu** was killed in 1913 during a test flight of one of his models.

The second, smaller airport in **Bucharest** is officially named "Aurel Vlaicu" Airport although it is still generally referred to as **Băneasa**.

His portrait currently appears on the **50 lei** note.

## Mihai Eminescu

If one individual could be said to possess the "soul" of Romania, it would be Mihai Eminescu, the most famous and respected poet of all time in the Romanian language.

As he spent much of this adult life writing and teaching in **Iaşi**, the city has many statues, monuments and dedications in his honor, including the famous linden tree that inspired him in **Copou Park**.

Translations of his most famous works (including *Luceafarul*) can be found but it is impossible to fully denote the masterful way in which Eminescu shaped and molded the Romanian language.

Because of the great respect Romanians have for his poems, Eminescu's portrait currently appears on the **500 lei** note, the largest in circulation.

### Nicolae Grigorescu

Considered the father of modern Romanian painting, **Grigorescu**'s name adorns many streets, plazas, schools and neighborhoods in honor of his talent.

His portrait currently appears on the **1 leu** note.

### Constantin Brancuşi

Probably one of the most famous sculptors of all-time, Brancuşi spent much of his adult life in France in the early part of the 20th century.

His most famous extant sculpture in Romania stands in the city of **Tîrgu-Jiu**[140] and is known as the "Endless Column".

### Ştefan cel Mare

Known as "Steven the Great" in English, he is easily the most famous and respected monarch in Romanian history, ruling the Kingdom of Moldova in the 15th century, the same period of time as Vlad Ţepeş (for more on him, see page 10).

**Ştefan cel Mare** (*shtef-on chel mar-aye*) founded a number of monasteries, built churches and solidified Romanian control over Moldova in the face of stiff opposition from the Turkish Ottoman Empire, Tatar invaders, the Polish-Lithuanian Commonwealth and the Kingdom of Hungary.

You can find street names, neighborhoods, monuments, statues and churches dedicated to him all throughout Moldova.

In 1992, the Romanian Orthodox Church canonized **Ştefan Cel Mare** as a saint. Because of this, he is sometimes referred to as **Ştefan cel Mare şi Sfânt** or Saint Steven the Great.

---

[140] Due to Romanian orthography, this city is sometimes spelled "Târgu-Jiu". For much more on this, see page 303.

### Mihai Viteazu/Bravu

In **Bucharest** and **Wallachia** (page 244), he is generally referred to as **Mihai Bravu** but in the rest of the country he is known as **Mihai Viteazu**. In both cases, the appellation means "brave" or "courageous".

Living about 100 years after **Vlad Ţepeş** and **Ştefan cel Mare**, Mihai Bravu/Viteazu is most famously known for being the very first monarch to unite the three major Romanian principalities (**Transylvania, Wallachia** and **Moldova**) under a single rule for the first time in history.

This unification in 1600 lasted briefly (about one year) but was the inspiration for later nationalist sentiments that led to the creation of the modern nation of Romania that we have here today.

### King Mihai

Still alive today (born in 1921), **Regele Mihai** (English: King Michael) was and is the last king of Romania, although today he has no governing power. He is related to other royal houses in Europe, including the British royal family, as his great-grandmother was Queen Victoria.

Forced to abdicate by the Communists in 1947, **Mihai** spend most of his life living in Britain and Switzerland. After the Revolution of 1989, **Mihai** has been allowed to return to Romania and has had several formerly royal properties returned to him, including the family castle at **Peleş** (see page 170).

Today he remains solely a figurehead with no power or throne, although there is a small percentage of Romanian citizens who remain solidly dedicated to him, urging a return of the monarchy.

# Famous Hungarians

### Saint Stephen the King

Known in Hungarian as *Szent István*, this was the legendary first king of the modern Hungarians, who settled the previously semi-nomadic tribes *and* introduced them to (Catholic) Christianity.

Although he spent little (if any) time in Romania, he is the number one most venerated figure in Hungarian history and it is important to know who he was.

The date celebrating his life is August 20, a national holiday in Hungary and celebrated by Hungarians in Romania as well.

## Elizabeth Bathory

Around the end of the 16<sup>th</sup> century, Elizabeth Bathory (Hun: *Báthory Erzsébet*) was a countess who ruled over a territory that is now in southern Slovakia although during her lifetime it was part of Hungary.

Whether due to misogyny, political intrigue or because it was actually true, Elizabeth Bathory was convicted of torturing and killing 80 women, supposedly drinking and/or bathing in their blood to "retain her youth".

While she never ruled in what is today Romania, the often-repeated stories of the "Blood Countess" clearly influenced later interpretations of vampire stories, including Bram Stoker's <u>Dracula</u> (see page 12).

## Mattias Corvinus

Known in Hungarian as *Hunyadi Mátyás*, this is one of the most famous and powerful kings in Hungarian history, born the son of John Hunyadi (see the following page).

Corvinus was born in what is today's **Cluj-Napoca** (page 158) and his house is still standing, a popular tourist attraction, along with the main central square with an enormous statue in his honor.

During the late 15<sup>th</sup> century, Corvinus expanded his empire, gaining rule over (what is now) Austria, Croatia and Bohemia as well as his lands in Hungary and (what is today) Transylvania, as well as parts of (today's) Ukraine and Poland.

Despite his vast territorial gains and numerous successful battles against the Ottoman Turks, Corvinus is probably best well-known in the west for being one of the princes who variously fought with, imprisoned and later allied with Vlad "Dracula" Țepeș (page 10).

One of the castles used by Corvinus is still standing today and is in excellent, although not original, condition (see page 169).

## Paul Chinezul

Sometimes his first name is written as "Pavel" but his last name "Chinezul" means "Chinese" in Romanian, which is a little confusing.

This man's Hungarian name was *Pál Kinizsi*, which was transliterated as "Chinezul" in Romanian and has nothing to do with being of Chinese origin.

Chinezul was a general fighting under Matthias Corvinus (page 255) against the Ottoman Turks, especially in several key battles in the Banat, where he is widely commemorated.

## John Hunyadi

One of the greatest Hungarian generals of all time, John Hunyadi's (Hun: *Hunyadi János*) achievements were only to be eclipsed by his son, Mattias Corvinus (page 255 above).

After fighting off the numerically superior forces of the Ottoman Turks and their allies several times, the Pope declared Hunyadi to be an "Athlete of Christ".

Although he himself never held royal power, he did end up becoming the largest private landowner in all of Hungarian history.

Romanian Language

**Basic expressions**

| Romanian | Pronunciation | English |
|---|---|---|
| Da | *dah* | Yes |
| Nu | *new* | No |
| Cine | *chee-neigh* | Who |
| Ce | *chay* | What[141] |
| Unde | *oon-day* | Where |
| Unde toaletă? | *oon-day tow-ah-lettah* | Where is the WC/bathroom? |
| Când | *kund* | When |
| De ce | *day chay* | Why |
| Cum | *koom* | How |
| Vorbiti engleza? | *vor-beets englaze-uh?* | Do you speak English? |
| Vorbiți mai puțin repede | *vor-beets my poots-een ray-pay-day* | Speak more slowly |
| Nu înțeleg | *new untzeh-leg* | I don't understand |
| Nu vorbesc românește | *new vor-besk romuhn-eshtay* | I don't speak Romanian |
| Vă rog | *va rawg* | Please |
| Mersi | *mare-see* | Thank you |
| Pardon | *par-doan* | Excuse me |
| Cât costa | *cut coast-uh* | How much does it cost |
| Cât e ceasul? | *cut eh chass-ool* | What time is it? |
| Bine | *been-eh* | Fine/okay |
| Îmi pare rău | *eem par-eh rouw* | I'm sorry |

For asking directions and starting conversations with strangers, see page 135.

For meeting and greeting people, see page 258.

The phrase **la mulți ani** (*lah-moolts-on*) is used to greet someone on New Year's Eve, New Year's Day, the person's birthday, their wedding anniversary and generally just about any holiday.

It literally means "to many (more) years".

---

[141] If you didn't hear someone and want them to repeat what they said, say "**Poftim?**" (*poaf-team*).

## Time Expressions

| Romanian | Pronunciation | English |
|---|---|---|
| mic dejun | *meek day-june* | breakfast |
| prânz | *pruhnz* | lunch |
| cina | *chee-nuh* | dinner/supper |
| astazi | *ost-uz* | today |
| azi | *uz* | today |
| mâine | *mwee-neh* | tomorrow |
| ieri | *yer* | yesterday |
| poimâine | *poy-mwee-neh* | day after tomorrow |
| ziuă | *zee-wuh* | day |
| săptămână | *supt-eh-moon-uh* | week |
| lună | *loo-nuh* | month |
| an | *awn* | year |
| secunda | *seh-coon-duh* | second |
| minut | *mee-noot* | minute |
| ora | *oh-ruh* | hour |
| ceas | *chass* | hour |

## Meeting and Greeting

As mentioned in the chapter on rudeness (page 134) and getting good service, it's very important to be *polite* in this country.

One of the most important things to know is how to greet people.

The first thing is to know the three "time of the day" openers. Although I am going to give you the translations below, in effect, all of these combined are just the way Romanians say "**hello**" and are a generic greeting:

**Buna dimineață** – *boo-nah dee-me-KNOT-za* – Good morning

**Buna ziua** – *boo-nah zee-wah* – Good day

**Buna seara** – *boo-nah se-AH-rah* – Good evening

When these times actually exist:

| Time Period | Romanian |
|---|---|
| Anywhere from after midnight to roughly 10-11 am | Buna dimineața |

| | |
|---|---|
| All day until it starts to get dark | Buna ziua |
| From dark until about midnight | Buna seara |

There is a fourth greeting – **noapte buna** (*nwop-tay boo-nah*) which means "goodnight" and is only said when the person in question is going to sleep.

Let's take these "hello" greetings for a test run:

| Scene | Time of Day Greeting |
|---|---|
| To a store clerk at 8:00 am | Buna dimineața |
| Get in a taxi at noon | Buna ziua |
| Pass an old neighbor you know at 9:00 pm | Buna seara |
| Buy a bottle of water at 3:00 pm | Buna ziua |
| Enter a restaurant at 11:30 am | Buna ziua |
| At a hotel reception desk at 6:00 pm | Buna ziua (if light out)<br><br>Buna seara (if dark) |

Note: <u>Any time you can use the correct time of day greeting in any formal situation, do so</u>.

Like many languages, Romanian has both a formal and informal set of ways to indicate what your social relationship is to the person you are addressing. In Spanish this is **tu** and **usted**, Italian **tu** and **lei**, French **tu** and **vous**, etcetera.

Therefore it's important to know when to use the formal and when to use the informal. The good news is that Romanians are not ultra huffy sticklers for when to use which form of address but you'll ruffle a lot fewer feathers if you get the hang of doing it the right way.

As you might expect, whenever you're in doubt, just use the formal mode when addressing people.

**Formal Relationships**:

- Anyone 20 years older or more than you
- Your romantic partner's parents
- Anyone working for the government
- Anyone you have a professional relationship with
- Any clerk, waitress, bartender or other employee
- Neighbors
- Any stranger who is not a young child or a gypsy

It's very important to understand that (in order to be polite) you must greet everyone with a "hello" in the proper way when you speak to them. This includes people in stores (shops) or taxi drivers or anyone you have a "commercial" relationship with.

If you do not have a commercial or other kind of relationship with them and they are total strangers, like someone you're stopping on the street to ask for directions, it is not necessary to say "hello", but only to use the phrase "excuse me" (see page 135).

**Informal Relationships**:

- Young children
- Punk teenagers
- Someone who is the age of your own children, or younger
- Gypsies
- Your romantic partner
- Your friends
- The friends of your friends
- Work colleagues who are at the same pay level as you
- Anyone you're flirting with

Now that you know the difference, let's look at some *informal* greetings or ways to say "hello":

**Servus** (only in Transylvania by Romanians and by Hungarians everywhere)

**Ciao** – (mostly only in the Banat)

**Salut**[142] – (any time of day)

**Buna** – (any time of day)

---

[142] You might know this one from "Dragostea Din Tei", the most famous Romanian-language song of all time. It is also called the "Numa Numa" or "Maya Hi" song by some people.

'**Neatza** – (*knot-za*, short form of *buna dimineata*)

Now let's mix and match the two together:

| Scene | Greeting |
|---|---|
| You walk into a museum at 3:00 pm | Buna ziua |
| You see your friend Farkas in a Hungarian village | Servus |
| Your good buddy Pete calls you on the phone | Buna |
| You wake up your lazy boyfriend | 'Neatza |
| You run into your friend Cristi in Timişoara | Ciao |

If all that seems complicated, the good news is that saying goodbye is super easy.

The formal way is always the same: **la revedere** (*lah ray-vay-day-ray*)

Again, as with all formal relationships, including commercial ones, if you want to be polite it is obligatory to say goodbye. It might seem weird to say "goodbye" to your taxi driver but that is how it is done here.

Please don't freak out about this because these greetings are for people you actually speak to. If you enter a store and put a candy bar on the counter and she rings you up and you hand over money and you don't speak then none of this *buna ziua* stuff comes into play.

Likewise you don't need to say "la revedere" to the lady who just sold you a bus ticket either. But with taxi drivers and waitresses (amongst others), you've been speaking to them during the course of your commercial transaction so the whole "hello/goodbye" thing does come into play.

Furthermore, since all telephone conversations count as speaking (duh), using "hello/goodbye" is similarly mandatory to be polite, especially in formal situations. This means if you call to order a pizza you say "la revedere" before you hang up.

Saying "goodbye" in Romanian for informal relationships is again variable:

**Servus** – (Transylvania Romanians and Hungarians again)

**Ciao** - nationwide

**Pa** – more akin to just "bye"

**Szia** – (*see-ah* – Hungarians only)

One other thing to note is that when answering the telephone, Romanians have one additional informal greeting, which is **alo?**, sort of like saying *AH-low.*

Hungarians likewise answer their phone (informally) with **szia** (*see-ah*).

All telephone goodbyes are the same as listed above.

Again, all of the above about greetings is how to be *polite* in this country. It is not, however, in any way mandatory if politeness isn't your goal. I see and hear Romanians every day speak to each other with very little politeness at all.

That being said, politeness goes a *long way* here and I truly mean that. If you comport yourself as a polite gentleman/lady that will be of enormous help in receiving better service and treatment here.

After I had been in Romania a while I noticed that I had become a lot politer when speaking to people, primarily because I had learned this kind of rote way to greet people and yet Romanians around me were shouting "**auzi?**" to get the attention of the waitress, which means "hey you hear me?" and sounds unbelievably disrespectful.

This worked to my advantage precisely because most Romanians feel there is a chronic *shortage* of politeness and good comportment in this country and so therefore most people are quite appreciative of a polite interaction.

### Vocabulary – Food/Drink

Meat/Eggs

| | **ouă** | *oh-ah* | eggs |
|---|---|---|---|
| | ou | *oh* | egg |
| | **pui**[143] | *pwee* | **chicken** |
| pulpe | de pui | *pul-pay day pwee* | chicken legs |
| piept | de pui | *pyept day pwee* | chicken breast |
| aripi | de pui | *ah reep day pwee* | chicken wings |
| pui | de balta | *pwee de bawl-tuh* | **frog's legs** |
| (carne de) | **vita** | *vee-tah* | **beef** |
| friptură | | *freep-tour-ah* | steak |

---

[143] In Romanian *pui* also means the baby of any animal, not just chickens (and their meat). If this is the case, it will usually be specified.

| | | | |
|---|---|---|---|
| biftec | | *beef-take* | steak |
| hamburger | | *hum-boor-ghare* | hamburger |
| burtă[144] | de vacă | *burt-ah day vock-uh* | tripe (stomach) |
| | **porc** | *pork* | **pork** |
| şunca | | *shoon-kuh* | ham |
| ciolan | de porc | *cho-lawn* | pork loin |
| cotlet | de porc | *coat-let* | chop |
| creier | | *cray-air* | brain |
| jumari | | *jew-mar* | rinds |
| ceăfa | de porc | *chof-uh* | rib roast |
| salam | | *sah-lam* | salami |
| kaizer | | *ky-zare* | bacon |
| mezeluri | | *mezzle-lure* | sausages |
| crenvurşt | | *kren-voorsht* | hotdogs |
| | **miel** | *me-el* | **lamb** |
| drob | de miel | *drobe day me-el* | (see page 56) |
| | **peşte** | *pesh-tay* | **fish** |
| crap | | *crop* | carp |
| pastrăv | | *puh-struv* | trout |
| somon | | *so moan* | salmon |
| ton | | *tone* | tuna |
| somn | | *soamn* | catfish |
| | **fructe de mare** | *frook-tay day mar-eh* | **seafood** |
| caracatiţa | | *cah-rock cah teets-uh* | octopus |
| crevete | | *cray-vay-tay* | shrimp/prawns |

Drinks

| | | | |
|---|---|---|---|
| suc | | *sook* | juice[145] |
| suc | de mere | *day may-ray* | apple juice |
| fresh | | | fresh-squeezed juice[146] |
| fresh | de portocale | *day port-o-call-eh* | fresh-squeezed orange juice |
| cola | | | Coca-Cola[147] |
| cola | light | | Diet Coke |
| lapte | | *lop-tay* | milk |
| lapte | batut | *lop-tay ba-toot* | buttermilk |

---

[144] For the famous soup *ciorba de burta* see page 87.
[145] The word "suc" in Romanian refers to any kind of non-alcoholic beverage, not just juices. For more on this, see page 71.
[146] As in not pasteurized. For much more on this, see page 89.
[147] If you want Pepsi or another brand, you have to order it by name. See page 90.

263

| | | | |
|---|---|---|---|
| sana | | *suh-nuh* | yogurt drink |
| iaurt | | *yah-oort* | yogurt |
| bere | (la sticla) | *bear-eh la steek-luh* | (bottle of) beer |
| bere | la halba | *bear-eh la hall-buh* | stein or mug of (draft) beer |
| beri | | *bear* | beers |
| vin | alb | *veen owlb* | white wine |
| vin | roşu | *veen roe-shoe* | red wine |
| gin tonic | | *jean toe-neek* | gin and tonic |
| martini | | - | vermouth |
| gin cu martini | | *jean coo martini* | a martini[148] |
| şampanie | | *sham-pagny-eh* | champagne |
| ţuica | | *tsweeka* | plum brandy[149] |
| palincă | | *puh-link-uh* | See page 74 |
| horincă | | *hoe-rink-uh* | See page 74 |
| vişinată | | *vee-shee-naught-uh* | cherry liquor |

Vegetables/Grains

| Romanian | Pronunciation | English |
|---|---|---|
| cartofi | *car-toaf* | potatoes |
| castravete | *cost-ruh vet-tay* | cucumbers |
| castraveţi muraţi | *cost-ruh vets moor otts* | pickles (cucumbers) |
| ceapă | *chop-puh* | onions |
| ciuperci | *chew-perch* | mushrooms |
| conopide | *cone-oh-peed-eh* | cauliflower |
| dovlecei | *doav-lay-chay* | see page 67 |
| fasole | *fah-soul-eh* | beans |
| gogoşari | *go-go-shar* | see page 67 |
| grâu | *grew* | wheat |
| malai | *muh-lie* | cornmeal |
| mâsline | *muzz-lee-neigh* | olives |
| mazare | *maz-zah ray* | peas |
| morcovi | *more cove* | carrots |
| muraturi | *moor-ah tour* | mix of pickled vegetables |
| orez | *oh-rez* | rice |
| porumb | *poh-roomb* | corn/maize |

---

[148] The confusion here is that "Martini" is a brand of vermouth. The mixed drink has to be specified therefore as gin AND (Martini brand) vermouth.
[149] For much more on this, see page 83.

| | | |
|---|---|---|
| praz | *proz* | leek |
| roşii | *roe-shee* | tomatoes |
| sfeclă | *sfek-luh* | beets |
| spanac | *spon-ock* | spinach |
| ţelina | *tsell-ee-nuh* | celery[150] |
| usturoi | *oost-ooh-roy* | garlic |
| varză | *var-zuh* | cabbage |
| vinete | *veen-eh-tay* | eggplant/aubergine |

## Fruits

| Romanian | Pronunciation | English |
|---|---|---|
| ananas | *ah-nah-nuss* | pineapple |
| banane | *buh-non-eh* | bananas |
| capşuni | *cop-shoon* | strawberries |
| cirese | *chee-ray-say* | cherries |
| coacaze | *co-ah-kazee* | currants |
| gref | *gref* | grapefruit |
| gutui | *gut-twee* | quince |
| lamâie | *luh-muh-eh* | lemon |
| lebeniţa | *leh-ben-itza* | watermelon |
| mere | *meh-ray* | apples |
| pepene | *pay-pay-neigh* | melon |
| pere | *pay-ray* | pears |
| piersici | *pee-air seetch* | peaches |
| portocale | *port-oh-call-eh* | orange |
| prune | *proo-neigh* | plums |
| struguri | *stroo-goor* | grapes |
| vişine | *vee-shee-neigh* | black cherries |

## Foods/Dishes

| Romanian | Pronunciation | English | Page |
|---|---|---|---|
| ardei copţi | *ar-day coapts* | roasted peppers | 72 |
| biscuiţi | *beese-cu-eets* | biscuits[151] | |
| biscuiţi saraţi | *sar-otts* | crackers | |
| budinca | *bood-in-ka* | pudding[152] | |
| ciocolată | *chock-oh-lottah* | chocolate | |
| ciorbă | *chore-buh* | (sour) soup | 76 |

---

[150] In Romania, it's the *root* of the celery plant being eaten while in many western countries it's the *stalk* growing abovethe ground that's eaten. That has a different name here (**aspic**) in Romania and is only found in specialty stores.

[151] In the British sense, meaning a sweet flour creation, rather than the American "bread" food.

[152] As in the sweet, creamy dessert not meaning any sweet treat whatsoever in the British sense.

| | | | |
|---|---|---|---|
| ciorbă de burtă | *chore-buh day boor-tah* | tripe soup | 76 |
| colac | *coe-lock* | "ring" bread | 236 |
| covrigi | *coe-vreej* | (hot) pretzels | |
| drob | *drobe* | haggis | 56 |
| fursecuri | *foor-seck-oor* | cookies | |
| iahnie (de fasole) | *yah-neh-eh day fah-soul-eh* | beans in sauce | 71 |
| inghetata | *in-ghetz-at-uh* | ice cream | |
| langoşi | *lun-goash* | fried dough | 54 |
| mămăligă | | boiled cornmeal | 46 |
| mâncare de post | *day post* | vegan food | 71 |
| mici | *meetch* | sausages | 43 |
| mititei | *meaty-tay* | sausages | 43 |
| mujdei de usturoi | *mooj-day day ooster-oy* | garlic sauce | 48 |
| placinte | *plah-cheent-eh* | fried dough | 54 |
| salată de icre | *sal-otta day eek-ray* | caviar/fish eggs | 71 |
| salată de varză | *sal-otta day var-zuh* | shredded cabbage | 72 |
| salată de vinete | *sah-lotta day vee-neigh-tay* | eggplant spread | |
| shawarma | *shah-warm-ah* | grilled meat | 57 |
| slănină | *slah-nee-nah* | cured pork fat | 45 |
| smântână | *smun-tuna* | sour cream | |
| tocană | *toe-con-ah* | stew | 76 |
| tochitură | *toe-key-tour-ah* | meat platter | |

Be aware that all Romanian nouns (see page 279) have multiple forms, including for gender and number and declension. The nouns listed above are all in their most common form.

## Vocabulary – Stores and Businesses

Because all Romanian cities (including **Bucharest**) are heavily pedestrian, you're going to do a lot of walking around and see a wide variety of stores and shops. Some are self-explanatory (computer stores always say "computer", for instance) but others are not.

In alphabetical order:

**Amanet** – A pawnshop. Trades a lot more in gold and silver than electronic items and the like. If you don't speak Romanian and aren't desperate, don't go in these!

**Anticariat** – Meaning the sale of used books, many of which look far older than that really are due to Communist-era (poor) printing techniques.

**Anvelope** – Automobile tires (tyres).

**Apicultura** – Honey and other bee products.

**Autogară** – The inter-city bus station for a given city. Not all inter-city buses stop here though.

**Bar de Zi** – A really crappy, seedy establishment that sells beer and alcohol (and coffee) and has nothing in the way of entertainment (besides maybe a TV overhead). While not dangerous, these places are dingy and only recommended for the alcoholic on a very, very tight budget.

**Benzinărie** – A gas/petrol station, often with an attached mini-mart.

**Biblioteca** – A library.

**Bistro** – I've been seeing the use of this word cropping up a lot as of late but it doesn't mean anything. It just sounds fancy.

**Brutarie** – Bakery, often selling literally nothing but bread. Most bakeries sell both sliced (*feliata*) and unsliced (*nefeliata*) bread.

**Cabinet** – This means a private *medical* office of some kind, usually small.

**Cabinet Stomotologic** – This has nothing to do with stomachs but instead refers to *dentistry*. The person is a *dentist* in Romanian but the business is called a *cabinet stomotologic*.

**Café** – See **Cafenea** below. Occasionally though "Cafe" doesn't mean anything at all, it's just a name people use for their place to sound cool.

**Cafenea** – Sometimes "stylishly" shortened to **Café**, this is a place whose main focus is on coffee (page 81). Sometimes there are a few food items. Tea is usually of the green/fruit variety (page 80).

**Cafeteria** – Usually (but not always) a place that sells a lot of pastries, fancy cakes, other desserts and coffee. Almost always has places to sit down and a large, illuminated display case so you can point at the sweeties you want.

**Carne şi produse de carne** – Meat and meat products.

**Ceainarie** – A teashop.

**Coafoară** – Women's hair styling/cutting salon.

**Cofetaria** – This is essentially the same as a **Cafeteria** in most cases.

**Covrigerie** – A small place selling pretzels for not much money.

**Farmacie** – Pharmacy/chemist. Note, in every large town the law mandates a **Non-Stop** aka 24 hour pharmacy. If you're coming from the United States, medicines are insanely cheap. This is where you also can get anything related to *babies* (diapers, etc).

**Fast Food** – In Romanian it's a noun, as in "a fast food" and almost always refers to walk-up service to a window where a variety of, you guessed it, fast food is sold. Occasionally there are chairs and tables in the interior for customers. For much more, see page 56.

**Fornetti** – A Hungarian company with an Italian name. This is the nation's largest **Patiserie** chain selling a wide variety of pastries with different fillings, from salty cheese to sweet cherries or chocolate. I've never met a foreigner who didn't find these incredibly tasty.

**Frizerie** – This is the equivalent of a men's barbershop although occasionally they are unisex.

**Fructe şi Legume** – A stall/store selling fruits and vegetables.

**Gara** – Train station, occasionally referred to as the "gara de tren".

**Hypermarket** – If you're American, think "Wal-Mart." If you're British, think "Asda" or "Tesco". If you're Mexican think of "Gigante". If you're French, think "Carrefour". A large retail store that also has a complete grocery store inside as well.

**Incalţaminte** – A shoe store. The actual shoes are called *pantofi* though, confusingly enough.

**Lactate** – Milk and other dairy products from ice cream to yoghurt, cheese and sour cream.

**Langoşerie** – A place selling fried, semi-crunchy slices of dough with various toppings, primarily sour cream and cheese. Virtually identical with a **Placinterie**. See page 54 for more.

**Librarie** – A bookstore selling new books, quite often with some in English and other foreign languages.

**Magazin Alimentar** – Refers to a corner store (occasionally bigger) where food items are sold, usually including both some fresh and the rest pre-packaged goods, including beer, liquor and cigarettes.

The smaller the store, the higher the likelihood that a worker is going to be behind the counter and you have to name every item you want to buy and then she goes and fetches it for you. Be prepared to point if you don't speak Romanian!

Literally the name translates to "food store" as *magazin* is the generic Romanian name for any store/shop.

**Magazin Mixt** – Technically different than a **Magazin Alimentar**, they're virtually identical.

**Mezeluri** – This means "sausages" and often sold alongside other cuts and preparations of meat. If you see the word **Brânzeturi** as well, this means cheeses are sold.

**Mobila** – Furniture.

**Muraturi** – Pickles and other pickled vegetables.

**Nature/Natura** – Sells a wide variety of herbs, "alternative" medicines and natural teas to cure or alleviate a wide selection of ailments. Also a place to get *bio* products (USA English: "organic").

**Nightclub** – This always, always, always refers to a strip club, titty bar, gentleman's club or whatever other term you know it as. It never refers to a "disco".

**Non-Stop** – Hilariously this does not always mean 24 hours a day. Just sometimes. Almost all stores named "non-stop" are an all/late night **Magazin Mixt**.

**Papetarie** – Stationary store.

**Patiserie** – Selling a wide variety of baked goods, mostly pastries either with a sweet filling or else something else (cheese, cabbage, etc).

**Placinterie** – Usually identical (or nearly so) with a **Langoşerie**.

**Popas** – Literally a "rest stop" and only found alongside the inter-city roads, it's a place to pull over, use the bathroom and get some snacks. It usually also has a restaurant with hot food.

**Schimb Valutar** – A place to exchange money.

**Second Hand** – Practically always refers to second-hand *clothes* unless otherwise specified.

When someone donates clothes to a charity (Oxfam, Goodwill, etc) in another country, the charity sells off the clothes (by weight) to dealers who then turn around and sell them in Romania. You can get some incredible deals if you don't mind pawing through mountains of clothes (and shoes, belts, etc).

**Solar** – A tanning salon.

**Spital** – Just hospital. It sometimes goes along with the international "H" sign, making it H – spital.

A few ones that are easy to understand:

Aeroport (Airport)
Banca (Bank)
Bar

Casino
Cinema
Dealer(ship)
Hotel
Mall
Pizzerie
Posta (Post Office)
Restaurant
Showroom
Taxi

## Phrases - Food/Drink

| a fost delicios | *ah fawst day-lee-choase* | it was delicious |
|---|---|---|
| aş dori | *osh-door-ee* | I would like |
| cât costa? | *cut coast-uh* | How much does it cost? |
| cu gheaţă | *koo gay-otza* | with ice[153] |
| este loc? | *yest-eh loak* | Is there a free space/table? |
| îmi aduceţi | *eem a-doo-chets* | bring me... |
| mersi | *mer-see* | thank you |
| nota | *note-uh* | the check (bill) |
| oţet | *ots-et* | vinegar |
| pâine | *pwee-neh* | bread |

---

[153] See page 86.

| | | |
|---|---|---|
| piper | *pee-pear* | (black) pepper |
| sare | *saw-ray* | salt |
| şervețele | *share-vets-el-eh* | napkins |
| ulei | *ooh-lay* | oil |
| un pahar de | *oon pa-har day* | a glass of |
| unde toaletă? | *oon-day tow-ah-lettuh* | where is the WC/bathroom? |
| vă rog | *vuh rawg* | please |

For a list of words for drinks, see page 263.

For a list of food items, see page 262.

**Phrases - Transportation**

For taxis, see page 113.

For riding a bus, see page 91.

For how to ask for basic information, see page 135.

**Phrases - Hotel rooms and lodgings**

| English | Romanian | Pronunciation |
|---|---|---|
| lodgings | cazare | *ka-zar-aye* |
| room | camera | *cah-me-rah* |
| single | (persoana) singura | *pair-swannah seen-goorah* |
| double (2 people) | dublu | *doo-blew* |
| bed | pat | *pot* |
| 2-person bed | pat matrimonial | *mah-tree-moany-all* |
| an extra bed | un pat suplimentar | *oon pot souply men-tar* |
| two beds | doua paturi | *dough-ah pot-oor* |
| Is there... | Este... | *yes-tay* |
| a room available? | o camera libera? | *oh cah me rah lee bear ah?* |
| parking? | parcare? | *par-car-eh* |
| internet? | internet? | *internet* |
| smoking allowed? | se fumeaza? | *say foomy-ozzah* |
| for non-smokers? | pentru nefumatori? | *pen-true neigh-foom ah tour* |
| breakfast included? | mic dejun inclus? | *meek day-june in-cloose* |
| hot water | apă caldă | *ah-paw called-ah* |
| pillow | perna | *pear-nuh* |
| towel | prosop | *pro-soap* |

| towels | prosoape | *pro-swap-eh* |
|---|---|---|
| remote control | telecomanda | *tell-he com-and-uh* |
| television | televizor | *tell-he vee-zore* |
| price of | preț de | *prets day* |
| broken/ruined | stricat | *stree-cot* |
| cleaning | curațenie | *coo-rots and-ye* |
| I would like... | Aș dori... | *osh door-ee* |
| extra cost | cost suplimentar | *cost souply men-tar* |

## Pronunciation Guide

If you look at a sea of printed Romanian, it can be quite intimidating to try to pronounce. One time I was with a group of Polish tourists and I asked them to try and pronounce the cities on a destination board at the bus station and it sent me into gales of laughter.

I wasn't laughing at them but at myself and remembering all my struggles to get a handle on how to pronounce Romanian.

If you want the complete list on how to pronounce Romanian, I suggest you read the entire wikipedia article,[154] which includes this little fun nugget:

*Romanian spelling is mostly phonetic.*

Nope, afraid not[155].

So here are a few shortcuts that will make things about 10 times easier for you. Mind you this isn't how a Romanian would speak nor is it 100% correct, this is just to get you started and most importantly, *understood*.

Vowels are the same (generally) as in Spanish, Latin or Italian.

**A** is "ah" like "father" if you're super British

**E** is "a" like the letter A or the last word in every sentence if you're Canadian, eh

**I** is "ee" like the letter E or the word bee

**O** is "oh" like oh say can you see; and

**U** is "ooh" like "boo, I'm the letter U!"

---

[154] http://en.wikipedia.org/wiki/Romanian_alphabet

[155] Literally every single Romanian you will ever meet will argue the opposite, that Romanian is almost entirely phonetic.

The last **i** in any Romanian word is always silent (i.e. unpronounced) in the vast majority of cases. Some Romanians will give you a song and dance about how it's kind of aspirated and semi-pronounced and what not and blah, blah. No.

If there's two i's at the end of the word (ie *copii*) then the next to last i IS pronounced. And yes there are a couple exceptions[156] to this but it's mostly when otherwise the word would be unpronounceable without it (ex: *aflî*).

If you ever see the vowels **ea** together just forget the "e" and pronounced it as just plain "a" (ex: *seara* doesn't have 3 syllables *se-ah-rah* it's more akin to "sara" *sah-rah*)

**ă** or "a with a little bowl on top", just say it like a normal "a" sound. Yes they're actually different than a regular "a" to be completely accurate but for now just say it like a normal "a" sound and you'll be fine.

The **ului** at the end of some nouns can be a murderous tongue twister, such as the word *controlorului* – WHEW! Ok here's the secret – first off, just break it away from the rest of the word in your mind (using the above example it'd be "controlor" and then "ului") and then **ului** itself is "ooh-lwee" like "woo weee" but "ooh-lwee" and not three syllables "ooh-loo-ee".

Basically if you can say the word "controlorului" then you're set for life in terms of pronouncing Romanian (it's the name of a famous song and means "of the controllers").

**â** otherwise known as "a with a hat" is the one sound that doesn't exist in English.

It's a super guttural "uuuh" sound from way down in your diaphragm. Just have a friend or loved one punch you right in the stomach and the sound that gets expelled from your gut as you bend over in pain is the **â** sound. So when pronouncing România (the name of the is country) just say Rom(friend punches you UUUH)nia. Yay, you did it!

**î** otherwise known as "i with a hat" is just the old Communist-era way to write **â** and is pronounced <u>exactly the same</u>. (For more on this, see page 275).

**ț** otherwise known as "t with a tail" is just the sound of the letters "ts" combined. It's also known as the sound the Dog Whisperer uses to gain obedience.

---

[156] It's also pronounced in the infinitive form of verbs. But if you have to guess, generally speaking the last I is SILENT.

ș otherwise known as "s with a tail" is just the sound of the letters "sh" combined, exactly like the sentence "I should and shall learn to pronounsh the letter ș shuccesshfully."

Because of heavy Slavic influence, the letter "e" is pronounced as "ye" in a few situations. These are:

**ești** meaning "you are" – did you pronounce it *yesht*? Awesome!

**este** meaning "he/she/it is"

BUT NOT **est** meaning "east" as in the direction

**ele** which means "they"

**ei** which means "they" or hers" (pronounced *yay*).

**ea** which means "she" (pronounced *yah*).

BUT NOT **el** which means "he".

See? Super simple. That's the entire list.

Note: If you're in Moldova, pretty much EVERY "e" has the "ye" pronounciation.

The letter "R" is as rolled or "trilled" as you can get it, unless your first language is Spanish and then you're probably "over-rolling" the R, your R rolling bandito!

The letter "J" in Romanian is also borrowed from Slavic languages (Ж in the Cyrillic alphabet) and is more like a "zhhhh" sound. It tends to always be the last letter in a word or the name of a town (like **Cluj**, where I live). Therefore **Cluj** rhymes with the word luge.

The letter **C** has a number of unique variants, identical with Italian.

**C with anything else** – just like the English letter K

**CHE** – kay

**CE** – chay rhymes with neighbor and weigh

**CHI** - key

**CI**– chee rhymes with monkey glee

Likewise, the letter **G** has a couple of variants.

**G with anything else** – just like English "G" for "guppy".

**GE** – jay

**GHE** - gay

**GI** – jee

**GHI** - ghee

And there you go! The rest is easy and my little guide should get you cracking on about 99% of the language and you'll be understood in no time.

### Hijinks in Romanian Spellng

Romanian orthography[157] has changed significantly over the years and can be quite confusing to the modern visitor as many words still use a variant of the older spellings, including the names of cities (see page 164).

To illustrate the differences, I'm going to spell out the same word in the different formats, that word being **pâine** (*pwee-neigh* - bread).

VERY IMPORTANT: All of these spelling ways are pronounced exactly the same. Only the spelling has changed.

Current Official Super Looper Accurate Way

**pâine** – Enough said. If you're writing a letter to a Romanian (and really, I have to ask why you're doing this) government official, then this is how you do it.

Internet Style aka Lazy Style

**paine** – Most times, most people (myself included) don't have a Romanian keyboard with the special letters so you get to "skip" them. Some words, like pâine, do just fine as "paine" but other words like "gasca" can be confusing because they mean two different things when spelled (correctly) two different ways.

Printed Sign Style

**pãine** – The other problem is that for a long time the idiots over at ISO (whatever that stands for) didn't even make it POSSIBLE to write the a with

---

[157] The official way to spell words.

the hat (otherwise known as â, the correct letter) and so to distinguish regular "a" from "â" without being able to type it properly, Romanians sometimes were/are forced to use ã with a squiggly line over it.

The letter ã doesn't ACTUALLY even exist in Romanian but it's all you got when your print shop doesnt have â. Dig it?

<u>Communist Era Style</u>

**pîine** – This is the one that messed me up because my dictionary was printed during the Communist era and so I'd keep looking up words that had an â in 'them and find only the î with a hat.

There's a long and complicated (and boring) reason[158] why the Communists switched up the spelling like this and some Romanians still prefer it and it can be very confusing EVEN NOW because, just for example, on the CFR (Romanian railways) web site all the city names are spelled Communist Era style.

So if you're looking for tickets to **Târgu-Mureş** for instance, you have to search under **Tîrgu-Mureş**. SUPER FUN!

<u>Lazy Communist Style</u>

**piine** – Mostly used in Youtube comments by Romanians who moved out of the country during the Communist days and so continue to write this way.

<u>Cyrillic</u>

**пуйне** – This is only used in some parts of Republic of Moldova (as in the country of Moldova) but prior to about 1860, regular Romanian was written this way too. You won't really have to deal with this in Romania but it's interesting if you look at the writing on old churches and what not because it's all in the Cyrillic alphabet.

Note: Just for "extra fun", the Cyrillic alphabet historically used for Romanian is slightly different than the one currently used in Moldova.

<u>THINGS TO KNOW:</u>

Be aware sometimes signs and printed material have a combination of both lazy and official and/or lazy and communist style all mixed in together.

---

[158] Having to do with which sounds were considered "Slavic" and which ones weren't.

Reading signs and posted things essentially require that you already super secretly masterfully know the language and "fill in the blanks" for yourself if the spelling isn't correct or accurate.

## Numbers

Romanian numbers can be extraordinarily complicated. However a few basic forms for your use:

| 1 | un/una | *oon/oon-ah* |
|---|---|---|
| 2 | doi/doua | *doy/dough-ah* |
| 3 | trei | *tray* |
| 4 | patru | *pah-true* |
| 5 | cinci | *cheench* |
| 6 | şase | *shosh-aye* |
| 7 | şapte | *shop-tay* |
| 8 | opt | *awpt* |
| 9 | noua | *no-ah* |
| 10 | zece | *zay-chay* |
| 11 | unsprezece | *oon spray zay-chay* |
| 12 | doisprezece | *doy spray zay-chay* |
| 13 | treisprezece | *tray spray zay-chay* |
| 14 | paisprezece | *pie spray zay-chay* |
| 15 | cincisprezece | *cheench spray zay-chay* |
| 16 | şaisprezece | *shy spray zay-chay* |
| 17 | şaptesprezece | *shop-tay spray zay-chay* |
| 18 | optsprezece | *awpt spray zay-chay* |
| 19 | nouasprezece | *no-ah spray zay-chay* |
| 20 | douazeci | *dough-ah zaych* |
| 30 | treizeci | *tray zaych* |
| 40 | patruzeci | *pah-true zaych* |
| 50 | cincizeci | *cheench zaych* |
| 60 | şaizeci | *shy zaych* |
| 70 | şaptezeci | *shop-tay zaych* |
| 80 | optzeci | *awpt zaych* |
| 90 | nouazeci | *no-ah zaych* |
| 100 | o sută | *oh sue-tah* |
| 1,000 | o mie | *oh me-eh* |
| 1,000,000 | un milion | *oon meel-yawn* |

Numbers bigger than 20 use the word **şi** (*she*) meaning "and" before the last number.

277

Therefore the number 42 is **patruzeci şi doi** (literally 40 and 2).

The number 142 is therefore **o sută patruzeci şi doi** (literally 100, 40 and 2).

You might notice that the words for 1 and 2 have two forms – this is because they match the grammatical gender for the item in question, the forms ending in "a" for female and the other for male.

Unfortunately, there are also several slang or regional ways to say some of these numbers. While none of these are "official" they are used extremely often in some places when talking (but never written down).

A few examples:

| 3 | tri | *tree* |
|---|---|---|
| 7 | şepte | *shep tay* |
| 14 | paişpe | *pie shpay* |
| 15 | cincişpe | *cheench shpay* |
| 25 | doşcinci | *doash-cheench* |
| 32 | treişdoi | *traysh-doy* |
| 50 | cinzeci | *cheen zaych* |

All of these are either modified pronounciations (like 3 and 7) or else shortened versions of the official version (like *cinzeci* instead of the official *cincizeci*).

Romanians do not generally use ordinal numbers (first, second, third) etcetera except for the word for 1st (first), which is **întâi** (*un-tie*), especially when referring to days of the month (see page 117).

When writing ordinal numbers, Romanians often just add "-a" to the end of the number. Therefore in a newspaper article talking about someone coming in third place in a competition, it would be written "3-a".

Note: Due to a currency shift in 2005, the Romanian currency (**leu**) had four zeroes removed. In other words, 10,000 **lei** in 2005 became just **1 leu**. Likewise one million **lei** in 2005 became just **100 lei** now.

Prices that are written down invariably show the new prices[159] but often people, while speaking, refer to them in the old style, which can be

---

[159] This means if you speak no Romanian, you don't need to worry about this as items in the store are priced normally. It's only when you begin to talk to people out loud that this becomes an issue.

confusing. Especially when referring to salaries, people in Romania often refer to their income in "millions" of **lei** because of this.

## Romanian grammar

It took me over a decade to be able to properly converse and write in Romanian and it's true – Romanian grammar is an exceedingly tough nut to crack for most people.

That being said, most Romanians are quite tolerant and indeed happy to hear any foreigner even *attempt* to speak their language and won't be sticklers about grammar until you gain fluency.

If you really want to learn this language, I recommend you buy a series of good textbooks as well as check out my website, as I often write on these thornier issues.

## Romanian nouns

Romanian nouns are "declined", a term that is roughly analogous to the way verbs are conjugated. This means that all Romanian nouns have a wide variety of forms and you can't learn just one word for each thing.

Examples:

**Oraş** = city[160]

**Oraşul** = the city

**Oraşului** = of the city

**Oraşe** = cities

**Oraşele** = the cities

**Oraşelor** = of the cities

And many, many more....

These nouns also change depending on gender and number and it's a complicated process.

For much, much more on this, see my website or consult proper textbooks and learning materials.

---

[160] See page 33 for more.

## Converting Metric Measurements

Some of the following have been rounded up for convenience.

Weight:

| Metric to U.S. | U.S. to Metric |
|---|---|
| 450 g = 1 lb | 1 lb = 450 g |
| 1 kg = 2.2 lbs | 10 lbs = 4 kg |
| 28 g = 1 oz | 1 oz = 28 g |

Distance:

| Metric to U.S. | U.S. to Metric |
|---|---|
| 1 km = 0.6 miles | 1 mile = 1.6 km |
| 10 km = 6 miles | 16 miles = 10 km |
| 1 meter = 1 yard | 1 yard = 1 meter |
| 1609 meters = 1 mile | 1 mile = 1609 meters |
| 30.5 cm = 1 foot | 1 foot = 30.5 cm |
| 2.5 cm = 1 inch | 1 inch = 2.5 cm |

Fluids:

| Metric to U.S. | U.S. to Metric |
|---|---|
| 5 ml = 1 tsp | 1 tsp = 5 ml |
| 15 ml = 1 tblsp | 1 tblsp = 15 ml |
| 250 ml = 8.5 oz | 12 oz = 355 ml |
| 500 ml = 17 oz | 16 oz = 473 ml |
| 1 liter = 33 oz | 32 oz = 976 ml |
| 4 liters = 135 oz | 1 gallon = 3.8 liters |

Temperature conversion between Celsius and Fahrenheit can be done in your head with a simple algorithm.

To convert **F to C** = (temperature − 32) divided by 2

To convert **C to F** = (temperature multipled by 2) + 32

A few examples using the "in your head" calculations:

| Temperature | Roughly | Precisely |
|---|---|---|
| 0 C | 32 F | 32 F |
| 10 C | 52 F | 50 F |
| 20 C | 72 F | 68 F |

| | | |
|---|---|---|
| 25 C | 82 F | 77 F |
| 30 C | 92 F | 86 F |
| 35 C | 102 F | 95 F |

Please note that in terms of shoe size (and occasionally clothing size) the measurements used are the common European ones, different from either U.S. or British indices.

## Index of Romanian words used in this book

| Romanian | English | Page |
|---|---|---|
| 7 ani de acasa | a proper upbringing | 228 |
| anunțuri | classified ads/adverts | 181 |
| apă | water | 77 |
| autostop | hitchhiking | 106 |
| auzi | hey you | 262 |
| bal de absolvire | graduation party | 237 |
| bancomat | ATM/cash point | 39 |
| bani gheața | cash | 40 |
| benzină | gasoline/petrol | 107 |
| bio | organic | 269 |
| bip | the "beep" | 129 |
| bon fiscal | receipt | 112 |
| borș | a sour broth | 49 |
| boschetar | beggar | 216 |
| botezul | baptism | 236 |
| brad crăciun | Christmas tree | 122 |
| buletin | Romanian ID card | 230 |
| cântar | scale (for weighing) | 64 |
| cabane | cabins | 35 |
| cabinet medical | doctor's office | 239 |
| cabinet stomatolog | dentist's office | 239 |
| canicula | dog days of summer | 9 |
| carnet de conducere | driver's license | 231 |
| cartela | (telephone) card | 28 |
| cărucior | shopping cart/trolley | 133 |
| casa de piatra | "house of stone" | 235 |
| casa de schimb | currency exchange | 38 |
| cash[161] | cash | 40 |
| ceas | clock/meter | 111 |
| centru | downtown/city centre | 31 |
| chiflă | (bread) bun | 58 |
| clinici | medical clinics | 239 |
| cobariți? | are you getting off at this stop? | 91 |

---

[161] Generally pronounced "kish" by Romanians.

| comună | town | 29 |
|---|---|---|
| corect | proper/correct | 137 |
| coş de mână | hand basket | 133 |
| Crăciun | Christmas | 122 |
| cresa | pre-school | 229 |
| curent | drafty/moving air | 128 |
| cuşeta | sleeping car (train) | 100 |
| daca n-ai tupeu, stai acasa | If you have no guts, stay home | 185 |
| de toate | with everything | 59 |
| diavola | spicy meat combo | 52 |
| etno | folk/traditional | 179 |
| fără | without | 51 |
| feliata | sliced | 267 |
| fresh | fresh-squeezed juice | 79 |
| ghichitoară | fortune teller | 205 |
| gradină botanică | botanical garden | 151 |
| gradinița | "kindergarten" | 229 |
| horă | a traditional dance | 180 |
| hypermarket | very large retail store w/food | 268 |
| iarbă verde | "green grass" | 130 |
| îmi pare rău dar ați greşit numarul | Sorry but you've dialed the wrong number | 131 |
| la farfurie | a meal on a plate | 61 |
| la mână | no wrapping for a sandwich | 61 |
| la mulți ani | (many things) | 257 |
| la pachet | to go/take away | 61 |
| la revedere | goodbye | 130 |
| liceu | high school | 237 |
| luna de miere | honeymoon | 234 |
| magazin mixt | corner store | 269 |
| majorat | "age of majority" – 18 years old | 237 |
| mare | big | 51 |
| Marea Neagră | Black Sea | 159 |
| martişor | A Romanian holiday/amulet | 116 |
| mediu | medium | 51 |
| mic | small | 51 |
| miere | honey | 68 |
| motorină | diesel fuel | 107 |
| Muştruluială Justificată | Scolding of Righteousness | 137 |
| muzică populară | updated folk songs | 180 |
| naş | godfather | 233 |
| ness | instant coffee | 81 |
| nume | first name | 132 |
| nume de familia | last (sur)name | 132 |
| nuntă | wedding | 233 |
| o porție de | a portion of | 61 |

## Index of Hungarian words used in this book

| puliszka | polenta | 49 |
|---|---|---|
| Székely | Szekely | 199 |
| Romániai Magyar Demokrata Szövetség | Hungarian political party | 251 |

## Index of Cyrillic words used in this book

| Cyrillic | English | Page |
|---|---|---|
| закуска | (zacusca) | 72 |
| Липоване | Lipoveni | 209 |
| пуйне | bread | 276 |
| Приднестровская Молдавская Республика | Transnistria | 191 |
| Превед медвед! | hello, sir | |

# Final Note

All those years ago when I first step foot on Romanian soil, I knew next to nothing about this country. I considered my ignorance about this wonderful land and amazing people to be a personal shortcoming – something I thankfully soon remedied.

But over the years I came to meet hundreds of visitors here and I began to realize I wasn't the only one arriving here without knowing much – I'd safely wager the image most people have of Romania is scarcely more than vampires, poverty and starving orphans.

Romania has certainly had a difficult "childhood" as it were but this country is full of amazingly bright, resilient and tough people. Perhaps it hides its charms beneath a grey veil of endless Communist era *blocuri* but once you open to your eyes to what's all around you, Romania blooms like a wildflower with a fierce, remarkable beauty.

Whether for business, duty, curiosity or sheer traveler's whimsy, millions of people arrive in this, my newly adopted country, every year. I wrote this book in the hopes that it would allow them to enjoy their (too brief) time here just as much as I do.

This book is an entirely self-published affair, which means it was conceived of, written and edited entirely by myself. As the era of self-publishing is still rather new, this means that a lot of what is available today is not of the highest quality.

I have spent years collecting and writing anecdotes and observations about this fascinating country and it took me untold, painstaking hours to edit and re-write this guide.

Yet for all of the errors, omissions and shortcomings in this book, I take full responsibility.

Over the years I have been amazed and astounded by the seemingly limitless generosity of the heart and spirit by the Romanians I have known while living here.

Many thousands of more Romanians have treated me exceedingly kindly and well, including giving me valuable criticism and insight on my website.

To them, and to the timeless beauty that seems steeped in every pore of every rock and and tree and field in this amazing country, I am eternally grateful for my life here.

---Sam R.


Email: samcelroman@gmail.com

www.kingofromania.com

Made in the USA
Lexington, KY
10 April 2015